PRAISE FOR RAYE

"Jimmy Raye likely would have never had the opportunity to launch his coaching career at Michigan State if not for the so-called "Underground Railroad" that marked the legacy of the late coach Duffy Daugherty."
—Jarrett Bell, *USA Today*

"What Texas Western, with its all-black starting five, was to the integration of college basketball in 1966, the Spartans, in my mind, were to the integration of college football: a great leap forward."
—Dan Daly, *Pro Football Daily*

"Raye of Light" reveals a story of social evolution, not revolution, while at the same time dispels the myths of southern black participation in college football. In Jimmy Raye's career and ascension at all levels of football, he demonstrates how achievement really works and why shared opportunities for all races are the right answer. Be prepared to learn a lot about what really happened!"
—Jim Proebstle, author of *Unintended Impact: One athlete's journey from concussions in amateur football to CTE dementia*

"The next couple years are going to see plenty of reminiscing about Daugherty's great 1965-66 teams, considering that this fall is the 50th anniversary of the 1965 national title and the following November will see the 50th anniversary of the 'Game of the Century.' "
—Joe Rexrode, *Detroit Free Press*

"Great book! Informative and well-written, by a great writer. I recommend it to any sports fan, and especially to any Big Ten football fan, or Spartan fan."
—Thomas Kaulukukui Jr., Michigan State alumnus, Managing Trustee of the Queen Lili'uokalani Fund

Raye of Light

RAYE OF LIGHT

Jimmy Raye, Duffy Daugherty, the Integration of
College Football, and the 1965-66 Michigan State
Spartans

Tom Shanahan

 **August Publications**

Middleton, WI

For my wife Taosheng and daughter Jai Jai,
the inspirations for my second act

CONTENTS

COPYRIGHT

Raye of Light: Jimmy Raye, Duffy Daugherty, The Integration of College Football, and The 1965-66 Michigan State Spartans

August Publications
3543 John Muir Dr.
Middleton, WI 53562
608.836.3730
augustpublications.com
rayeoflight.com

Print ISBN: 978-1-938532-19-1
eBook ISBN: 978-1-938532-22-1

9 8 7 6 5 4 3

Designer (cover): Natalie Nowytski

Index available at *rayeoflightbook.com* website.

FOREWORD

By Tony Dungy

Growing up as a boy in the early 1960s in Jackson, Michigan, I was a Michigan State Spartans fan. Jackson is located about 30 miles south of East Lansing, and I kept up with how the Spartans were doing. In 1963, I got one of the biggest blessings God could have given me. My Dad, who was a college professor, decided to attend Michigan State to work on his PhD. Our family lived on campus in University Village the next three years, and I couldn't have been happier. Dad took me to a lot of MSU football and basketball games. I can remember the "Dollar Days" when Dad and I sat in the end zone at Spartan Stadium for $1 each.

Football Saturdays at Michigan State were special events for me. I was a sports nut, and I tried to attend as many games as possible. I had always rooted for Michigan State, and now that we were living in East Lansing it seemed everyone was a fan.

But there was one other reason I became so enamored with the Spartans. When I went to watch them play, there were African-Americans on those teams—and they were not just simply on the team, they were playing major roles. As a 9- or 10-year-old, I couldn't really tell you at the time why that had such an impact on me. I just knew that there were guys going to school and playing at Michigan State who looked like me. I also knew from watching college football on television that wasn't the case everywhere. But now, in my boyhood dreams I could visualize myself one day playing in Spartan Stadium.

One of the stars on that team who I was drawn to was Jimmy Raye. Jimmy was unique to me because he was not just a talented African-American player. He was the *quarterback*. I know that's not very newsworthy in this day and age, but in 1965, his sophomore year, it was stunning. Jimmy also played the game with a flair that caught your eye. He could throw and he was a great athlete, but I also noticed, even at my young age, that he was **the leader**. There was no question who was in charge out on the field and who his teammates looked to in clutch situations. That's the biggest reason why, in all the backyard games, I was Jimmy Raye.

Jimmy had a great career at Michigan State. He helped lead the Spartans to a Rose Bowl berth and the No. 1 national ranking in college football. But this story is about more than on-field performance. It really tells the story of how the game of football was reshaped during the Civil Rights era. How did major college football become integrated to the point where today we don't even think about the color of the players? How did the landscape change so that today African-American quarterbacks Robert Griffin III and Russell Wilson are able to compete for Rookie of the Year honors and Super Bowl rings in the NFL? How did we arrive at the point where African-Americans would have an opportunity to coach teams in the Super Bowl?

I believe it all stems back to the Big Ten in the early 1960s and the influence those players had on the rest of the country. This book documents the efforts of Duffy Daugherty and his staff in recruiting black players from the South. For many of those players, their only other choices were the historically black colleges and universities, but suddenly the world of major-college football was opening up to them. As you will read, it wasn't all smooth, and it certainly wasn't easy, but soon the whole country would get to see just how talented some of these players were. It not only made college football more exciting, it also gave hope to a whole generation of young people—including a young, impressionable boy in Jackson, Michigan.

As I mentioned, I was Jimmy Raye in the backyard games, and that feeling continued when I played quarterback at Parkside High in Jackson. By my high-school years in the early 1970s, the landscape of college football changed. African-American quarterbacks played at many schools across the country. Changes took place in the Big Ten as well. In fact, two coaching changes would dramatically impact my college plans. Duffy Daugherty retired after my senior season in 1972. Former Michigan State assistant coach Cal Stoll, who had recruited Jimmy for the Spartans out of Fayetteville, North Carolina, had taken over as the head coach at the University of Minnesota.

Although it had always been my dream to play at MSU, Coach Stoll recruited me much the way he recruited Jimmy. He sold me on doing something uncommon. He challenged me to create a legacy rather than building on someone else's. That was the beauty of what Jimmy Raye had started; young black quarterbacks felt they could go anywhere and play.

I headed off to Minnesota. By my junior year in 1975, I was one of seven African-American starting quarterbacks in the Big Ten. One of the highlights of my college career came in 1976 when I finally fulfilled that dream of playing quarterback in Spartan Stadium and led my Gophers to a 14-10 win over Michigan State.

Because I grew up in Michigan, I was aware of the impact Jimmy Raye and those Spartans teams had on college football. But the influx of African-American players in the 1960s had another effect on the game beyond impacting the speed and style of play. It changed things off the field as well. As players like Jimmy became team leaders, it opened the door for African-Americans to go into the coaching ranks. Again, Jimmy became one of the pioneers when, in 1977, he became one of the very few African-American assistant coaches in the National Football League with the San Francisco 49ers. Four years later, when I started my coaching career with the Pittsburgh Steelers, there was still only a handful of minority coaches in the NFL. Jimmy was one of my role models, helping pave the way for so many young minority coaches over the next two decades.

My journey through the National Football League culminated with coaching the Indianapolis Colts to a victory over the Chicago Bears in Super Bowl XLI. The Bears were coached by Lovie Smith, another African-American coach, who had started his NFL career coaching for me in Tampa. I was proud to have helped Lovie, but as I walked up to the victory podium after the game, I couldn't help but think of how many people had helped me along the way. One of those people I wanted to personally thank for opening doors was Jimmy Raye. This book tells how some of those doors got pushed open. I'm sure you will enjoy reading about the journey!

Tony Dungy *played three seasons in the NFL before ascending the coaching ranks to head coach of the Tampa Bay Buccaneers and Indianapolis Colts. He is currently an analyst on NBC's* Football Night in America.

INTRODUCTION

This book may be viewed as a companion to *The Biggest Game of Them All*, albeit with a different ending. Perhaps that sounds strange to you, but the Notre Dame-Michigan State 1966 Game of the Century was a de facto national title contest with two storylines and two endings.

One ending saw Notre Dame win the AP and UPI national championships despite the Irish and Spartans compiling identical 9-0-1 season records and playing to a head-to-head 10-10 tie. That's how the late Mike Celizic's excellent 1992 book finishes, while told largely through the memories of Notre Dame's players.

Michigan State's storyline included the Underground Railroad and the Civil Rights era as a backdrop. The ending, viewed through Michigan State's players, includes the Spartans' sharing of the national title when the National Football Foundation presented the MacArthur Bowl Trophy to the Spartans and Irish as national co-champions at the Waldorf Astoria in New York. The MacArthur Bowl was a prestigious crown in the 1960s, and it gave the Spartans a share of the national title they felt they were unfairly denied by the AP and UPI. In addition to identical records and the tie on the field, the teams split the No. 1 national ranking five weeks each over 10 weeks. The schools flip-flopped their 1-2 positions midway through without Michigan State losing a game.

The idea for this book was formulated the first time I met Jimmy Raye III, the son of Michigan State's pioneer black quarterback of the same name. I was writing for *Chargers.com* and Jimmy III worked in the Chargers' front office during a tenure that included his time as the No. 2 man in player personnel to general manager A.J. Smith. We were talking in a hallway at Chargers Park when Jimmy III told me his father and the Spartans have always believed they were national champions despite the 10-10 tie and AP and UPI polls.

By 2012, I had the time to tackle the book project and asked Jimmy III to introduce me to his father. We met at the 10th annual Jimmy Raye Youth Foundation dinner in Jimmy's hometown of Fayetteville, North Carolina. We began working together in an all-day session (that seemed to fly by) in a conference room at his high-school alma mater, E.E. Smith. We were in agreement that this was more than a sports story; this book should be about Michigan State's trailblazing in the Civil Rights era. Every step of the way, the research proved more fascinating than expected. The best part was learning and informing Jimmy, Gene Washington, Clint Jones, or others of something they hadn't recalled or never knew.

Other college football seasons have ended with disputed national championships, but there was none other like 1966. The season saw a year-long buildup to the November 19 showdown, Michigan State's tenth of 10 games and Notre Dame's ninth of 10. Adding to the anticipation was the recognition neither team would play in a bowl game. Michigan State had played in the 1966 Rose Bowl, and at the time the Big Ten prohibited repeats in the New Year's Day classic; Purdue, instead, represented the Big Ten. Notre Dame at the time adhered to a no-bowl policy that wasn't lifted until the 1969 season.

The Game of the Century was, in essence, a BCS Championship Game before the BCS.

Fortunately, the 1966 circumstances that created the year-end controversy won't be duplicated. First, the final polls were based on votes taken before bowl games. Next, the tiebreaker rule was implemented to negate playing for a tie to preserve a ranking. And now, a national champion is determined with the advent of the Bowl Championship Series, giving way to the College Football Playoffs in 2014.

In a calculated move, Notre Dame coach Ara Parseghian chose to let the clock run out and play for a tie while Michigan State, on defense, called timeouts. The move ultimately paid off with the national title. The Fighting Irish routed USC 51-0 the next week and won the AP and UPI voting. Explain the circumstances and how events played out to people too young to remember the Game of the Century and you get the same response then as now: 1) Ara's strategy worked, so he was right; 2) Parseghian "Tied one for the Gipper," and Michigan State deserved better for playing to win.

With time, Michigan State's players realized the 10-10 tie made the Spartans immortal despite finishing second in the polls. Actually, Parseghian gave them that notion in a gracious letter he wrote to the Spartans on the occasion of a 30th anniversary, telling them they should be thanking him. He was right. Name another team that finished second in the polls with a more favorable standing in college football annals than Michigan State's 1966 Spartans.

The scoreboard at Spartan Stadium told the story of the Game Of The Century. [AP Photo/Michigan State University via the Johnstown Tribune Democrat]

The Game of the Century is the sports story. The Michigan State team with a progressive head coach, a pioneer black quarterback, and the first fully integrated roster in college football is the history tale.

This is the first book to fully explain Duffy Daugherty's Underground Railroad. History has not accorded Daugherty, Raye, and the Spartans proper credit for their roles in the integration of college football. Too many view Daugherty as recruiting a couple of All-American players from the South, winning a bunch of games with his 1965-66 teams, and then having it all come to an end.

In reality, Daugherty recruited 44 black players from the segregated South to Michigan State between 1959 and 1972. The 20 black players the Spartans had on their 1966 roster does not sound like much compared to the 61 black athletes on Alabama's first national championship roster of the 21st century (2009), but in 1966 Notre Dame had only one black player, USC's 1967 national championship team had only seven black players, and USC's 1970 squad—the first integrated roster to play Alabama at Legion Field—had only five black starters among 17 black players on the team.

Myths have bloated and revised the history surrounding the 1970 USC-Alabama game, overshadowing Michigan State's more significant role in the integration of college football.

Among the myths is the idea that Alabama coach Bear Bryant scheduled the game to shame Alabama's segregationists into allowing him to recruit black athletes. Bryant had already signed Wilbur Jackson as his first black player by 1970, and Jackson watched the game as a member of the freshmen team when NCAA rules prevented freshmen eligibility. Jackson had arrived on the Tuscaloosa campus from recently desegregated Alabama high schools; his all-black high school had closed down following his junior year. With the integration of Alabama high schools, there was no reason for Bryant's college teams to remain all white. The university's student body had been peacefully integrated since 1963. The Alabama student newspaper wrote editorials in the late 1960s supporting the integration of the football program. Bryant was not leading in the late 1960s—he was merely catching up to the rest of the nation by the 1970s.

Another myth is Bryant supposedly parading USC fullback Sam Cunningham through the Alabama locker room to show his players an example of a prized fullback, but Alabama's players say it didn't happen. Cunningham himself won't confirm it happened—preferring the myth to live on in legendary lore. The game also was not on television. Its overnight impact was limited to black fans in Alabama listening on the radio and taking delight in Bryant's all-white team losing to a school with black players.

Another point to make: Daugherty's Underground Railroad did not end with the 1966 season. He continued to recruit the segregated South throughout his final season in 1972. There were still plenty of black players in the South to recruit, as Alabama didn't dress its first black player in a varsity game until 1971, while LSU and Georgia didn't field their first black players in a varsity game until 1972.

Daugherty's win-loss record declined after 1966, but more important was the overall graduation record of his Underground Railroad players. He didn't bring them North just to play football. Of the 44 players, 68 percent graduated—an African-American graduation rate that embarrasses most other national championship teams.

History is not alone in failing to give Daugherty his proper credit. Michigan State named a series of outsiders as presidents and athletic directors with little understanding of the Underground Railroad's impact upon college football. They overlooked Daugherty and his trailblazing players. Michigan State named its football facility for Daugherty, but other campuses have erected statutes to coaches merely for winning a single national championship. Daugherty won multiple national titles and accomplished much more. USC has a statue on campus of Tody Smith, a member of the famed 1969 USC defense's Wild Bunch, but Michigan State does not have a statue of Tody's more famous big brother Bubba Smith, a College Football Hall of Famer. Bubba remains one of the largest figures in college-football history, dominating as one of the five All-Americans on the Spartans' 1965 and 1966 championship teams. San Jose State erected statutes that honor Olympic track medalists Tommie Smith and John Carlos, who were students at the school, for their Civil Rights protest at the 1968 Mexico City Olympics. Michigan State has a historical marker on campus recognizing the 1963 "Game of Change" played in the NCAA tournament at Jenison Fieldhouse that involved two basketball teams from other schools—Mississippi State and Loyola Chicago.

A fitting tribute to the Underground Railroad would be a bronzed mural wall replicating the iconic 1966 photo of Michigan State's five All-Americans—Bob Apisa, Clinton Jones, Bubba Smith, Gene Washington and George Webster—as the background to a statue of Daugherty and Raye huddled on the sideline.

The Big Ten office also has failed to recognize both Daugherty and Minnesota coach Murray Warmath for their combined roles in the integration of college football. Warmath won a national title at Minnesota with Sandy Stephens as the first black quarterback of a national championship team. Daugherty won a national title with Jimmy Raye as the first black quarterback from the South to win a national title.

The Big Ten honors Ohio State's Woody Hayes, Michigan's Bo Schembechler, and Wisconsin's Dave McClain with its Coach-of-the-Year award. There is no denying the conference records that Schembechler and Hayes built dominating the Big Ten in the 1970s, but their abysmal failings in the Rose Bowl launched the popular national sport of Big Ten bashing that continues to this day. In the New Year's Day Rose Bowls of the 1970s, Schembechler was 0-5 and Hayes was 1-4. Hayes' career ended in disgrace after he was fired for punching a Clemson player in the 1978 Gator Bowl. Schembechler finished his career without a national title.

One reason Daugherty's teams are not better remembered as the leaders of the integration of college football: the Game of the Century ended in a 10-10 tie and followed a crushing Rose Bowl upset loss a year earlier. As a consequence there is some missing romance.

Another reason is that, at least as of yet, the Underground Railroad has failed to inspire a movie or documentary similar to recent ones about the 1963 Loyola Chicago and 1966 Texas Western basketball teams that won national titles: *Game of Change* about Loyola Chicago debuted in 2008, and the movie *Glory Road* about Texas Western opened in 2006. The legend of Bear Bryant has plenty of momentum to propel the myths surrounding the 1970 USC-Alabama game without a movie, but the story also was part of a 2008 HBO documentary, *Breaking the Huddle*.

Raye's career, which included coaching 40-plus years in college and the NFL, would be better remembered if he had received an opportunity as a head coach that so many in the business say he deserved. He would be grouped among pioneer black head coaches Art Shell, Dennis Green, Tony Dungy, and Tyrone Willingham.

With time, Michigan State's 1966 team came to be viewed as immortal. The hope is that eventually Raye, his teammates, and Daugherty will be likewise revered as the men who broke down barriers and led the way to changing the face of the game. They raised the profile of black athletes in college football more than any other group in history.

ACKNOWLEDGMENTS

One of my favorite Michigan State classes was United States History with Madison Kuhn, author of *Michigan State—The First Hundred Years*. I proudly cited his book in Chapter 5 when summarizing Michigan State's history as a land-grant university. Kuhn, who was appointed university historian by the Board of Trustees, required a paper that taught me how to immerse oneself into newspaper microfilm.

His class was at least one time in my academic career I truly enjoyed holing up in the library every night after dinner at Wonders Hall. On two recent trips to campus to research this book, I hiked between Michigan State's main library and the University Archives—enjoying every step and taking a different path each time to enjoy the scenery and reminisce. The first visit was in the fall when Clinton Jones was inducted into the Michigan State Hall of Fame. Thanks to Michigan State sports operations assistant Julee Burgess, I had access to Hall of Fame events and picked up information I otherwise would not have come across to add to the chapters on Jones, Bubba Smith, and Gene Washington.

I have to thank University Archives assistant director Portia Vescio and her staff. They never tired of another request and tracked down media guides and other resources. I could not have identified and researched the 44 Underground Railroad passengers between 1959 and 1972 without their help.

The media information and university archivist offices at Ferris State University also helped me fill in holes on Gideon Smith's odyssey from Virginia to Big Rapids before his arrival at Michigan State. I grew up in Big Rapids, home of the Ferris campus, and took special delight in learning about his experiences prior to arriving at Michigan State, where he is better known as the school's first African-American athlete.

A special thanks to *Roanoke Times* librarian Belinda Harris. She found the final piece I needed to punch a hole in the long-standing myth that Bear Bryant sent Charlie Thornhill to Duffy Daugherty in exchange for Duffy sending Joe Namath to Bear. It's a nice story, but it's not true. I did not intend to go down that avenue, but as the facts gradually accumulated, they did not add up with the myth that I, as well as others, had long accepted.

As I explained to Kaleb Thornhill, Charlie's son, debunking the myth does nothing to diminish his father's All-Big Ten career at Michigan State. However, the myth certainly does unfairly diminish Duffy Daugherty's legacy. Daugherty built a fraternity among southern black high-school coaches that resulted in the Underground Railroad. The myth portrayed him as simply picking up the phone and receiving tips from Bryant, a profound irony since Bryant was a man who in reality had little to no knowledge of black talent in the segregated South or contact with black coaches.

Interviewing the Michigan State athletes and coaches reminded me of a comment from Presidential historian Doris Kearns Goodwin. She said she felt like she lived with President Lincoln during the 10 years spent researching the book upon which the movie *Lincoln* was based. I felt I relived the 1965 and 1966 championship seasons, but this time with much more social understanding than I had as an elementary school kid when I first became a Michigan State fan.

All of the Spartans gave me plenty of time. Jimmy Raye had many of the phone numbers, and ones he lacked Pat Gallinagh and Ernie Pasteur either had or tracked down. The easy access and time granted was an example of the immense respect they held for Raye and Daugherty. In addition to Raye, Gallinagh, and Pasteur, other Michigan State athletes and coaches to thank for their time are Kale Ane, Bob Apisa, Charlie Baggett, Tony Banks, Hank Bullough, Daswell Campell, Vince Carillot, Larry Cundiff, Billy Joe DuPree, Johnny Green, Jud Heathcote, Clinton Jones, Carter Kamana, Sherman Lewis, Arnold Morgado, Jim Nicholson, Clifton Roaf, Craig Raye, Bob Steele, Jimmy Summers, George Syzpula, Kaleb Thornhill, Gene Washington, Tyrone Willingham, Doug Won, and Tom Yewcic.

Other interviews were with Julian Brown, Mike Burgener, William Carver, Melody Chalmers, Donna Clayton Lloyd, Dan Daugherty, Dree Daugherty Hudson, Father Jake Foglio, Linda Garrett, Jimmy Harvey, Stanley Johnson, Tom Kaulukukui Jr., Ernest Green, Richard Lewis, Bobby Mitchell, Ken Niumatalolo, Coley O'Brien, Edwena Raye, James Raye Sr., Jimmy Raye III, Pat Raye, John Robinson, Nick Vista, Ike Walker, Doug Wilkerson, Ken Willard and Wallace Wright.

Jimmy's sister Pat, the oldest of the five siblings, was a big help with information on the family before she passed away in September 2013. Jimmy took a sabbatical from coaching with the Tampa Bay Buccaneers in the 2013 season following back surgery in the offseason and his sister's death.

In 2014 the NFL named Raye a senior advisor to NFL executive vice-president for football operations Troy Vincent.

There were a few unreturned calls, but one special response came from Jesse Jackson. He emphasized to me the importance of black athletes simply being seen on television in positive roles—particularly a black quarterback such as Jimmy Raye—in an era when they were otherwise non-existent or portrayed negatively. This was a theme validated throughout the book. Clarence Underwood was inspired by watching Michigan State's integrated team in the 1954 Rose Bowl. Jimmy Raye was stirred when he watched Minnesota's black quarterback in the 1962 Rose Bowl. It was also a pleasure to discuss the era with Ernest Green, a Michigan State grad and Civil Rights icon as a member of the Little Rock Nine, and Bobby Mitchell, the Pro Football Hall of Famer who was the Jackie Robinson of the Washington Redskins.

Others who helped in various ways were Tom Apostle, Mark Baric, Robert Bentley, Heidi Bleazey, Chae Castillo, David Cornwell, Doug Doughty, Trajan Dubiel, John Glionna, Robin Greene, Ted Halm, Bob Hammel, Kim Henderson, Mark Hollis, Jackie Holtenstein, Charles Hurt, Melinda Isler, Neil Iwamoto, Lia Kamana, Jeff Keag, Chris Lamb, Laurie Langland, Matt Larson, Paulette Martis, Ali Marumoto, Mark Moore, Doug Miller, Vanessa Mitchell, Bill Nemesi, Jeff Neuman, Barb O'Brien, Michael Oriard, Chandra Owen, Mike Perry, Jim Pignataro, Shelly Poe, Paul Rovnak, Rex Schuberg, Kami Silk, Scott Strasemeier, Tim Tessalone, Steven Travers, Kim Winkel, and Rachel Zylstra.

I need to thank my bosses Mark Baric and Sam Pasquale for allowing me to time to work and travel to research and finish this book.

Finally, thanks to Pam Whitten and Steve Smith. Whitten, the dean of Michigan State's College of Communications Arts, and Smith, a Michigan State basketball legend and now a broadcaster, organized the first Michigan State Sports Journalism Classic on in April 2013. I received an invitation among the alums to meet with students, and that event led me to my publisher, Kevin Reichard, and editor, Jesse Goldberg-Strassler, of August Publications. I learned of them through a relay of former sports editors of *The State News* (Michigan State's student newspaper) who were present at the forum—Rick Gosselin (1971-1972), Lynn Henning (1974), and myself (1978).

I lamented to Henning I was still seeking a publisher when he told me of Gosselin's success working with August Publications. Henning and Gosselin were two sports journalism heavyweights to trust. Henning has written the two definitive books on the ups and downs of Michigan State sports in the post-World War II years, *Spartan Seasons* and *Spartan Seasons II*. His books are cited liberally here with his permission. Gosselin fulfilled a passion by publishing his excellent book, *Goodfellows*, a story of St. Ambrose and Catholic high school football in Detroit.

Thankfully, Reichard and Goldberg-Strassler recognized the special story that combined the lives of Jimmy Raye, Duffy Daugherty, and the Underground Railroad. They added polished editing and had the same eye to history that I'm sure Madison Kuhn would have had. This was meant to be more than a sports book, and I like to think Kuhn would have considered this the history book it was intended to be on Michigan State football's trailblazing role in the Civil Rights era.

1

MICHIGAN STATE'S
UNDERGROUND RAILROAD

"I just figured Michigan State had a history of playing blacks. Michigan State had played a black quarterback. Willie Thrower hadn't been a starter there, but there was some history that they would entertain the thought of playing a black quarterback."—Jimmy Raye

Summer turned to fall in September 1963 as Michigan State University's freshman football recruits arrived to a postcard scene with 5,000 acres of rolling green grass, towering trees, and the Red Cedar River running through campus. The varsity players already were practicing for their September 28 opener at Spartan Stadium when the freshmen gathered for the first time.

Michigan State University football coach Duffy Daugherty loaded his 1963 football recruiting class aboard what came to be called the Underground Railroad. The class included black athletes from the segregated South who were denied a chance to attend their home-state university simply because of their skin color, and it featured no fewer than three future College Football Hall of Famers—Bubba Smith of Beaumont, Texas; George Webster of Anderson, South Carolina; and Gene Washington of La Porte, Texas.

Daugherty, himself a College Football Hall of Famer, combined his southern recruits with his northern prospects to form his grandest haul in 19 years as the Spartans' head coach. In all, the class produced four two-time All-America players who were also first-round picks in the 1967 National Football League draft: Smith, Webster, Washington, and Clinton Jones of Cleveland, Ohio. Smith was selected No. 1 overall by the Baltimore Colts; Jones No. 2 to the Minnesota Vikings; Webster No. 5 by the Houston Oilers; and Washington No. 8 to the Minnesota Vikings. No school has come close to matching four picks among the top eight.

MICHIGAN STATE UNIVERSITY
1963 FRESHMAN FOOTBALL TEAM

FIRST ROW [L-R]: First player, Reuben Marshall; SECOND ROW [L-R]: Third player, Jerry West; sixth player, Pat Gallinagh; ninth player, Ernie Pasteur; THIRD ROW [L-R]: First black player, Clinton Jones; next to Jones, Phil Hoag; FOURTH ROW [L-R]: First coach, Wayne Fontes; second coach, head coach Burt Smith; fourth player, Dick Kenney; first black player, Maurice Haynes; FIFTH [BACK] ROW: First black player, Jeff Richardson; next to Richardson, Gene Washington; next to Washington, George Webster; next to Webster, Bubba Smith.

A year after the 1963 recruiting class, the Underground Railroad delivered a pioneer black quarterback from segregated Fayetteville, North Carolina. Jimmy Raye proved to be ahead of his time—decades ahead. In his junior season in 1966, he was Michigan State's first black starting quarterback and the first black quarterback from the South to win a national title.

The Underground Railroad is a football story, but it also is a drama of heartless racism that forced players to look north for opportunity, and of decent-hearted people who helped them reach Michigan State to play Big Ten football and earn a college degree.

Raye led Daugherty's national powerhouse in an era when the quarterback position, the most important in football and perhaps the most difficult to play in sports, was reserved for white players in the North as well as the South. He was one of 11 black starters in 1966—an unheard-of number for the time—with four on offense and seven on defense.

Raye followed his playing days, including two years in the NFL as a defensive back, with a coaching career of 40-plus years in the college and NFL ranks. He was often the only black coach on the staff early in his career at both levels and as a result has been an active voice in minority hiring as president of the NFL Coaches Association. Add up his playing and coaching careers, and he is the most socially significant player among the Underground Railroad recruits.

Although Raye was not one of Michigan State's five All-America players—he was second-team All-Big Ten to Purdue's All-American Bob Griese—the coaches realized he was indispensable to their offense and national championship shortly before the 1966 season opener. A practice squad player ran into Raye as he held the ball for an extra-point kick, sending him to the university infirmary with knee and lower leg injuries on the Saturday before facing North Carolina State. Michigan State quarterbacks coach Al Dorow revealed the code-red level of concern when he spoke a month after the season to a Jimmy Raye Day audience in Fayetteville. They fretted their season was going up in smoke.

"Well, we thought we'd had it," Dorow said. "Not another solid quarterback on the squad, and Jimmy on crutches. Tuesday before the game, he was still hobbling around. The next day, though, he couldn't stand seeing another guy at his position and decided to give it a whirl.

"It was painful, but he stayed with it. But that's the difference in good ball players and great ball players. The great ones never miss a game, and from that day on, we knew we had winner in Jimmy Raye."[1]

Raye directed four touchdown drives for a 28-3 lead before N.C. State scored a late touchdown in Michigan State's 28-10 victory at Spartan Stadium. MSU was fortunate that Raye started all 10 games in that historic 1966 season, including playing through the Ohio State and Purdue victories with a bruised shoulder that he suffered in a win over Michigan.

Michigan State coach Duffy Daugherty, left, gives last-minute instructions to Jimmy Raye before rushing him into the second quarter of the game with Purdue in East Lansing, Oct. 22, 1966. [AP Photo]

A loss early in the year without Raye and there would have been no showdown with Notre Dame in The Game of the Century. With no national title chase to create headlines and draw a record television audience, the legacy of the game's first fully integrated roster from the 1965 and 1966 Underground Railroad seasons would have been diminished.

The significance of Michigan State's success became more than a sports story. African-Americans and any American favoring Civil Rights causes joined forces with Spartans fans. The Underground Railroad recruits of the 1960s did not confront the surreptitious, dangerous journey American hero Harriet Tubman faced when she guided escaped slaves to freedom a century earlier on the genuine Underground Railroad. They did not participate in protests. But Civil Rights leader Reverend Jesse Jackson said it was important to the cause simply for them to be seen in stadiums, newspapers, magazines, and on television in America's living rooms: "These athletes redefined race relations in many ways. Why do we do so well in baseball, football, basketball, and track? On the ball field the playing field is even. When the rules are objective and public, and the referees are fair, we can win. The ball field is so unique. These athletes made it to the top because fair rules lend themselves to achieving."

Jackson had experienced his own journey as a black quarterback from the South to a Big Ten school. Raye accomplished what Jackson hoped to achieve when he attended the University of Illinois as freshman team in 1959 from Greenville, South Carolina.

"Jimmy Raye was one of my heroes," Jackson said. "We pulled for him. There weren't many black quarterbacks in the pipeline then. We knew that people like him had tremendous pressure on them. They had to not just play but perform better than their competitor. We knew there would be alumni pressure to play the white quarterback and Jimmy would have to sit. We knew there were two sets of rules."

In 1966, Raye was one of only two black quarterbacks who was a starter at a major conference school. The other was Stanford University's Gene Washington, though Washington was switched to receiver for his junior and senior years. Two starting black quarterbacks—like two black head coaches in the future—was enough progress to prompt *Ebony* magazine to devote a story in its December 1966 issue to the football exploits and campus life of Raye and Washington.

Raye led Michigan State's 1966 march to the de facto national championship showdown with Notre Dame. The Game of the Century was the Bowl Championship Series before there was a BCS. The debate for identifying the top two teams in America was reduced to whether No. 1 Notre Dame and No. 2 Michigan State was the correct order. (Later in this book we'll address the claims from Crimson Tide diehards that undefeated Alabama deserved the top spot.)

Football came of age when The Game of the Century was played on November 19, drawing the sport's largest television audience at that time with 33 million viewers and a staggering 22.5 Nielsen rating on ABC. The nation saw Raye and the rest of the Spartans, to borrow a line from the TV marketing of the era, in living color.

The monumental game ended in a then-controversial and now immortal 10-10 tie. At the time multiple organizations named national champions. The most recognized were the Associated Press and United Press International polls that voted Notre Dame No. 1 and Michigan State No. 2 despite both schools finishing with 9-0-1 records, and these AP and UPI tallies are still debated to this day. Two other recognized major national titles were the Football Writers Association of America (FWAA) and the National Football Foundation (NFF). The FWAA agreed with AP and UPI, but the NFF departed course and named Michigan State and Notre Dame national co-champions. The NFF presented its MacArthur Bowl Trophy to the Michigan State and Notre Dame head coaches and team captains on December 6 at the Waldorf Astoria in New York City (the NFF still awards the MacArthur Bowl Trophy, but instead of picking a champion the trophy is presented to the winner of the BCS title game).

Michigan State's national title allowed Raye to follow in the footsteps of his inspiration, the University of Minnesota's Sandy Stephens of Uniontown, Pennsylvania. In 1960, Stephens was the first black starting quarterback to lead a team to a national title and the first black quarterback named an All-American pick.

Another 19 years would pass before a black quarterback matched Stephens and Raye as the starter on a national championship team. Oklahoma University's Jamelle Holloway directed the Sooners' wishbone offense to the national title in 1985.

Jimmy Raye carrying the ball in the Game of the Century. Photo courtesy Jimmy Raye.

Raye's 1966 and 1967 seasons as a starter and his Rose Bowl performance in relief as a sophomore backup in 1965 defied the stereotype
that black athletes could not play a "whites-only" position requiring
intelligence and leadership. He possessed both qualities in abundance
and continued to earn the respect he gained in his coaching career. By
1983, Raye was one of the NFL's first black offensive coordinators, serving on the Los Angeles Rams' staff under head coach John Robinson.

The genesis of the Underground Railroad that opened Raye's career
path was Duffy Daugherty's selection as the 1955 American Football
Coaches Association Coach of the Year, the same season the Spartans
won the 1956 New Year's Day Rose Bowl. Daugherty was a national figure who was on the cover of *Time* magazine's October 8, 1956, issue.
The 1950s was an era that *Time* publisher Henry Luce dubbed "The
American Century," and he considered a *Time* cover the most coveted
honor in American culture.[2]

When Daugherty spoke in the South, he was disturbed by the
"whites-only" clinics. On return trips he fulfilled his obligation to speak
at the white coaches clinic and then staged his own second clinic for
black coaches to attend.

Daugherty passed away at the age of 72 in 1987, but Vince Carillot
and Hank Bullough, the last two surviving assistant coaches on Daugherty's mid-1960s staffs, say the black coaching clinics were designed
to fill a void in the coaching fraternity—not to recruit black players.
Daugherty was the only white coach from a major conference school
sharing a fellowship with African-American coaches in the South.
Prominent southern coaches like Paul "Bear" Bryant at the University of
Alabama had little to no interaction with black high-school coaches in
their states or throughout the South, according to the black high-school
coaches of their era and a lawsuit filed against Bryant in July 1969 by the
Alabama Afro-American Student Association.

Raye learned from Texas black high-school coaches the same was
true of University of Texas coach Darrell Royal when Raye hit the Texas
high-school recruiting trail as a Longhorns assistant in 1977 under
Royal's successor, Fred Akers.

"They hated Darrell Royal," Raye said. "They said he didn't care
about their players. He said he could win national titles without black
players."

Daugherty, though, enjoyed the coaching fraternity.

"Duffy spent time with the black coaches," said Carillot, an assistant under Daugherty from 1960 to 1968. "They trusted Duffy and had faith in him. They knew Duffy viewed their players as individuals and not football freaks. The coaches started coming up to Duffy. They'd say, 'I've got this player for you.'"

A recruiting network, the Underground Railroad, was born.

The Spartans' 1966 roster included 20 black players, with 12 from the South. There were 11 black starters with seven from the South. Six of the southern black starters earned All-American or All Big Ten honors, and all seven were drafted by an NFL or an American Football League team. In addition to Smith, Webster, and Washington as the All-American choices, the All-Big Ten picks were first-team safety Jess Phillips, Beaumont, Texas; first-team linebacker Charlie Thornhill, Roanoke, Virginia; and Raye as a second-team quarterback. Jimmy Summers of Orangeburg, South Carolina, was a two-year starting cornerback.

Steve Garvey was a white athlete Daugherty recruited from the South as a football-baseball talent out of Tampa, Florida. He started games for the Spartans as sophomore defensive back in 1967 (there is a noted photo of him tackling USC's O.J. Simpson in a game at Spartan Stadium) and was an All-American baseball player in the spring of 1968 before he signed with the Los Angeles Dodgers.

"I think Duffy was a Renaissance man when it came to the integration of college sports," Garvey said. "It's one thing to try to implement something like that and it's another thing to make it happen. It's one thing to influence your sport and it's another to make societal change. The ultimate compliment I can give him is he's a Renaissance man for making it happen."

Another key building block to the Underground Railroad was Michigan State's established reputation for integrated teams. Daugherty and his predecessor Biggie Munn had recruited black athletes from Michigan factory towns throughout the 1950s. The Spartans' first four black All-Americas were tackle Don Coleman (1949-51), halfback James Ellis (1951-53), halfback Leroy Bolden (1951-54) and end Ellis Duckett (1952-54). Coleman, Ellis, and Bolden were from Flint—Buick City—and Duckett from Saginaw, an auto-parts town.

Michigan State's black pioneers were seen on TV in the 1954 and 1956 New Year's Day Rose Bowl wins.

Watching the 1954 Rose Bowl changed the life of Clarence Under-wood, a future black Michigan State athletic director. Underwood was an Army paratrooper at Fort Bragg in Fayetteville, North Carolina, when he watched the 1954 Rose Bowl between guard duty shifts. Until then, he had planned to attend Tuskegee Institute (now Tuskegee University), the historically black school in Alabama founded by Booker T. Washington, but he was struck by the number of black players on the Spartans' roster.

"Having been raised in Alabama where segregation laws prevented socializing among blacks and whites, the game really caught my attention," Underwood said. "It was the first time I had seen blacks and whites play together on the same collegiate team. Michigan State appeared to have 10 or 12 different black players. UCLA had fewer, but it was obvious that all of the blacks were impact players. I was so interested and amazed by those integrated teams that I decided that night I would research MSU in the Army library and apply for admission." [3]

Underwood, the son of an Alabama sharecropper, became a trail-blazer—first as an athletic administrator at Michigan State and later in the Big Ten office in Chicago. He served as Michigan State's athletic director from 1999 to 2002 before he retired.

The 1954 Rose Bowl also influenced Jesse Jackson as a wide-eyed 12-year-old youth in South Carolina. He took particular note of Bolden and Duckett. Bolden scored a touchdown on a one-yard run, and Duckett blocked a punt and returned it six yards for a touchdown in Michigan State's 28-20 victory.

Jackson, a quarterback at Greenville's Sterling High, accepted a scholarship to Illinois over a pro baseball contract, but he was switched to halfback when he played on the freshmen team in the NCAA era of freshmen varsity ineligibility. He left Illinois after one year and finished his college career as a quarterback at North Carolina A&T, the historically black school in Greensboro. The NCAA ranked Jackson No. 15 on its list of 100 most influential NCAA-student athletes to commemorate its 100th anniversary in 2006.

Raye also understood the integration history of Big Ten schools. He was aware a black quarterback had played for Michigan State under Munn when Daugherty was an assistant in the early 1950s. The quarterback's name, fittingly, was Willie Thrower, a native of New Kensington, Pennsylvania. Thrower later was the first black quarterback in the modern NFL era (per the Pro Football Hall of Fame), in 1953 with the Chicago Bears.

"I just figured Michigan State had a history of playing blacks," Raye said. "Michigan State had played a black quarterback. Willie Thrower hadn't been a starter there, but there was some history that they would entertain the thought of playing a black quarterback."

Munn and Daugherty worked under the progressive voice of John Hannah, Michigan State's president from 1941 to 1969. In addition to the athletic program, Michigan State's faculty members understood that Hannah viewed the school as a vanguard to integration.

"It was very clear where Hannah stood," said Richard Lewis, a Michigan State business professor in the 1960s and the dean of the College of Business from 1974 to 1993. "He was committed to integration and it pervaded throughout the campus."

In 1966, Lewis worked closely with Hannah when the president of Nigeria, Nnamdi Azikiwe, asked Hannah for help to establish a college in Nigeria that followed Michigan State's model as land-grant school. Hannah and Azikiwe went before the U.S. Agency for International Development in Washington, D.C., to secure funding. Hannah then appointed Lewis as the founding dean of the University of Nigeria business school.

In the same time frame, Hannah served as the first chairman of the Civil Rights Commission when he was appointed by President Dwight Eisenhower in 1957. That was the year of the Little Rock Nine, when Eisenhower sent federal troops into Little Rock, Arkansas, to enforce the desegregation of Central High School.

Michigan State graduate Ernest Green was among the nine black students known as the Little Rock Nine when they enrolled at Central. Green was the lone senior and thus the first black student to graduate from Central in the 1957-58 school year. He attended Michigan State on a scholarship anonymously provided by Hannah—a fact Green did not learn until after Hannah's death in 1991, when the secret was discovered in Hannah's papers.

"Michigan State has a long history of African-American achievements in sports and other endeavors," Green said. "It was an atmosphere I found very invigorating. The accomplishments of all the people made it the vibrant place it was. We had our problems, certainly. There was segregation in East Lansing in terms of housing and some of the white students had to adjust to having never been around people of color. But basically the school was a real launching pad for many people."

When Green finally learned that Hannah had funded his scholarship, it provided him with ironic amusement. He thought back to his days as president of the school's National Association for the Advancement of Colored People chapter.

"Hannah was very progressive, but I was president of the campus NAACP for a couple of years, and we of course were very active," Green said. "We picketed outside of Hannah's house, but I didn't know at the time he was responsible for my scholarship." Green learned Hannah was his benefactor when he was invited to be a speaker at Michigan State's 1995 commencement ceremony along with President Bill Clinton.

With Hannah for a boss, Daugherty was empowered to accept recruiting tips from southern black high-school coaches. Two men, color-blind and proactive in the Civil Rights movement, came together at the right time to generate steam for the Underground Railroad.

By the 1962 season, the Associated Press reported that Michigan State's 17 black players formed "the largest delegation of Negro players in the history of major college football." But Michigan State's 1962 varsity roster had only five black players from the South. By the 1965 Rose Bowl season, the Spartans' 20 black players included 11 from the South. The 1966 team also had 20 black players, with 12 from the South.

As the 1960s progressed, Daugherty had brought along combinations of assistant coaches to his southern clinics—Bullough, Carillot, Danny Boisture, and Cal Stoll. One year Bullough and Boisture put on a three-day clinic at Alcorn A&M, a historically black college (now known as Alcorn State University) in Lorman, Mississippi.

"Duffy decided if we're going to be down there for the clinics we might as well be recruiting," Bullough said. "In those days, the number-one guy for a high-school kid was his coach. They listened to their high-school coach about picking a college a heck of a lot. Duffy was good with a lot of high-school coaches because he treated them fair at the clinics. That's the type of person Duffy was. He wasn't doing it to just to gain an advantage. He wanted to give those clinics for the black coaches. He was a unique guy. Duffy was way ahead of people."

Among these southern high school coaches was Willie Ray Smith Sr., a highly successful Texas coach at Beaumont Pollard near Houston. He understood the perils of college football recruiting. His oldest son,

Willie Ray Smith Jr., had chosen Iowa over an offer from Michigan State and Daugherty in 1961.

Willie Ray Jr., a running back, had early success before he re-injured a knee that he first hurt in high school. Academic issues also developed for a young student-athlete who was far from home without a support system or football as an anchor. He lettered only once at Iowa, in the 1962 season, and was never the same player. He transferred to Kansas before completing an undistinguished college career.

Willie Ray Sr. began to regret not steering his oldest son to Daugherty. With his second son graduating in 1963, he decided Charles A. "Bubba" Smith would play for Michigan State. Willie Ray Sr. also tipped off Daugherty to Gene Washington, who played at Baytown Carver, a Pollard rival.

"Duffy befriended Bubba's father and he helped out Duffy a lot," Bullough said.

Willie Ray Sr. ultimately steered nine players within a 10-year period from the Houston area to Michigan State. Six were from Pollard, including Bubba's younger brother Tody Smith (he later was injured and transferred to the University of Southern California). Pollard supplied two starters in the Game of the Century with Smith and Phillips.

Daugherty was tipped off to George Webster by a black high-school coach at an Atlanta clinic the summer of 1962 before Webster's senior yrar. Daugherty learned about Raye through an old friend, North Carolina State head coach Earle Edwards. Daugherty and Edwards were assistants on Munn's Michigan State teams from 1949 to 1953.

Before Daugherty built his network in the South, the first southern black athletes in the Big Ten began as a trickle in the mid-1950s. The contacts were anecdotal and isolated. As an example, Pro Football Hall of Famer Bobby Mitchell of Hot Springs, Arkansas, was one of the first black players to migrate north when he was at Illinois from 1954 to 1957. He said Hot Springs federal judge Henry Britt was an Illinois alumnus and college roommate of Illinois assistant coach Mel Brewer. Britt told Brewer about Mitchell after the U.S. Supreme Court's decision on May 17, 1954, in *Brown v. Board of Education*. The decision held "separate but equal" education to be an unconstitutional practice.

Mitchell said he planned to play at Grambling State University for a young Eddie Robinson, who grew into a legendary coach at the historically black school in Louisiana from 1941 to 1998.

"Eddie Robinson and I laughed about that for years," Mitchell said. "He said, 'I had you before that ruling.' I decided I would go out and try Illinois. Eddie Robinson had so many great players from the South, I probably wouldn't have made his team."

That is unlikely, and Mitchell said it with a chuckle, but it is true that many players from historically black colleges in the 1950s went onto successful NFL careers, some even earning a place in the Pro Football Hall of Fame.

Illinois learned about Jesse Jackson through the Furman University coach. At Minnesota, head coach Murray Warmath had contacts in western North Carolina that led to Bobby Bell of Shelby and Carl Eller of Winston-Salem playing for the Gophers in the early 1960s and Charlie Sanders of Greensboro in the mid-1960s. But Warmath's network was limited. Raye, from eastern North Carolina, was not recruited by Warmath.

What made the Underground Railroad a force of social progress was the South's geographical breadth of segregation and Daugherty's contacts that covered the wide spectrum. It spanned 13 states from Maryland to Texas and encompassed three major conferences—the Atlantic Coast Conference, the Southeastern Conference, and the Southwest Conference.

The number of black players on major college rosters in the 1960s—other than Michigan State and a few other major programs—could be counted on one hand. Michigan State's two primary rivals for the 1966 national title were Notre Dame and Alabama. Notre Dame had only one black player, future College and Pro Football Hall of Famer Alan Page. Alabama, staunchly segregated, remained all-white until the 1971 season.

With the exception of Page arriving at Notre Dame in 1963 as a freshman, Notre Dame's rosters were nearly as segregated as southern teams until the late 1960s. Notre Dame relied on the South as part of its national recruiting base and an integrated roster was a threat to the Irish's success with commitments from southern athletes, according to Michael Oriard, an Oregon State University professor and former Notre Dame and NFL player who has written books on sports and American culture. Notre Dame recruited one black player in 1966 on its freshman team, two in 1967 and five in 1968.

Michigan State's 1966 varsity roster was 29.9 percent black with 20 of 67 players. Within a decade the Spartans' influence on college football's changing face was discernible from national championship team photos. On Minnesota's 1960 national title team, Sandy Stephens and Bobby Bell, a College and Pro Football Hall of Famer, were two of five black players. On the University of Southern California's 1967 national championship roster, there were only seven black players. USC's number jumped to 23 just five years later when the Trojans won their 1972 national title.

The NCAA did not begin to track official statistics on race until 1999, when the percentage of black players at all NCAA levels was recorded at 34.5 percent. The NCAA reported its first black plurality in 2011 with 45.8 percent (45.1 white and 9.1 others).

The number of black players on college football's current elite teams is much higher than 45.8 percent. On Alabama's first national championship team of the 21st century, the 2009 Crimson Tide listed 61 black scholarship players—70.1 percent. The grandfathers of those 61 black players could not have played for Bear Bryant prior to the 1970s.

One of those grandfathers, in a profound irony, was Art Johnson, a Michigan State halfback (1956-58). Johnson's grandson, Mark Ingram Jr., won the 2009 Heisman Trophy as a member of the Crimson Tide. Alabama recruited the Michigan State legacy out of Southwestern Academy in Flint, Michigan. His father, Mark Ingram Sr., played at Michigan State (1983-86) and Flint Northwestern. Johnson played his high-school ball at Flint Northern.

In addition to Michigan State's 20 black players in 1966, the Spartans' melting pot included college football's first Samoan All-American player, fullback Bob Apisa of Hawaii.

These days, Raye encounters football players and younger coaches who view segregation as ancient history, but it was within the lifetime of Raye and his athletic contemporaries. Their experiences run parallel to Jackson, Green, and other Civil Rights icons.

"It's a constant education process," Green said. "It's a different world now. It's hard for younger people to even fathom the segregation that took place just 50 years ago."

There was another vital reason Michigan State's Underground Railroad athletes helped push college football integration forward. They felt a responsibility to take advantage of opportunities to set the table for future black college students and athletes.

However, coping with the pressure accompanying the integration of college athletics demanded more than athletic skill. Success also required a level of maturity and awareness on the level of Jackie Robinson. Brooklyn Dodgers general manager Branch Rickey chose Robinson, a college graduate and athlete at integrated UCLA, as the candidate best able to handle the pressure of breaking Major League Baseball's color line in 1947. Jesse Jackson says young black athletes who have squandered their lottery-like contracts lacked appreciation for their athletic pioneers.

"They are so detached from the history that made them possible," Jackson said. "That's why they blow their chances with foolishness—their style and comportment. You have but a moment or two in the sun. When you have that uniform on, you're one kind of guy. When that uniform comes off, you're a citizen so fast."

Bubba Smith was and remains the most famous of the Underground Railroad players. His thread runs through every chapter of the 1965 and 1966 Spartans thanks to a mammoth physique matched only by an outsized personality. Smith's fame was cemented with his Hollywood career in the *Police Academy* movies and popular Miller Lite beer television commercials that set advertising industry standards. But, as with any tale involving Hollywood fame, there is a deeper underlying story more difficult to distill into scripted punch lines or commercial snapshots.

Jimmy Raye remains the more socially significant story. He faced more obstacles than anticipated to finally emerge as Michigan State's first starting black quarterback, but by the time he graduated and moved into coaching he transcended segregation. He was the first black quarterback from the South to wear a national championship ring.

Notes

1. *Fayetteville Observer*, Dec. 20, 1966.

2. Maureen Dowd, *The New York Times*, March 10, 2013.

3. Clarence Underwood, *Greener Pastures*, 2005, p. 63.

2

JIMMY RAYE DAY

"I wanted so much to come through for this young man, but at the same time I didn't know what to expect. I had been through those areas in the South. On my way down there, I was curious if there would be any white people attending."—Bobby Mitchell

Fayetteville, North Carolina, a city in the early phases of shedding segregation, took the rare—if not unprecedented—step of honoring an African-American man on December 19, 1966 by celebrating the first Jimmy Raye Day.

Pro Football Hall of Famer and integration groundbreaker Bobby Mitchell was living in Washington, D.C., when he received an invitation to speak at Jimmy Raye Day. Normally, the then-Washington Redskins flanker would have turned down such a request to venture 320 miles into the South. Mitchell and other African-Americans of his generation traveled through the segregated South only when necessary. They knew the risks of stopping in the wrong place at the wrong time for something as mundane as using a restroom, eating, or filling up a car's tank with gasoline. In 1959, Mitchell was forced to plan such a trip when his brother died. He was in the second season of his NFL career playing for the Cleveland Browns and made the long drive to his hometown of Hot Springs, Arkansas.

"I had to map out exactly where I could stop all the way from Cleveland to Hot Springs," Mitchell said. "I had to know how far I could go on a tank of gas before I could get more gas. It might be I could have gotten gas at other places, but you didn't know what would happen if you stopped. Driving through the South was frightening. You had to worry about the police pulling you over—all those things. You had to be careful all the way and that was a long trip."

Retired General Colin Powell, whose service to his country included serving as Secretary of State, tells similar stories as a young U.S. Army officer driving through the South in the 1960s from Fort Benning in Georgia to military assignments in Washington, D.C. Powell explained that he and a white Army officer once debated states' rights and property rights after President Lyndon B. Johnson signed the 1964 Civil Rights Act. The white officer argued that citizens should be able to invoke property rights to protect long-standing discriminatory practices. Powell countered that human dignity was behind Johnson's legislation.

"If you're a soldier and you're black, you'd better have a strong bladder, because you won't be stopping much between Washington, D.C., and Fort Benning," he said.[1]

Those were the predicaments African-Americans faced, but Bobby Mitchell was eager to accept this invitation for Jimmy Raye Day. He considered it unlike any other invitation he had received.

Raye was 20 years old and had graduated just 30 months earlier in June 1964 from Fayetteville's black high school, E. E. Smith. He returned to a city that was united, blacks and whites alike, in its support of a nationally known homegrown college quarterback playing at Michigan State. Mitchell and other NFL black players were well aware of Raye's pioneering role. They rooted for Raye's success.

"I wanted so much to come through for this young man, but at the same time I didn't know what to expect," Mitchell said. "I had been through those areas in the South. On my way down there I was curious if there would be any white people attending."

Mitchell's own history of breaking racial barriers in the NFL made him an ideal choice to speak on Jimmy Raye Day. He was the Jackie Robinson of the Washington Redskins, the last NFL team to integrate when avowed racist owner George Preston Marshall finally gave in to pressure from President John F. Kennedy's administration.

The Redskins were at the time the NFL's southern-most franchise and Marshall wanted an all-white team to protect his radio and TV advertising base among southern fans. However, he had a 30-year lease

Bobby Mitchell (l) and Jimmy Raye (r). Photo courtesy Jimmy Raye.

for D.C. Stadium (now RFK Stadium), which was located on federal land. He finally gave in when he was informed that his lease would be revoked if the Redskins did not integrate their roster. Marshall subsequently acquired Mitchell from Cleveland as the most prominent of four black players on the 1962 Redskins.

Jimmy Raye Day was organized by three prominent Fayetteville citizens: Dr. Art Butterfield, a white veterinarian and 1960 graduate of Michigan State; Don Clayton, a white businessman who supported integration; and Bill Hennessee, a black local radio station program director. Clayton served as master of ceremonies and extended the invitation to Mitchell as the keynote speaker.

Clayton was an insurance man in town until 1954 when he founded Putt Putt Fun Center, which grew into a world-wide miniature golf franchise. He was a sportsman right down to his involvement in the Fayetteville High athletic booster club (Fayetteville High is now named Terry Sanford High), even though he did not have a son playing for the high-school teams.

"Don Clayton was an astute businessman," said Ike Walker, one of Raye's high school coaches and a teacher and coach at E.E. Smith. "When the right people take the initiative on something, people take note. Don knew how unusual it was for a black quarterback in 1966. He was profoundly influenced by Jimmy's success."

As Raye began making a name for himself at Michigan State, Clayton noted that Fayetteville's white and black football fans alike enthusiastically followed the hometown kid. First there was the 1965 season that finished with Michigan State's Rose Bowl appearance. Then there was the Game of the Century in 1966, the immortal 10-10 tie with Notre Dame. There also had been Michigan State's 1966 season-opening win when Raye made his first career college start against North Carolina State, a game Michigan State soundly won 28-10.

"Jimmy put Fayetteville on the map when he went to Michigan State and played in the Rose Bowl," said William Carver, one of Raye's high-school coaches and teachers at E.E. Smith. His career later included serving as the athletic director at Fayetteville State University. "People who didn't have a TV would find someone who did. Man, it was phenomenal when he played in the Rose Bowl game. And then the next year there was the 10-10 tie game with Notre Dame. Everybody in Fayetteville—black and white—followed him."

During the 1966 season, the *Fayetteville Observer* adopted Michigan State as a hometown team. The paper ran frequent stories updating readers on the Spartans' unbeaten season and highlighted Raye's role in each victory.

Jimmy Raye Day took place on a Monday when Michigan State was on Christmas break during Raye's junior year. On the Friday before the Monday events, a proclamation from Mayor Monroe E. Evans was read at City Hall.

"WHEREAS, Jimmy Raye has, through his efforts and ability, brought success, fame and honor to himself, to Michigan State University and to Fayetteville, North Carolina; and;

WHEREAS, Jimmy Raye has become a stellar quarterback and exemplifies the top in collegiate sports activities;

NOW, THEREFORE, I, Monroe E. Evans, Mayor of the City of Fayetteville, do hereby proclaim Monday, December 19, 1966, Jimmy Raye Day."

The Monday afternoon events began with a parade and motorcade through downtown streets. The parade began next to the Market House, a memorial to slaves sold a century earlier on the site. The parade was followed by a luncheon at the Downtowner Motor Inn.

The evening dinner program drew 450 people to Horace Sisk Junior High. In addition to Bobby Mitchell, distinguished guests included former North Carolina Governor Terry Sanford and Fort Bragg commanding general Joe Lawrie, a former Louisiana State University quarterback. Michigan State coach Duffy Daugherty was unable to attend due to his commitment to coach the East-West Shrine Game in San Francisco. Assistant coach Al Dorow represented the Spartans instead.

"I was impressed to see black and white people coming together to honor him," said Mitchell. "It was unusual, but I felt so comfortable. Everybody was so nice. You knew he had to be a great player for the town to honor him, but at the same time it said a lot about what a good person he was."

Mitchell's keynote speech objective was to help Raye understand he should trust his talent and endure any tribulations and setbacks.

"My message was that others had gone off to school from the South and if we could make it he could do it," Mitchell said. "I couldn't go to the University of Arkansas, so I went off to Illinois. But you're going to have ups and downs no matter where you go, and you have to make the best of it. He had the additional challenge of being a quarterback when people weren't ready for it, but I reminded him he had the ability to make it or Michigan State wouldn't have taken a chance on him."

In the eyes of Fayetteville denizens, Raye's success was multilayered. He was a hometown athletic hero in addition to a pioneer. E. E. Smith was long known for sending players to historically black colleges under their legendary coach, D.T. Carter, but Raye was the first player from the Golden Bulls' highly successful program to earn a scholarship to an integrated major conference school. Jimmy Raye Day was his triumphant return.

Two Western Union telegrams were delivered. Raye's mother Peggy kept a scrapbook from her oldest son's career and years later the yellowed paper telegrams could be found tucked away in an unmarked envelope.

One telegram was from Daugherty: *"I want to convey my warmest congratulations on Jimmy Raye Day. We are thankful that you have one year left as a Spartan. We could not have been national champs without you."*

The other telegram was from George Romney, Michigan's sitting governor. Michigan's capital city is Lansing, bordering East Lansing, and Romney was a big fan of the Spartans. He sometimes visited the locker room after games, including consoling players after their upset loss at the Rose Bowl in Pasadena: "You had a great season. We're all proud of you."[2]

Romney's telegram to Jimmy Raye came at a time when he was considered a viable candidate for the 1968 Republican presidential nomination. The bid was later thwarted by his 1967 gaffe when he said he was "brainwashed" by generals during a fact-finding trip to Vietnam. But in 1966, Romney was known as a supporter of the Civil Rights movement. He had marched with Martin Luther King Jr. in 1963 in Detroit. He had pushed for a Civil Rights plank at the Republican Party's 1964 convention. When 1964 Republican nominee Barry Goldwater opposed Civil Rights, Romney declined to support Goldwater's campaign. Ironically, by the time George Romney's son Mitt Romney was a presidential candidate in 2008 and 2012, Mitt Romney and the Republican Party had turned back toward views closer to Goldwater's than his own father's. George Romney was a moderate. Decades later Mitt Romney ran as a plutocrat with less support from African-Americans and Hispanics than previous Republican candidates.

Unlike some football fans, George Romney's enthusiasm for the Spartans was not dimmed when Daugherty played Raye as his starting quarterback. Traveling to North Carolina for a sports banquet would have been more than could be expected from a Michigan politician, but Romney's telegram suggests he understood the social significance of a Southern city honoring a black man in 1966: *"Unable to attend tonight's dinner in honor of Michigan State's mighty-might, Jimmy Raye. Congratulations to Jimmy for his inspiration, leadership and outstanding play as MSU achieved its fabulous gridiron achievement two years in a row. MSU is still number one in my book and Jimmy Raye helped make it so. Best regards to Jimmy and to all others at tonight's dinner."*

Coach D.T. Carter [l] with Jimmy Raye on Jimmy Raye Day. Photo courtesy Jimmy Raye.

The dinner program opened with comments from E.E. Smith head coach D.T. Carter, whose reputation in the community was as a hard-nosed football coach. Carter, a quarterback at Virginia Union University, trusted Raye with play-calling unlike any of his previous quarterbacks. Jimmy Raye, Carter told the assembled audience, was "[a]n athlete's athlete, and a coach's athlete. Because he works so hard, he inspires others to work hard."[3]

Dorow, an assistant coach under Daugherty from 1965 to 1970, explained how Raye earned the starting job. Daugherty's primary concern about Raye was his arm strength, which came as a surprise to the Fayetteville audience since Raye had been known as a passing quarterback at E.E. Smith. Dorow told the crowd Raye was self-motivated and went to work as soon as the Rose Bowl ended and school resumed. "All winter long, you'd find Jimmy down by the gym throwing that football during his spare hours," Dorow said. "He'd corral anybody to do the catching, and if he couldn't find anyone he'd throw into a net."[4]

Raye, who always has been an understated man, thanked the Jimmy Raye Day audience at the end of the night. "No thrill has so elated me before, and never have I been so full of joy," he said. "From the bottom of my heart, I pray that I will never let any of you down."[5]

To paraphrase a tongue-in-cheek line told in different pockets of the South about pioneering black athletes breaking barriers, you could say Jimmy Raye did more for integration in Fayetteville than Martin Luther King.

The dinner took place only three years after the peak of the Civil Rights movement in Fayetteville—the demonstrations led by students at Fayetteville State Teachers College (now Fayetteville State University).

Fayetteville State history professor Dr. Stanley Johnson was a student at the school from 1959 to 1963. Johnson also was a leader in a black group known as the Demonstration Committee. The student group organized the first marches and sit-ins staged downtown, echoing similar civic turmoil from the era throughout the South. Johnson participated in one sit-in where a business owner poured ammonia on the floor, forcing demonstrators to abandon their protest. He remembers when the police broke up another protest and the next day's newspaper printed a photograph of the police arresting a black protester. In the background, a then-segregated movie theater marquee advertised its latest film, *The Ugly American*, the 1963 movie starring Marlon Brando.

But, for the most part, the city police and mobs of white citizens did not respond to protesters with the brutal tactics of fire hoses and police dogs infamously used in Birmingham, Alabama, by Bull Connor and his policemen in 1963. Johnson said there were several factors working to temper the response from Fayetteville's city officials, police, mobs, and even the Ku Klux Klan. For one, resistance to desegregation was stronger in Deep South states, such as Alabama and Mississippi, which had large slave populations prior to the Civil War. North Carolina never had the number of sprawling cotton plantations or large slave populations found in the Deep South. A second reason: the presence of integrated Fort Bragg, the U.S. Army base bordering the city. Fort Bragg brass made it clear to city officials if there was violence in Fayetteville, city businesses would be declared off-limits for Fort Bragg personnel.

City officials understood the possible consequences—a severe financial impact on the local economy. The city attorney at the time was J.O. Tally, whom Johnson says met with the Demonstration Committee about their concerns. Tally's family had been long established and invested in Fayetteville. He began a Fayetteville law firm in 1948, Tally and Tally, still run by family members. Stanley Johnson remembers Tally advised then-mayor Wilbur Clark "that change was coming" and the city needed to progressively plan for it.

A third reason, Johnson said, was the significant number of white people in Fayetteville supporting desegregation. They asked to meet with the Demonstration Committee.

"A group came to the campus and wanted to know what they could do to help," Johnson said. "I remember I asked one of the persons, 'Since a number of you feel this way, why haven't we heard these voices before?' They said because in the past they didn't see indications from African-Americans—although we weren't called African-Americans then—that they wanted to do anything about it. They said a number of people didn't believe in segregation, but they didn't see an initiative from the African-Americans to stop it."

As the demonstrations and sit-ins gained traction, Mayor Clark formed the Mayor's Bi-Racial Committee on June 19, 1963. The mayor and city council began applying subtle pressure on business owners to desegregate during the summer and gradually increased the pressure. It was a slow process and demonstrations continued, but by the time the President Johnson signed the 1964 Civil Rights Act on July 2 of that year, Fayetteville's downtown hotels and theaters had been desegregated and most restaurants and lunch counters were desegregated.[6]

"I can remember when I was a senior in high school," said Raye of the 1963-64 school year. "We no longer had to go around to the back of the theater to get in and then have to sit in the balcony."

Some segregated pockets held out as long as possible. The country club where Don Clayton's daughter Donna planned to be married in the summer of 1968 was one. The invitation list included a longtime employee of her father's business who was black, Alvin Taylor. When the Claytons learned Taylor and his family would not be permitted by the country club to attend, they moved the wedding to a church.

A young Jimmy Raye at his parents' house. Photo courtesy Jimmy Raye.

"I'm so grateful I had eyes to see how unfair the structure of society was to so many people," said Donna Clayton Lloyd, who lives and works in Fayetteville in the real-estate business. "I believe my father helped push those integration discussions."

Jimmy Raye Day was tangible evidence the Michigan State quarterback had followed the urging of his teachers and mentors at E.E. Smith and Seabrook Park to take advantage of new opportunities previously denied people of color. Break barriers and set an example, they urged. Use the changing mood of the country to push the cause of integration.

"The teachers at E.E. Smith had gotten their education at historically black schools, and they were leaders in the community," Raye said. "They impressed upon us to go forward and diversify. I wasn't the only guy in my class who went to a white college. Our mindset was to expand and to go forward so those coming behind us could see that they had opportunities. I had friends who went to North Carolina Chapel Hill and North Carolina Greensboro who became lawyers."

Raye's success at Michigan State inspired Clyde Chesney, who graduated from E.E. Smith after Raye, to take the next step in his football career at North Carolina State—which by then had begun accepting a handful of African-American players. Chesney had originally enrolled at N.C. State as a student before making the football team as a walk-on athlete. He earned varsity letters in the 1969, 1970, and 1971 seasons.

N.C. State's first black player had been Marcus Martin as a walk-on in 1967, but Chesney was N.C. State's first black starter as a defensive end. He also was the Wolfpack's first black player voted All-Academic Atlantic Coast Conference honors as a senior in 1971.

Chesney earned BA and MA degrees at N.C. State, but he later completed his PhD at Michigan State in 1980. He was an administrator at Tennessee State University at the time of his death in 2012.

Michigan State's Underground Railroad players acknowledged that their Civil Rights role was limited to their presence on the football field, but Raye's inspiration of Chesney is an example of how they influenced the future. They were not actively involved in the protest movement, but the fact that they were written about in newspapers and seen on TV blazing trails was a significant contribution. They helped turn civil wrongs right.

"It was important for anybody, and certainly for younger people, to see that Jimmy was leading Michigan State's squad," says Ernest Green of the Little Rock Nine. "Jimmy is an achiever."

Ike Walker, who was an E.E. Smith assistant coach in both football and basketball when Raye played, was among those in the audience at Jimmy Raye Day. He says Raye has paid back his community many times over with the Jimmy Raye Youth Foundation. Raye began the foundation in 2003 with his longtime friend and mentor, Ronnie Chalmers.

Chalmers passed away in 2005, but once a year in late June it is essentially Jimmy Raye Weekend in Fayetteville. He returns home to host a free football clinic and put on a dinner to raise scholarship funds for Fayetteville youth. The funds also provide registration fees for under-privileged children to play on youth sports teams.

Raye's clout around the NFL can be measured by the friends who make the trip to appear at the clinic and the dinner. The keynote speakers have included Super Bowl champion coaches Tony Dungy of the

Indianapolis Colts and Mike McCarthy of the Green Bay Packers. The former players have included Pro Football Hall of Famers Marcus Allen to Mean Joe Greene, as well as former Michigan State athletes and Fayetteville high school graduates that made it to the NFL. Also prominent is Jimmy's son, Jimmy Raye III, a vice-president for player operations with the NFL's Indianapolis Colts.

Marcus Allen was the 1981 Heisman Trophy winner, Super Bowl XVIII MVP, and 1985 NFL MVP. He played for the Kansas City Chiefs when Raye was the Chiefs' running backs coach in the 1990s. Allen not only attends Raye's event every year, he serves as the master of ceremonies.

"He's a man of honor, a man of integrity, and excellence," Allen said. "As players, we always knew that he cared about us. That's why so many of us care so much about him."[7]

Former NFL quarterback Sean Salisbury and former NFL fullback Lorenzo Neal did not play for Raye, but like Allen they hold him in high regard.

Salisbury was at the peak of his ESPN commentary tenure when he appeared in the early days of the clinic and dinner in 2006. "He's one of those guys who speaks softly," Salisbury said, "but when he speaks, you listen. I've been a fan of his for a long time, as a coach and even more important as a person."[8]

Neal, one of the best blocking fullbacks in NFL history, rescheduled plans in 2006 in order to travel to Fayetteville after an invitation from Raye.

"He just has an aura about him," Neal said. "When a man of that caliber calls you up and asks you to help him out, you rearrange your schedule and say, 'I'll do whatever I can.'"[9]

Wallace Wright was a New York Jets wide receiver from Fayetteville's Pine Forest High when Raye was a Jets assistant coach. Wright said the name Jimmy Raye still resonates among kids in the city decades after he left for Michigan State.

"We knew who Jimmy Raye was when I was growing up," Wright said at the 10th anniversary clinic. "He played at Michigan State. He was a college football hero. That's why all these NFL players come to his clinics. He's not only a great football coach, but a great individual and asset to the community. It was an honor for me to be on the same team with him when we were with the Jets."

In the course of a half-century of achievement and influence, Jimmy Raye Day evolved into the Jimmy Raye Youth Foundation.

"Over the years, untold numbers of people have told me they identified with me and they have gone forward because they saw me play quarterback at Michigan State," Raye said. "We were predominantly a black team. We changed things for the black athlete. When you're going through it, you don't always think of it that way. But we changed the face of college football."

On Jimmy Raye Day, Bobby Mitchell, a football icon with his own Jackie Robinson label, saw black and white citizens of Fayetteville gather to honor a favorite son. Jimmy Raye Day is an example of what happens when a group gets to know the person and not the stereotype.

Notes

1. Colin Powell with Joseph E. Persico, *My American Journey*, Random House, 1995, p. 114.

2. *Los Angeles Times*, Jan. 3, 1966.

3. Ed Seaman, *Fayetteville Observer*, Dec. 20, 1966.

4. *Ibid.*

5. *Ibid.*

6. Brian Suttell, *Countdown to Downtown: The Civil Rights Protest Movement in Downtown Fayetteville, North Carolina.* M.A., NCSU, 2007.

7. *Fayetteville Observer*, June 28, 2006.

8. *Ibid.*

9. *Ibid.*

3

SEABROOK AND E.E. SMITH

"My grandmother told my mother, 'That boy is going to play ball for a living one day.' That impacted my mother. My mother felt if the Lord gives you talent, you should not squander it. She thought you should be able to express your talent, so she allowed me to play on Friday nights in high school."—Jimmy Raye

James Arthur Sr. and Peggy Raye raised five children in the segregated city of Fayetteville, at a house on 1610 Murchison Road with a backyard bordered by the grounds of a dynamic recreation facility, Seabrook Park.

Seabrook Park featured ball fields, outdoor basketball courts, a swimming pool and—most significantly—mentors to teach fundamentals and sportsmanship and to emphasize education. From a young age, Jimmy, the second oldest child, stepped out the back door, crossed the backyard in a few strides and waded into his playground, where he found everything he needed to shape his future. He played in endless pickup games and on organized youth league teams.

Raye was still a regular at Seabrook in his high-school years at E.E. Smith. He was an all-state quarterback and two-time all-state basketball guard for the Golden Bulls in what was known as North Carolina Negro High School Athletic Association. Early in his high-school career, he was better known as a high-scoring guard than a quarterback.

Anyone looking for Raye knew three places to search—home, school or Seabrook. In fact, that's how Raye first met James Harris, another pioneering black quarterback, destined to embark upon a groundbreaking path.

Raye was home sleeping when word spread across Seabrook that a big kid had shown up and dominated the basketball courts. "Shack"—as Harris was known in his 13 years as a National Football League quarterback—and his family were visiting Fayetteville from Louisiana to see his older brother stationed at Fort Bragg, the nearby U.S. Army base.

Allen Cole, Ronnie Chalmers, and Jimmy Raye at the Fayetteville Sports Club Hall of Fame induction.

"Some friends came over and said I had to see this guy who could really shoot," Raye said. "When I met Shack, he says, 'Let two great hands meet'—and he shook his own hands. We started playing games. Word started to spread and more and more people kept coming to watch. We had a thousand people watching."

Raye and Harris became lifelong friends from that first meeting, and would meet again at Michigan State. Raye was going through spring drills preparing for his sophomore season in 1965 when he served as Harris' host on his recruiting trip.

Despite their epic showdown in Seabrook lore, the park was about more than big kids holding court. Watching over Raye and thousands of others over the years were Art "Monk" Smith and Ronnie "Chase" Chalmers. Smith began working in the parks department in 1946. Chalmers, who was only three years older than Raye, worked under Smith as early as his high-school years. He was later a teacher and coach in the Fayetteville public schools in addition to working 40-plus years as a youth sports advocate.

Seabrook Park was renamed Smith Recreation Center, and the Seabrook pool was renamed Chalmers Pool. Smith was 85 when he died in 2011, and Chalmers was 61 when he passed away in 2005.

"My father worked hard to keep that pool open when there were budget cuts or political initiatives to close it," said Chalmers' daughter Melody, who was named E.E. Smith's principal in 2011. "My father felt providing recreation sports was so important to helping kids stay out of trouble. Jimmy Raye's family had a lot to do with the pool being named for my father."

In Seabrook's nurturing environment, Raye, like many kids in their youth, began to dream of playing college and then professional sports. The early footprints Raye hoped to follow were E.E. Smith athletes who went off to college and returned to Seabrook on school breaks to hold court. Raye watched the games, always on the lookout for tips.

Fortunately for Raye, his grandmother, Georgia Harper Monroe, saw his love of sports at a young age and recognized sooner than anyone he had a future in athletics. The Rayes were Seventh-Day Adventists and Jimmy's mother Peggy was devout. Seventh-Day Adventists consider the Sabbath a time of rest at home from Friday sunset to Saturday sunset. It may well have presented a looming conflict for a teenager intending to play Friday night high-school football and basketball.

Jimmy's father was a boxer in the military, but his mother pulled no punches. There were no sports conflicts with the Sabbath in her mind.

"My grandmother told my mother, 'That boy is going to play ball for a living one day,'" Raye said. "That impacted my mother. My mother felt if the Lord gives you talent, you should not squander it. She thought you should be able to express your talent, so she allowed me to play on Friday nights in high school."

Raye and so many others gained their athletic foundation on youth sports teams coached by Smith and Chalmers. One year during Raye's Pee Wee football days, Smith took the team out to Fort Bragg to play an integrated squad of military dependents. It was the first and only time Raye played against white kids until he arrived at Michigan State as a freshman.

"Monk Smith used to say they put air in the ball the same as we do," Raye said. "The ball's dimensions are the same. Just go do what you do."

Smith influenced many youths before and after Raye's era, including Charlie Baggett, who lived next door to the Raye family at 1612 Murchison Road. Baggett, seven years younger than Raye, was a 1971 E.E. Smith graduate. He followed Raye to Michigan State and was a three-year starting quarterback (1973-75) for the Spartans, playing one pro season in the Canadian Football League with the Hamilton Tiger-Cats before tracing Raye's coaching footprints with a 35-year career in both the college ranks and NFL.

"Monk Smith was instrumental in our early development," Baggett said. "It was not only sports, it was in life. Monk exposed us to everything kids learn now at places like the Boys and Girls Club. We played everything—football, basketball, baseball and ran track. Now kids want to specialize in sports. We did it all. We lived at Seabrook."

Smith's influence was broader than sports. He had the kids work odd jobs, such as cutting grass to raise money to rent a bus for field trips. There were camping trips into North Carolina's eastern beaches and western mountains.

"It was something we looked forward to every year," Baggett said. "Monk Smith would take us different places to expose us to different things. He prepared us for life. He was way ahead of his time."

Other beneficiaries of Smith and Chalmers were the coaches at E.E. Smith. The Seabrook youths were taken to another level by Golden Bulls head football coach D.T. Carter and head basketball coach D.S. Kelly. Ike Walker and William Carver were assistants who succeeded their bosses, with Walker a longtime head basketball coach and Carver a longtime head football coach.

"One of those reasons we did so well in sports is they did such a good job introducing kids to sports at Seabrook," Walker said. "They were like godfathers to those kids."

Raye was a three-sport high-school athlete: a three-year starter at quarterback, a three-year starter in basketball, and cleanup batter and catcher in baseball.

In football, D.T. Carter introduced Raye into a sophisticated game for the high-school level in the early 1960s. Carter was a demanding coach—in essence, he was the original "Coach Carter" before actor Samuel L. Jackson played the role in a movie about a California basketball coach—and he knew football from having played quarterback at Virginia Union University, a historically black school. He ran a split-T offense that lined up a receiver wide and a tight end. (In those days receivers were called offensive ends and lined up shoulder to shoulder with the tackle.) Carter's offense balanced running and passing in an era when most high schools stuck to basic run-oriented schemes with full-house backfields.

The Carter Stadium rock dedicated to coach Dennis T. Carter. Photo by the author.

His memory lives on to the present. There is a memorial rock in one end zone of D.T. Carter Stadium dedicated to the football coach's memory. The Golden Bulls players tap the rock as they run onto the field for pre-game warm-ups.

In Jimmy Raye's senior year in 1963, he threw for nine touchdowns and ran for eight in nine games. That might sound modest when viewed against today's game with rules designed to favor offense and scoring, but in that same 1963 college season, Navy quarterback Roger Staubach finished with nine touchdown passes and seven rushing touchdowns in 11 games—good enough to win the Heisman Trophy.

Coach Dennis T. Carter. Photo courtesy Jimmy Raye.

Among Raye's highlights, he threw 41- and 22-yard touchdown passes against Lumberton Hayswood, a 67-yard touchdown pass with a one-yard touchdown run against Raleigh Ligon and 66- and 45-yard touchdown passes against Henderson Institute.

For Raye to learn advanced football was beneficial to his future, but the bad news was Carter's background meant he was hardest on quarterbacks. Raye was around him as long as anyone as a three-year starter when he led the Golden Bulls to 21-3-4 overall record.

"I wouldn't know how to characterize our relationship as anything other than love-hate," Raye said. "He was an interesting person—an enigma. He was a very intense and demanding guy. He didn't give much and ran a dictatorial environment."

But Carter loosened the reins when he recognized the future college and NFL coach's football IQ. Jimmy Raye was the first quarterback Carter allowed to call his own plays.

"We were playing a team from Rocky Mount and we weren't playing very well," Raye said. "It was a team we should have been beating handily, and he was upset at halftime. Then he said, 'Jimmy, you got it.' From that point on, midway through my junior year, and through my senior year, I called all the plays."

On crucial plays, Kelly might call a timeout and confer with Raye. "Your number is a good number," he'd say, meaning keep the ball on a run or call a pass play.

Raye was just as reliable in basketball with a scoring average around 20 points. In his junior year, he scored 23 points against Greensboro Dudley, but he was outscored by Charlie Sanders; the future University of Minnesota tight end and Pro Football Hall of Famer went for 24 points in a win over Smith. A photo in the *Greensboro Daily News* depicted Raye and Sanders battling for a rebound.

E.E. Smith boasted of a rich athletic tradition, but Walker said it was the Smith administration's emphasis on the classroom that kept him teaching and coaching at the school for 31 years until he retired in 1989.

"I never knew of any coach at E.E. Smith who asked a teacher to give a kid a grade to keep him academically eligible to play sports," remembered Walker. "When our athletes left the football field or the basketball court, they had their books under their arms. The teachers did not let them get by with anything. The teachers were dedicated people. Academics came first at E.E. Smith. You name it, you'll find it among E.E. Smith graduates: doctors, lawyers, military men."

Raye, who graduated 21st in a class of 178, planned to become a lawyer until Michigan State coach Duffy Daugherty steered him into coaching following his two-year NFL career as a defensive back with the Los Angeles Rams and Philadelphia Eagles.

Education was emphasized to the Raye children—Pat, Jimmy, Donald, Pamela, and Craig—at home as well as at school. Pat was the oldest and went off to Fayetteville State University as the family's first to graduate from college. Four of the five siblings earned bachelor degrees, and Pat, Pamela, and Craig added graduate degrees. Craig followed his brother Jimmy to Michigan State a decade later as a walk-on wide receiver. He also earned a master's degree before launching his own college coaching career.

E.E. Smith was founded in 1927 as Fayetteville's black high school and has survived desegregation to maintain its standing in the community. With the end of segregation in the late 1960s, most black high schools with inferior facilities were closed down or converted to elementary schools. But E.E. Smith is one of only six formerly all-black North Carolina high schools that remain open, along with Durham Hillside, West Charlotte, Greensboro Dudley, and two Winston-Salem schools, Atkins and Carver.

The school was named for Ezekiel Ezra Smith, who graduated from Raleigh Institute (now Shaw University) in 1875. In 1883, Smith relocated to Fayetteville and began a 50-year association as president of Fayetteville State. His tenure was interrupted when he was named U.S. Ambassador to Liberia in 1888 by President Grover Cleveland, but he returned to the college. He later donated 45 acres to continue development of the school.

Melody Chalmers, an E.E. Smith graduate who began her career as a teacher at her alma mater, was only the 11th principal in E.E. Smith's then-84-year history when she was named to the position. In the 2012-13 school year, four of the five E.E. Smith administrators and 23 of 150 staff members were E.E. Smith graduates.

"It's truly an honor to return to the school and support the mission and vision of our predecessors," Chalmers said. "The alumni play an integral role in maintaining the standing of our school. They provide time and political support. We're no longer a black school, but we are dedicated to providing a safe learning environment for all of our students."

E.E. Smith lacked resources in its segregated school days, but it was never short on high standards. The administration and teachers were taskmasters—even at the expense of a scholarship to a Big Ten school. There is a story embedded in E.E. Smith lore about how future NFL player Doug Wilkerson lost his scholarship to Michigan State.

Wilkerson, a 1966 E.E. Smith graduate, was a sophomore on the Golden Bulls varsity when Raye was a senior. By Wilkerson's senior year he planned to join Raye at Michigan State until his scholarship was revoked—but not by the NCAA or Spartans head coach Duffy Daugherty. E.E. Smith principal E.E. Miller telephoned Daugherty and informed him that Wilkerson's punishment for an incident on campus included the loss of his Michigan State scholarship. Wilkerson instead attended North Carolina College (now North Carolina Central), a historically black school in Durham.

"That was Mr. Miller's decision—he was the principal," Wilkerson said. "It would have been nice to have gone up to Michigan State and played with Jimmy, but that's the way it came down. I never looked back and always kept moving forward."

The cause was an after-school incident on campus started by a student egging Wilkerson into a footrace with a wager. Wilkerson finally relented and won the race. The antagonist refused to pay up.

"Doug took him out behind the school and dropped him on his head," said Jimmy Harvey, who was then a junior at E.E. Smith and went on to play football and baseball at Winston-Salem State University. "The message was clear to the rest of us: If they could do that to Doug, the best athlete in the school, you better stay out of trouble."

Daugherty and Wilkerson, of course, could have ignored the principal's punishment since no NCAA rules had been broken and no legal authorities were involved. Wilkerson said Daugherty never tried to intervene and Wilkerson never asked him to do so.

"Society has changed," said Julian Brown, a 1971 E.E. Smith alum who works at the school as its community outreach coordinator. "At that time in the black community, principals and ministers were very respected. Mr. Miller was revered and feared. He was letting Doug know that behavior was more important than football in the Big Ten. Mr. Miller had an expression that all the students understood: 'Young man or young lady, count the telephone poles.' That meant you were suspended; count the telephone poles on your way home from school."

In the end, the principal's punishment hurt Michigan State more than Wilkerson. "Moosie," as he was known in his NFL days, was an NFL first-round draft pick in 1970. The 15-year veteran was a three-time Pro Bowler from his time with the San Diego Chargers, including the Air Coryell era. In addition to the Fayetteville Hall of Fame, he has been inducted into the San Diego Chargers Hall of Fame. Meanwhile, Michigan State could have used Wilkerson to help stem the program's decline in what were his college varsity seasons—3-7 in 1967, 5-5 in 1968, and 4-6 in 1969.

Despite the severe punishment, Wilkerson remained true to his school and coaches. He returned home from college and helped condition players. Harvey said Wilkerson worked them to exhaustion.

"We hated to see Doug come around," said Harvey, who now works on the alumni foundation. "During the morning workouts, we'd be saying to each other, 'Please, Mrs. Wilkerson, come get your son and take him home for lunch. Give us a break!'"

Wilkerson said he merely continued a tradition of past E.E. Smith athletes. He remembered his high school years, when Bishop Harris came home from North Carolina Central. Harris was later a teacher and coach at E.E. Smith before he moved on to college and the NFL. He coached at Duke, LSU, Notre Dame, and other schools before he became the head coach at his alma mater, North Carolina Central. He started his NFL career with the Denver Broncos under Dan Reeves.

"You always try to give back to Fayetteville," Wilkerson said. "That's the way it was when I was younger."

The school pride is evident every Memorial Day weekend for the annual E.E. Smith Alumni and Friends Reunion. It began in 1977 on the school's 50th anniversary and soon developed a college-like atmosphere. It is a three-day event that includes all graduating classes, with turnouts of 3,000 to 3,500 people. There is a golf tournament, alumni games, and a Saturday all-day festival at D.T. Carter Stadium.

The reunion weekend's Blue and Gold Gala raises money to annually present four scholarships. Other graduates have established scholarships related to the school. Charlie Baggett's family funded one to honor Charlie's uncle, longtime coach Ike Walker.

The predictable turnout of out-of-town visitors for the reunion eventually led to Fayetteville hotels, knowing they can count on a weekend sellout, to submit bids to the school's alumni association to gain the designation as the reunion headquarters.

"I don't think you'll find another school in the country with so many graduates working and volunteering for their alma mater," Brown said. "The passion and respect for this school's history is unique. I don't know of many high schools that can boast of an alumni association like ours that is like a college."

The Seabrook and E.E. Smith experiences and environments have remained linked by their proximity and the relationships of the mentors and students.

It was at the Seabrook pool now bearing Chalmers' name where he and Raye had a conversation that changed Raye's life. Raye worked as a lifeguard at the pool in June of his senior year in 1964. By then, college enrollment was rapidly approaching and Raye was undecided on his future. Chalmers asked Raye the latest on his college plans. Raye mentioned Johnson C. Smith University in Charlotte and other historically black colleges.

"What about Michigan State?" Chalmers asked.

"I haven't heard from them since December," Raye said.

Michigan State had actively recruited Raye only from early November to early December in 1963 before the communications lines mysteriously went silent. Spartans assistant coach Cal Stoll, who recruited the Carolinas, had discussed bringing Raye up for a recruiting trip, but that was before the world was turned upside down by the assassination of President John F. Kennedy on November 22, 1963 in Dallas.

The nation was in mourning and many plans were canceled, postponed, and rescheduled. Michigan State was supposed to meet Illinois on November 23 at Spartan Stadium in a regular season finale that would decide the Big Ten title and Rose Bowl berth. The game was postponed to November 28, and when the teams reassembled in the somber national mood, the Spartans lost 13-0. The Illini defense, led by All-American linebacker Dick Butkus, shut down Michigan State All-American halfback Sherman Lewis.

The previously discussed plans for Raye to visit Michigan State never developed, even though Stoll traveled to North Carolina to watch Raye play in the annual Black Shrine All-Star game on December 7 at County Stadium in Durham.

Stoll saw Raye earn the Most Valuable Player Trophy as he led the East to a 31-0 win over the West. Raye threw two touchdown passes of 8 and 4 yards and directed two more touchdown drives. Stoll was pictured presenting the MVP trophy to Raye in the next day's *Durham Morning Herald*, but Raye believed Stoll returned to Michigan State with a misperception that he was a running quarterback. The East coach of the all-star game ran a Wing-T run-oriented scheme that Raye was forced to learn in practices and direct in the game.

Instead of Raye receiving increased interest from Michigan State for his MVP performance, he was stumped by the lack of communication. Big-brother/mentor Chalmers was equally surprised, but he offered an idea.

"My dad and Jimmy were like brothers," Melody Chalmers said. "They were truly best friends. Anyone would be envious to have a friendship as close as they were."

Throughout Chalmers' life as an educator and youth sports advocate, he prodded Fayetteville kids to aggressively pursue opportunities. He did so here with Jimmy Raye.

"Let's write a letter," Chalmers advised.

The letter they crafted worked. Jimmy Raye was invited to Michigan State by assistant coach Vince Carillot on a recruiting trip. Raye boarded an airplane on July 27 for his first flight only weeks before fall camp opened in the era of nine-game seasons and late-September season openers. Raye toured Michigan State's campus with Charlie Thornhill as his host and learned about Michigan State academically and athletically. Duffy Daugherty, however, remained skeptical about Raye's passing ability. Daugherty told Carillot to take Raye out to Spartan Stadium and test his arm.

Carillot, Raye, and offensive end Gene Washington, a future two-time All-American who would lead the team in receiving in the fall for the first of three straight years, worked out on Spartan Stadium's lush turf. Daugherty was essentially leaving the final decision to Carillot.

"I had him throw me some balls and then I had him throw Gene some passes," Carillot said. "I told Duffy, 'Good Lord, he's got a great arm. Don't worry about that.' Jimmy just looked like he could be a good player. You could tell right away Jimmy was a special guy."

When Raye's scholarship was a reported in the *Fayetteville Observer*, Carter told the paper he was "one of the best athletes I've ever coached. He's a natural leader and was what made us go during his three years at Smith."[1]

Chalmers, who earned his bachelor's degree from Johnson C. Smith, later followed Raye to Michigan State. He earned his master's degree and served as a football team manager. He returned home and continued his 30-year teaching career, but he never wavered from his dedication to youth sports. Chalmers and Jimmy Raye's older sister Pat worked together to run a National Youth Sports Program with federal funding through nearby Fayetteville State University.

As adults Raye and Chalmers collaborated on their biggest project. Chalmers presented Raye with an idea to start the Jimmy Raye Youth Foundation, which celebrated its 10th anniversary in June 2012. Raye puts on a free football clinic every June with many of the biggest names in the NFL answering Raye's request to appear. The foundation funds scholarships and youth fees for under-privileged kids to enter youth leagues. Raye funds the foundation with sales from his non-profit Jimmy Raye Barbecue Sauce—which is found on sale at the E.E. Smith reunion weekend. There also is a Jimmy Raye Youth Foundation fundraising banquet the weekend of the free clinic.

Chalmers passed away in 2005 a little more than one month before the third JRYF clinic. The headline in the May 9 *Fayetteville Observer*: "Youth sports lose a friend." Raye was quoted in the article: "I speak with a very heavy heart about someone that never sought any limelight or praise for anything he did. He was always there for the community and the kids and anyone that needed a hand."

Raye was offensive coordinator with the Oakland Raiders at the time, but JRYF has thrived no matter what corner of the map his NFL coaching career has taken him. Raye's family and Chalmers' family and others in Fayetteville have carried the torch with Chalmers' spirit.

"We're proud to continue it every year with Jimmy and his family," says Melody Chalmers. "We all feel like family working on the foundation. My father worked hard to see it come to fruition and it is part of our father's legacy."

Those opportunities for others through the JRYF all hearken back to when Raye's grandmother recognized his love of sports. Raye's mother kept a scrapbook throughout his high-school and college playing careers. As his high-school days wound down and college beckoned, Peggy Raye wrote a message in the scrapbook. She did not forget her own mother's prophecy in her hand-written words.

My Dear Big Son:

I'm very proud of you and I am very glad I didn't let your talent go to waste. I hope wherever you go in life that you will always remember my motto: "Make something of yourself and use your talent to the highest because God gave it to you and with Him in everything you do you will always come out on top." Good luck, son. Be a good boy and always remember I am your #1 fan. I have pushed you as far as you are and now I believe you will make it.

Your mother

Notes

1. *Fayetteville Observer*, August 23, 1964.

4

SANDY STEPHENS AND THE BIG O

"I never got that image of Sandy Stephens out of my mind. Back then when they introduced the players on TV at the start of the games. The players would say their name, position and hometown and then step off. All of the sudden he came on and said, 'Sandy Stephens, quarterback, Uniontown, Pennsylvania.' I thought, 'Wow, I could do that.' I knew about him, but I didn't know he was black. I would have never thought there would have been a black quarterback."—Jimmy Raye

Television spotlighted the Michigan State's Underground Railroad football teams of the mid-1960s, sending a message to the nation that black athletes like quarterback Jimmy Raye could play leadership roles on a top-ranked team. Civil Rights leaders Jesse Jackson and Ernest Green say it was important for Raye, Bubba Smith, George Webster, and other prominent black athletes to be seen on television and in newspapers, magazines, and stadiums.

Their role was to clear a path. They could contribute to Civil Rights progress without taking part in protests. The positive image of black athletes portrayed on TV the past half-century has been an overlooked influence on American race relations.

Jimmy Raye was a high-school sophomore and starting varsity quarterback in segregated Fayetteville when television provided him a chance to see University of Minnesota quarterback Sandy Stephens play on TV in the 1962 Rose Bowl (following the 1961 season). When Stephens' image appeared on the screen and he introduced himself, it was a pivotal moment for Raye to understand what was possible for his future dreams. Stephens was college football's first black All-American quarterback and first black quarterback to win a national title, but Raye learned Stephens was black through the power of television.

"I never got that image of Sandy Stephens out of my mind," Raye said. "Back then they introduced the players on TV at the start of the games. You would say your name, your position, hometown, and then step off. All of a sudden he came on and said, 'Sandy Stephens, quarterback, Uniontown, Pennsylvania.' I thought, 'Wow, I could do that.' I knew about him, but I didn't know he was black. I would have never thought there would have been a black quarterback."

It's unlikely Raye was alone in this revelation when Stephens' face flashed across TV screens. Black athletes breaking barriers was not commonly reported in the print media prior to the Civil Rights movement.

Chris Lamb is a professor of journalism at Indiana University-Indianapolis who authored a book on Jackie Robinson breaking pro baseball's color line, *Blackout: The Untold Story of Jackie Robinson's First Spring Training*. The book details how little the mainstream press covered Robinson's first spring training.

"Sportswriters wrote little about race and less about the skin color of athletes for a number of reasons," Lamb said. "Editors didn't want their writers to write about race because it made readers and advertisers uncomfortable."

Television wasn't yet prevalent in college basketball in 1958 when the 10th annual Dixie Classic, a three-day, eight-team holiday tournament, took place at North Carolina State's famed Reynolds Coliseum over the 1958 Christmas break.

Without the benefit of TV games to watch, Raye, 60 miles to the south in Fayetteville, had to imagine the play of two black All-American players in the Classic. When the University of Cincinnati's Oscar Robertson and Michigan State's Jumpin' Johnny Green took the court, the only avenues to follow results were through the radio, the newspaper, or word of mouth, but the moments were nonetheless impactful on Raye.

"Oscar scored 30 points in all three games," Raye said with pride more than a half-century later, recalling the tournament on a summer afternoon back home in Fayetteville for his annual Jimmy Raye Youth Foundation free football camp.

That's how much it meant to an impressionable kid to see a black athlete performing and succeeding on an integrated stage. The Big O actually scored 29, 29, and 29, but that's a close enough memory for 50-plus years later.

Robertson put together his scoring barrage despite the Reynolds Coliseum fans, opponents, and referees heaping abuse upon him. In Robertson's 2003 autobiography, *The Big O: My Life, My Times, My Game*, he detailed the verbal abuse from the crowd and the rough play. He said he heard fans calling him "nigger," "porter," and "redcap." They also hurled pennies and hotdogs at him.[1]

The 1958 Dixie Classic was essentially the first time black players had been invited. Seton Hall brought one black player in 1957, but he was a backup player who saw limited playing time. Perhaps if television had been prevalent at the time, cameras could have shined a light with images of the physical and verbal abuse Robertson and Green endured. It could have re-shaped racial attitudes similar to the turning point in the Civil Rights movement in 1963 when TV cameras exposed Bull Connor and his Birmingham policemen beating protesters with fire hoses, clubs, and dogs.

Raye—and other youths like him of his generation—nearly missed the chance to see Stephens on TV. Some improbable machinations played out before Minnesota was invited as the Rose Bowl's third choice after Alabama and Ohio State, with the enlightening prose of the *Los Angeles Times* sports columnist Jim Murray playing an enormous role. The public response in Southern California to Murray's articles prevented Alabama coach Paul "Bear" Bryant usurping the Rose Bowl invitation from a Big Ten school.

Alabama was 8-0 and ranked first in the nation when Bryant learned a Rose Bowl invitation for his Crimson Tide was possible. There had been a contract between the Big Ten and the then-Pacific Coast Conference champions in place since 1947, but a lapse in the deal raised the specter of Rose Bowl officials departing from tradition. The agreement was declared invalid in 1961 due to a West Coast pay-for play scandal two years earlier that broke up the PCC.

In the PCC's place, the Big Five was formed among the University of Southern California (USC), University of California at Los Angeles (UCLA), University of California at Berkley (Cal), University of Washington, and Stanford University. A formal Rose Bowl agreement between the West Coast schools and the Big Ten was again in place for the 1962 regular season and 1963 Rose Bowl.

Sandy Stephens. Courtesy University of Minnesota Athletics Communications.

Reliable inside sources informed Bear Bryant that Alabama would be selected for the Rose Bowl if they remained unbeaten and top-ranked. Big Five commissioner Tom Hamilton was Bryant's commander in the Navy in World War II. Washington coach Jim Owens also told Bryant the Rose Bowl planned to invite Alabama.

The 1961 season was Bryant's fourth year of rebuilding his alma mater, which had fallen off the map before his return in 1958. Playing in "The Granddaddy of Them All" presented a television ratings bonanza unlike any other in the football landscape. Bryant also had a special affection for the Rose Bowl, dating to his own playing days for the Crimson Tide in the 1935 Rose Bowl. He lined up at end alongside Don Hutson, a College and Pro Football Hall of Famer. Alabama had a rich history in the Rose Bowl before the 1947 Big Ten-PCC agreement. The Crimson Tide played in six Rose Bowls—1926, 1927, 1931, 1935, 1938, 1946—and won five of the six.

When rumors leaked that the Rose Bowl was considering Alabama, Jim Murray was most prominent among Southern California sportswriters who questioned the social injustice of inviting a segregated team to play integrated UCLA. The West Coast, although not immune to racism, had an established history of fielding integrated teams at Southern California's two major universities, UCLA and USC. UCLA's history included Jackie Robinson wearing a Bruins uniform in football, basketball, baseball, and track and field.

Murray, whose brilliant career for the *Los Angeles Times* would be rewarded with a Pulitzer Prize in 1990, emphasized in his column Bryant's tacit approval of segregation. He traveled to the 1961 Georgia Tech-Alabama game on November 18 at Legion Field in Birmingham. Murray and the usual cast of Alabama sportswriters had the chance to meet with Bryant in his suite at the Bankhead Hotel to discuss his team.

Murray, who described Bryant reclining on his bed, wrote that he asked Bryant what he thought of UCLA's black players saying they wouldn't take the field in the Rose Bowl if Alabama was the opponent. An awkward silence fell over the room before Bryant spoke: "I would have nothing to say about that. Neither will the university, I'm sure." Murray also quoted an unnamed sportswriter who blurted out, "Tell them West Coast N-lovers to go lick your boots, Bear."[2] Two sportswriters Murray did identify, the *Nashville Banner's* Fred Russell and the *Birmingham Post-Herald's* Bill Lumpkin, apologized for their fellow reporter's disturbing remark. Here was a chance for Bryant to express embarrassment, but Bear was content with no comment. His tacit (at the very least) approval of segregation was slowing the progress and opportunities for Jimmy Raye's generation.

Alabama retained its No. 1 ranking by beating Georgia Tech 10-0 to move to 9-0.

Murray's column in the *Los Angeles Times'* November 20 edition was headlined "Bama and Bedsheets," and it was as on target as if he was a historian writing with the benefit of hindsight. He used a splendid mix of zingers and righteous prose asking for human decency and adherence to the U.S. Constitution.

Zinger: Murray wrote that he was in Birmingham, Alabama, "the place where, when they say 'Evening Dress,' they mean bring a bed sheet with eyeholes. And, bring your matches. We're lighting a cross."

Human decency: "Citadels of prejudice have been crumbled by athletics. It is the proudest chapter of its history. The prowess of the Alabama team threatens to turn the pages back."

Jim Murray liked to call Alabama's football team the "front-of-the-bus champions"—a reference to the 1955 Montgomery bus boycott sparked by Rosa Parks' refusal to give up her seat to a white passenger. Murray felt an all-white team that only played all-white opponents was undeserving of the No. 1 national ranking. He also pointed the blame for bombed-out houses in the South away from the Civil Rights movement: "White male Americans are the enemy of America here. The Constitution is being torn in half by people whose ancestors helped to write it."

Birmingham's Legion Field was labeled the "Football Capital of the South," but during this period the city also was known as "Bombingham." There were 17 black churches or black homes bombed between 1957 and 1963.

Rose Bowl officials read the public response to Murray's column and subsequently backed away from its flirtation with Alabama. As for the team, it beat Auburn 34-0 to finish 10-0 and No. 1. Bryant and Alabama may have been living in a bubble, but it was not a vacuum. Murray's columns and the Rose Bowl's reaction showed significant national sentiment supporting the Civil Rights movement already prevalent in 1961.

"In most cases sportswriters said nothing about race in their stories and columns because race made editors and sportswriters uncomfortable," Lamb said. "So silence became the path of least resistance. I once asked Shirley Povich, the great sportswriter of the *Washington Post*, why so few sportswriters called for the end of the color line in baseball. He said, 'I'm afraid sportswriters were like the club owners. They thought separate was better.'"

With that context, it's easier to comprehend how rare it was for Murray as a sportswriter to question Bear Bryant on a matter of race in 1961 in Birmingham. Bryant still blamed Murray 13 years later for costing Alabama a Rose Bowl trip. Bryant says Murray "made a fuss" and "wrote about segregation and the Alabama Ku Klux Klan and every unrelated scandalous thing he could think of ... " The iconic coach failed to realize that being denied the Rose Bowl—as opposed to Jimmy Raye and other black youths robbed of a chance to feel inspired when they saw Sandy Stephens play on TV—should have provided a wakeup call that segregated Alabama was on the wrong side of history.

Oddly enough, the Rose Bowl's decision to pull back from courting Alabama was followed by another unexpected development that modern football fans would have a hard time comprehending.

With Alabama out of the picture, the Big Ten was in play again. Ohio State, which finished the regular season 8-0-1 overall and 6-0 in the Big Ten, was the Big Ten champion and received a tentative invitation to the 1962 Rose Bowl, following a 50-20 win over Michigan on November 25 to finish the 1961 regular season.

"Tentative invitation" meant something in this case. On Monday, November 27, Ohio State's faculty voted 28-25 to decline the Rose Bowl bid. The faculty expressed concern over the academic calendar. There also was displeasure that Ohio State coach Woody Hayes' football machine was running roughshod over academics. It's a story that continues to boil over in college sports, but in those days a Big Ten rule gave the faculty such authority over the athletic department.

Minnesota, ranked No. 2 in the Big Ten with a 7-2 and 6-1 record, was offered a bid. The school's faculty voted to accept, even though they were essentially the Rose Bowl's third choice. The Rose Bowl announced the Minnesota-UCLA match-up on December 2. The Gophers were victorious in a 21-3 win over UCLA, featuring two short touchdown runs from Sandy Stephens.

Stephens, who passed away in 2000, once said of his ambitions, "I was going to be more than a Big Ten quarterback who was black. I was going to be the Big Ten quarterback who took his team to the Rose Bowl."

There was not another black quarterback in the Rose Bowl after Stephens until Raye appeared as a sophomore on New Year's Day 1966, literally following his inspiration. He also nearly led a Michigan State comeback victory from a 14-0 deficit, entering the game with less than seven minutes to play and directing two touchdown drives. Only a pair of failed 2-point conversions prevented a tie or a victory in a stunning 14-12 upset loss for the Spartans.

"Sandy was the reason I wanted to go the Big Ten," Raye said of leaving the segregated South. "He was the quarterback who took Minnesota to the Rose Bowl. When I saw him play on TV in the Rose Bowl, I thought it was possible. I thought, 'Yeah, I can play in the Big Ten. It's possible.'"

Raye might still have accomplished all that he did if Alabama or Ohio State had played UCLA, but Stephens' play and the presence of television allowed Raye to carry an image of Stephens guiding him on his trail-blazing path.

In another pivotal moment for a young Jimmy Raye, he became aware of Oscar Robertson's venture into segregated North Carolina through word-of-mouth from older players gathered at the Seabrook Park. They discussed the Dixie Classic, which included the four Tobacco Road teams—North Carolina State, North Carolina, Duke, and Wake Forest.

The Classic, as it was known locally, was played at N.C. State's Reynolds Coliseum, a 12,400-seat grand arena which for many years was the largest in the South. The tournament buzz was clearly about Robertson—The Big O—who was voted the national Player of the Year by UPI during his sophomore 1957-58 season in addition to All-American honors. Jumpin' Johnny Green had his own following as well. North Carolina fans remembered him from the 1957 Final Four, when Michigan State lost to North Carolina in the semifinals in an epic triple-overtime marathon. The Tar Heels went on to defeat Kansas and Wilt Chamberlain in the national-championship game.

After the first night of Dixie Classic games, Raye wandered from Seabrook's lower courts with the junior-high kids to the upper courts reserved for the best of the older players. The Christmas break meant Fayetteville-area athletes were home from historically black colleges:

North Carolina A&T, Johnson C. Smith University, North Carolina Central, and Hampton University.

Raye watched the older players imitate The Big O's distinctive one-handed jump shot. He returned each day and listened as the college players recounted Robertson and his latest performance in the three-day Dixie Classic.

"As a youngster at Seabrook," Raye said, "the guys who had gone on to college were all held in tremendous esteem. My dream was to be a college player and come home and play on the upper court. As a youngster you hung on every word that was said by the guys on the upper court. If they thought Oscar Robertson was worth talking about and emulating, we were trying to do the same."

The Tobacco Road teams facing Robertson were a formidable crew, but they meant little to Raye and his friends, loyal fans of the Central Intercollege Athletic Association's historically black schools. They rooted for Robertson against the Tobacco Road schools. As Raye pointed out, "I didn't pay attention to the ACC and Big Four because I couldn't go there." Such was a North Carolina teenager's limited picture of the world at the time, framed by Jim Crow laws.

Adding to the hype for Dixie Classic, four of the eight teams were ranked among the nation's Top 10 teams. Cincinnati came to town ranked No. 2 in the latest Associated Press poll (No. 1 in another poll). North Carolina was No. 4, North Carolina State No. 5 and Michigan State No. 7 (albeit 4th in another poll). The tournament was organized by North Carolina State coach Everett Case when he arrived in 1949 from Indiana, a man credited with bringing big-time basketball to the South, and it drew a record total attendance of 73,600 fans in 1958.

Robertson, a junior, and Green, a senior, were breaking ground, but it's important to understand the racial climate they experienced. Robertson had one black teammate and Green three black teammates. They felt unwelcome from the moment they stepped off the plane at Raleigh-Durham airport.

Cincinnati and Michigan State had separate housing arrangements from the other visiting teams, who customarily stayed at the segregated Sir Walter Raleigh Hotel, the finest hotel of the era in downtown Raleigh.[3] The Bearcats and Spartans bunked together at a North Carolina State fraternity house vacant for the Christmas break.

Jumpin' Johnny Green was from Dayton, Ohio, but he was an U.S.

Army veteran who had been through the South and knew what confronted him. He told Michigan State coach Forddy Anderson he would stay home.

"My first thought was, 'Where are we going to stay?' My second thought was, 'Where are we going to eat?'" Green said. "I told the coaches to go without me, and I would be here when they got back."

Anderson assured him that the team would travel, eat, and stay together, but Green was still uncomfortable.

"My teammates can't stay in the hotel and they can't eat in the restaurants because of me," Green said. "That arouses a lot of internal feelings. I didn't like it. It made me feel like I was the problem. I didn't have to deal with those feelings at Michigan State. We didn't have problems at Michigan State."

As it turned out, those were merely off-court problems. Robertson and Green were roughed up throughout the tournament—and those were just from the foul calls.

"I took a certain amount of punishment, but Oscar was the national Player of the Year," Green said. "He was the target. He was really punished. One play he went up for a jump shot and was pushed so hard he fell into the stands. I just tried to move on to the next play, but Oscar was bitter. We used to talk about the Dixie Classic when we would see each other over the years."

Once the tournament began, the next few days included an ironic juxtaposition of newspaper stories. Stories about the final days of a 102-year-old former slave overlapped with accounts of Robertson and Green staring down segregation in the South. The Jan. 3, 1959 *Raleigh News and Observer* edition included an AP story with a Washington, D.C., dateline: "Ex-Slave Dead at 102." The item said, "Mrs. William Kinard was born a slave as a Carrie Gray in Newberry, S.C., and that her husband had taken his slave owner's name."[4]

On the sports pages throughout the week, the play of Robertson and Green were lauded and singled out with photos and quotes of praise from the Tobacco Road coaches. There were no reports from the sportswriters of the racially motivated abuse they endured.

Cincinnati beat Wake Forest in its first game, 94-70, but the Bearcats lost to N.C. State the next night in the semifinals, 69-60, and fell again on the final day to North Carolina in the third-place game, 90-88.

The tone for exploiting physical play and non-calls against Robertson was set in the first contest against the Demon Deacons. Robertson was even involved in a tussle with Dave Budd. Budd had a reputation for physical play and possessed the talent to later play in the National Basketball Association, however, so Robertson accepted his opponent's rough style.

"Dave Budd and I were roommates on the road when we played for the New York Knicks," said Green. "I found out he was a nice guy."

The fouls that upset Robertson—both calls and non-calls—were committed by backup players in the N.C. State and North Carolina games. In three Classic games Robertson shot 51 free throws.

William Carver, one of Jimmy Raye's high-school coaches, attended the 1958 Dixie Classic for the chance to see The Big O. Carver had graduated from E.E. Smith and was playing football at the time at Hampton Institute; he was home on Christmas break.

"I'll never forget going to see N.C. State play Oscar Robertson," Carver said. "We were probably two out of 10 black people in there among 12,000. Oscar was killing N.C. State. But then ol' Everett Case went down to the end of the bench and got a guy who hadn't been in the ball game." The newcomer entered with a purpose—Carver remembers him abusing Robertson with rough play. The Big O finished with eight field goals and 13 free throws (in 16 attempts). N.C. State's Dan Englehart fouled out with 4 points, Don Gallagher failed to score with two fouls, and two other N.C. State players finished with four fouls apiece. Oscar Robertson himself was whistled for three fouls.

According to Robertson, Cincinnati coach George Smith "stormed into the officials dressing room and cussed them out something fierce" for the treatment he endured.[5]

"When I got back to the dormitory at the end of the night, I compared notes with Johnny Green and some of other guys from Michigan State," Robertson wrote. "Johnny said he'd gotten the hell beat out of him too, and that refs hadn't done a thing. The rest of the tournament was filled with tension and punctuated with verbal outbursts. Afterwards, when reporters asked me about one game I just had to bite my tongue. 'They won and we didn't was all I said.'"[6]

In Michigan State's Dixie Classic opener, the Spartans beat Duke 82-57 and Johnny Green scored 14 points. Green totaled 20 in the semifinal as the Spartans defeated North Carolina 75-58 to set up the final against N.C. State. But Green was held to 4 points against N.C. State.

The Wolfpack rallied from a 41-32 halftime deficit for the win, preserving the Big Four's distinction of never having allowed an outside team to win the Dixie Classic. "Sometimes a couple of calls can change the momentum of a game," said Green. "I remember there were a couple of calls that got us mad and the game went the other way."

Years later, Johnny Green was at a Las Vegas hotel for an NBA convention with other retired players. He was standing in the lobby when a fan, self-identified as a North Carolina State fan, singled him out. "He said, 'Aren't you Jumpin' Johnny Green?' He tells me about the Dixie Classic and how he was sitting under one of the baskets. He started laughing and said, 'You guys always thought you could come down and win the Dixie Classic. You didn't realize you were playing five against seven—the team and the referees.' He couldn't stop laughing."

Jimmy Raye was unaware of the racial pressures Oscar Robertson and Johnny Green faced. The Big O and Jumpin' Johnny provided him and other black youths a chance to dream. Sandy Stephens did the same three years later in the Rose Bowl.

The inspiration of such moments helped Raye follow Stephens' footprints to the Rose Bowl. Raye played in the 1966 Rose Bowl (1965 season) as a sophomore backup. He would have led the Spartans to a second straight Rose Bowl trip his junior season if not for the Big Ten's no-repeat Rose Bowl rule, in place until 1971.

Green later followed Raye's career as a pioneer black quarterback at his alma mater and then as a longtime NFL assistant coach. He also followed Sherman Lewis, another Michigan State black football player as an All-American halfback in 1963, who went onto a long NFL coaching career.

"I was proud of those Michigan State teams," Green said. "Those two men had tremendous careers in school and then in the NFL. They should have been head coaches."

Minority opportunities progressed with television exposure, but the true journey began half a century earlier.

Notes

1. Oscar Robertson, *The Big O: My Life, My Times, My Game.* p. 99.

2. *Los Angeles Times*, Nov. 20, 1961.

3. The hotel stills stands as a senior apartment building called the Sir Walter Apartments and is listed on the National Register of Historic Places.

4. Oscar Robertson, *The Big O: My Life, My Times, My Game.* p. 6.

5. *Ibid.*, 8.

6. *Ibid.*, 9.

5

MICHIGAN STATE'S EARLY PIONEERS

"There should be a revolution in the answer the United States has given to this question, 'For whom are the public schools intended?' For twenty-five years I have answered this question in the language of democracy—here is the answer—'For all of the people all of the time.'"—Woodbridge N. Ferris

Jimmy Raye began his journey as a pioneer black quarterback at Michigan State with a 36-hour train trip in from segregated Fayetteville to Michigan State in 1964. He boarded the train's Jim Crow car, but his mode of travel no doubt was luxurious compared to Gideon Smith's odyssey a half-century earlier to Michigan State from Hampton, Virginia, by way of Big Rapids, Michigan.

From 1913 to 1915, Gideon Smith was one of college football's first black players as well as Michigan State's first black athlete. The school was known then as Michigan Agricultural College. Smith helped MAC to a pair of David and Goliath victories over the mighty University of Michigan during the 1913 and 1915 seasons.

Smith cleared an integration path for future black college athletes that included Willie Thrower, who was Michigan State College's first black quarterback in 1952. Thrower in turn blazed a trail that led to Raye as Michigan State's first black starting quarterback and the first black quarterback from the South to win a national title in 1966.

Football remains a university's most visible symbol in American culture, and the Spartans broke more barriers once Michigan State joined the Big Ten in 1950 (1953 in football).

Jimmy Raye was a wide-eyed Michigan State freshman in the fall of 1964 when he first saw a portrait of Gideon Smith in the lobby of the Jenison Fieldhouse offices. "It was so remarkable to see a black football player from 1913, and my initial thoughts were to try to imagine what kind of support system he had in the environment that existed at that time," said Raye. "What a tremendous individual Gideon must have been, and couple that with the extraordinary talent he must have possessed to be issued a uniform. I realized what he faced must have been overwhelming, and later I felt the obstacles I faced were not as insurmountable."

It is unlikely Michigan State football was on Smith's mind as he made his first 800-mile trip in 1910 from Hampton to the small but then-vibrant lumber town of Big Rapids in northern Michigan. He attended Ferris Industrial School (now Ferris State University) for three years with a group of other black students from Hampton. Smith took college preparatory classes and played on the Ferris football team from 1910 to 1912 until he left to enroll at Michigan Agricultural College—and play some more football. (Eligibility rules were lax in those days.)

Woodbridge N. Ferris, who founded the school in 1884, arranged a unique working relationship with the Hampton Normal and Agricultural Institute (now Hampton University). The details of the Hampton-Ferris partnership are lost to history, but black students from Hampton Normal began to arrive at Ferris Industrial in 1910 after Woodbridge Ferris read Booker T. Washington's autobiography, *Up from Slavery*. Washington, one of the nation's black leaders in the late 1880s and early 1900s, graduated from Hampton before founding Tuskegee Institute in Alabama.

Ferris State archives note that between 1913 and 1928, the school had an annual enrollment of 1,000 students with 15 to 25 black students.

Woodbridge Ferris, who later served as Michigan's governor from 1913 to 1917 and a U.S. senator from 1923 to 1928, believed education was for all Americans—and all races. Ferris State uses a quote from its founder on the university website: *"There should be a revolution in the answer the United States has given to this question, 'For whom are the public schools intended?' For twenty-five years I have answered this question in the language of democracy—here is the answer—'For all of the people all of the time.'"*

Another one of Woodbridge Ferris's defining quotes paid reverence to the Great Emancipator, President Abraham Lincoln: *"If I had my way, there would be in every community a life-size statue of Abraham Lincoln."*

Woodbridge Ferris built his fledgling school on the land-grant model—the Morrill Act of 1862, signed by President Lincoln. The federal government dedicated land to establish college campuses. Michigan State's first president, Joseph R. Williams, campaigned in Washington, D.C., for the land-grant bill.

Williams wrote: "Surely, if it is legitimate to grant land for the promotion of classical and professional education, it is to do so for the promotion of education bearing directly on the industrial and agricultural pursuits of the people."[1]

Ferris State archives also show that Gideon Smith was one of many Ferris Industrial students in that time period transferring to MAC, Michigan, or other schools. Once Smith journeyed 110 miles from Ferris to MAC, he continued his football despite MAC coach John Macklin failing to welcome him, and declining to issue Smith a uniform or equipment. A MAC teammate loaned Smith an old football jersey and pads, and the new transfer quickly demonstrated his football prowess on the practice field.

Blake Miller, one of Michigan State's first two All-American picks in the 1915 season, team captain, and an MSU Hall of Fame inductee, played three years side by side with Gideon Smith, with Miller at end and Smith at tackle.

In 1983, the then 94-year-old Miller was interviewed by Michigan State's sports information office. "Oh boy, there was a football player," he said of Gideon Smith. " ... Gideon and I, I don't think we had 3 yards against us the whole season. I never saw a lineman that could stop players the way he did. He'd just reach out with his arm like that and boy if he could get his hand on them he'd bring them down. ... Oh, he was a terrific tackle. No one would get by him."[2]

Smith's impact on the Aggies (they became the Spartans in the 1920s) was immediate. MAC posted its first unbeaten season in 1913, finishing 7-0, including MAC's initial victory over Michigan, 12-7. The

Ann Arbor school avenged the loss with a 3-0 triumph in 1914, but MAC and Smith won again in 1915 with a 24-0 shutout.

Until the 1913 and 1915 wins, MAC had played in Michigan's considerable shadow. In 1902, the Wolverines were already a national power and had beaten MAC 119-0. The next three years MAC was resigned to playing Michigan's freshmen team. Michigan State's future as the equal of fellow Big Ten members would have to wait another four decades into the future.

Gideon Smith playing football for Ferris State in 1912 before he was Michigan State's first African-American athlete from 1913-15. He traveled from Hampton, Virginia, to Big Rapids in northern Michigan in 1910. Courtesy Ferris State University.

In MAC's initial 1913 victory, a *Detroit News* report written by Eddie Batchelor called Smith and Hugh Blacklock "two of the best I ever saw playing on the same team at the same time." Of the former, Batchelor wrote, "Smith had arms that seemed 10 feet long plus the agility of a cat. When a play came through his position he folded up the whole side of the opposing line as if he were playing an accordion."

In MAC's 1915 victory, Batchelor reported Smith contributed "tackle-around-plays" on offense "for good gains" and dominated on the line on defense. Of Smith's defensive play, the *Detroit News* account reported Smith repeatedly stopped Michigan's All-American halfback, Johnny Maulbetsch.

"When it came to defense, Gideon Smith, the big MAC tackle, was far and away the best man in the game. This large person is a decided brunette as to complexion, but as a football player is pure gold all the way through."

Despite Smith's star status among the Aggies, he endured racial prejudices and indignities. When the team traveled by train, he had to sit in a different car for black passengers. Upon arriving at their destination, Macklin would meet Smith on the train platform. Since Smith could not stay with the team, Macklin provided him with hotel and meal money. The team would not see Smith again until the next day. During the games, opponents taunted him with racial slurs.

"He used to have a lot of abuse on the line," Blake Miller said. "He was perfect gentleman, a wonderful fella...very smart in college."

Gideon Smith also played pro football briefly for the Canton Bulldogs before the National Football League was formed in 1920. The Pro Football Hall of Fame lists him as the fourth black player in the NFL and its precursors. In a Canton team picture reprinted in *The Spartans* (pages 44-45), Smith is pictured in the same row as the legendary Jim Thorpe.

After Smith's playing days, he returned to Hampton, where he served as a professor of physical education and the football coach from 1921 to 1940. He remains the winningest and longest-tenured coach in Hampton's history with a career record of 97-46-12. Smith led Hampton to its first black college national championship in 1922 and four conference titles, and later served as the school's assistant athletic director until he retired in 1955. He passed away 13 years later at the age of 78.

Smith's grandson is John Milton Belcher III, who is an educator and project leader for a nonprofit education organization in Cambridge, Massachusetts. The emphasis is math and science programs for minority students. Belcher, whose mother Mildred Smith was Gideon Smith's daughter, was an only child. Belcher was 14 when Gideon Smith passed away in 1968. In 1994, he attended the Michigan State Hall of Fame ceremonies when Smith was enshrined (his mother had passed away by then).

"She loved my grandfather to death and took a lot of pride in his history at Michigan State and the honors he received," Belcher said. "When we visited him, I looked forward to hearing stories from him and going through his collections in his study."

Belcher broke into tears when he thought about his grandfather clearing paths in the manner of a Jesse Owens, Jackie Robinson, and other more famous groundbreaking black athletes.

"What comes to mind is his gentle nature," he said. "I've spent a lot of time try to reconcile the experiences and indignities that I endured with racism compared to what he must have faced. I don't know how he came through that as a gentle person. The world doesn't know him like a Jackie Robinson or a Jesse Owens, but I put him on that plane with what he confronted and the trails that he blazed. And there were others like him. They are the silent heroes. They are a part of history."

A half-century elapsed between the college playing careers of Gideon Smith and Jimmy Raye, yet Raye empathized with Smith's experience. But, as Raye's experience reveals, the same does not necessarily hold true for those young African-American athletes separated by a half-century from Raye and his fellow Underground Railroad passengers. As Raye notes, "Most young black coaches and players I talk to can't relate to what we went through. We were helping push social vehicles forward. We were changing the face of college football."

Smith was an influential groundbreaker at Michigan State, a school that subsequently did more to integrate college sports than any other over a longer period of time. By 1940, eight black athletes had played football at Michigan State, a figure believed to be more than any other Big Ten school.

There is much more known and documented about Willie Thrower's career at Michigan State. He was Michigan State's first black quarterback and one of the first in college football. Thrower's history at Michigan State gave Raye hope it was the right school for him.

Willie Thrower took a more conventional route to Michigan State than Smith endured—a Duffy Daugherty pipeline.

Daugherty's first player pipeline connected Michigan State with his home state of Pennsylvania. The initial Keystone State recruits arrived when Daugherty was an assistant coach under Biggie Munn—led by 1952 All-Americans Frank Kush of Windber, Dick Tamburo of New Kensington, and Tom Yewcic of Conemaugh. Thrower and Tamburo were part of a group of five players from New Kensington on the 1952 Spartans squad that went 9-0 and captured a national title.

"It was a great venture for us at Michigan State," Thrower said. "We all enjoyed it."[3]

Willie Thrower's decision to attend Michigan State was basically made for him. "Every college in the country wanted me—schools like Miami, Georgia, Kentucky—but as soon as they saw I was black, that was end of it," he said. "So I went north to Michigan State, where we had a fellow in front of me named Al Dorow, who later went to the Washington Redskins. Our stadium held 50,000 fans and they would chant, 'We want Willie! We want Willie!'"

Thrower did not receive recognition for his trail blazing until many years later. In fact, his hometown was unaware he was the first black quarterback in the NFL's modern era. The mainstream media tended to avoid the subject of race in sports stories, rather than report historic moments like Thrower's pioneering appearance with the Bears, particularly prior to the Civil Rights movement. The young signal-caller's pro debut was reported in Chicago papers as just that—a simple pro debut and not a groundbreaking moment for black athletes at his position.

"This was standard operating procedure in the mainstream press," said Indiana University-Indianapolis professor Chris Lamb. "This was true in both the South and the North. It was worse in the South, where newspapers had policies against publishing photographs of blacks. Northern sportswriters gave their support for segregation by remaining silent on the issue. Baseball, or society for that matter, could not have maintained the color line as long as it did without what one black sportswriter called 'The Conspiracy of Silence.'"

With little media recognition of Willie Thrower's ground-breaking moment, Willie Thrower's son, Willie Thrower, Jr., said people in his hometown did not believe he was the NFL's first black quarterback.

"It was only after he passed away that they started hearing the stories on TV," Willie Jr said. "Until then, people didn't believe him, not even in his own hometown. That's the saddest thing about it."[4]

Another son, Melvin Thrower, added, "My parents owned this bar called The Touchdown Lounge. My dad had a big picture of himself on the wall. On the bottom, it said, THE FIRST BLACK QUARTERBACK IN THE NFL, 1953. People told him to take it down. You're lying," they said. "You're lying. That ain't you. Take it down."

Hometown recognition finally arrived in 1979, when Willie was elected to the Westmoreland County Hall of Fame. In 1988, the Pro

Football Hall of Fame honored Thrower as part of a display that recognized the NFL's first black players. He passed away at age 71 in 2002, and a year later an official state marker was placed at his high school, now called Valley High. The school unveiled a statue of him at the football stadium entrance in 2006.

That same season, 2006, Warren Moon became the first black quarterback inducted into the Pro Football Hall of Fame. Said Moon in his induction speech, "But I also remember all the guys before me who blazed that trail to give me the inspiration and the motivation to keep going forward, like Willie Thrower, the first black quarterback to play in an NFL game, like Marlin Briscoe, who is here today, the first to start in an NFL game. Like James Harris, who is here today, the first to lead his team to the playoffs."

Thrower once told the *Valley News Dispatch* of Tarentum, Pennsylvania, "I look at it like this: I was the Jackie Robinson of football. A black quarterback was unheard of before I hit the pros."

During Thrower's high school days, New Kensington High gained national attention by winning back-to-back Western Pennsylvania Interscholastic League (WPIAL) titles in 1946 and 1947. The football team was invited in 1947 to Miami to compete with other top schools from around the country in a football festival. However, the organizers withdrew the invitation when they saw a photo of the New Kensington quarterback.

Thrower's time at Michigan State overlapped a period when two Spartans quarterbacks earned All-American honors: Al Dorow (1951) and Tom Yewcic (1952). Both also later played pro football. Dorow began in the NFL and later played in the Canadian Football League and American Football League through 1962. Yewcic, after a minor-league baseball career, played in the American Football League with the Boston Patriots from 1961 to 1966.

"Willie was a great teammate," Yewcic said. "I was competing against him for the starting job and it was a tough fight to beat him out. There were other areas where he was limited, but he could really throw the ball. He had a great arm."

In Michigan State's 1952 season, Thrower completed 29 of 43 passes for 400 yards and five touchdowns with three interceptions in a backup role in a run-oriented offense. Thrower's numbers compare impressively, considering total attempts, to Yewcic's All-American statistics as a starter: 41 of 95 passes for 941 yards and 10 touchdowns with five interceptions.

Thrower counts Michigan State's 48-6 rout of Texas A&M in the third week of the 1952 season as his "greatest moment in football." The October 11 game at Spartan Stadium (then called Macklin Stadium) was played before a full house of 50,000 and was nationally televised by NBC. Thrower entered the contest with four-and-a-half minutes to play and made it clear in the huddle what he planned.

"I said, 'What we're going to do is play pass and catch. That's all I'm going to do is throw the ball. I don't care if it's two yards for a first down. I'm going to throw it.'"

Thrower proceeded to complete seven of nine passes for 107 yards and two touchdowns. The performance gained the admiration of Texas A&M coach Raymond George, whose team was better known than the Spartans for a passing attack. George, Bear Bryant's predecessor at Texas A&M, defied unwritten rules in the segregated south by scheduling his all-white teams against integrated schools, including UCLA in 1951.

"After the game," said Thrower, "the Texas A&M coach came to our locker room. He says, 'Where's this Willie Thrower guy?' The players say, 'Over there, No. 27.' We were the No. 1 team in the nation, and he comes over. 'You know what?' he says. 'I was proud of my team today—until you stepped into the game. I'll tell you what,' he says. 'If they don't give you the game ball, you come to my locker room. I got one for you.'

"They didn't give me the game ball and I didn't go over and get one. I was just satisfied to get in there and play a little ball."

In the season's eighth week, Thrower helped save the national championship season against Notre Dame. Yewcic was injured with the Spartans clinging to a 7-3 lead in a home game. Thrower took the field and threw a touchdown pass en route to a 21-3 win. The victory extended the longest winning streak in the nation to 23 games. It ultimately reached 28 before ending in mid-1953.

"Notre Dame was always a tough game and he played well," Yewcic said. "Willie was a great teammate. He never complained about playing time but when he was called upon to play he delivered. He always played hard."

Thrower helped wrap up the 1952 season in a one-sided season finale, connecting on seven of 11 passes, including a touchdown, and adding a touchdown on the ground as the Spartans beat Marquette University, 62-13.

"All in all, I'd like to be remembered as a great passer," Thrower said of his legacy. "I loved throwing the football."

It is an interesting sidenote to Willie Thrower's limited playing career that he was known as a passing quarterback. As more black quarterbacks played college football in the 1970s and 1980s, the knock against them in their NFL projections was they were primarily running quarterbacks with limited passing ability. There was no mistaking Willie Thrower's identity.

"If we were ahead, they'd put him in and he'd call all pass plays," said Vince Pisano, one of Thrower's teammates at both New Kensington and Michigan State. "The whole student body would holler, 'We want Willie!'"[5] Yewcic added, "That was Willie. He had a great sense of humor. Everyone on the team liked Willie."

Thrower's arm strength took on mythic proportions. One day at practice, Michigan State's kickers were having trouble booting into the stiff wind when the Spartans practiced kickoff coverage. No matter. Head coach Biggie Munn had Thrower stand at the opposite 40-yard line and launch the ball into the end zone to simulate kickoffs.

"We couldn't practice kickoffs because of the wind," Thrower said. "They said, 'Willie, get in there and throw that ball.' I'd get back there on the 40 like a kickoff. I'd throw all the way to the end zone and they'd catch it and run back. I could throw it 80 yards. If you talked to people in New Ken, they'd say I could throw it 100 yards, but 80 yards was the most I ever threw it."

Thrower moved on to his historic NFL season in 1953 when Chicago Bears coach and owner George Halas signed him as a free agent. Thrower's roommate was starting quarterback George Blanda, who was inducted into the Pro Football Hall of Fame in 1981. Both quarterbacks were from western Pennsylvania, which later in the century gained fame as a cradle of quarterbacks. Other famous western Pennsylvania quarterbacks enshrined in Canton include Johnny Unitas, Joe Namath, Joe Montana, and Dan Marino.

Thrower became a sudden fan favorite in his pro debut on October 18, 1953, against the San Francisco 49ers. Blanda was struggling or briefly hurt when Halas replaced him with Thrower. The *Chicago Tri-*

bune wrote, "In the 10th minute of the period, [San Francisco's Joe] Perry fumbled and [Chicago's Dick] Hensley recovered on the 49ers' 16. Willie Thrower, former Michigan State Negro quarterback star making his major league debut, passed 12 yards to [Jim] Dooley, putting the ball on the 4."

But Willie didn't have a chance to finish the possession.

"Blanda and (Fred) Morrison came into the game with a resounding raspberry," continued the *Tribune* report. "They wanted Willie to put it over. But Morrison did it on a blast off tackle. The boos changed to cheers."

Thrower played in only two games for the Bears, but he remembers a conversation with Blanda while traveling by train to Baltimore.

"George told me, he said, 'You know what, Will? If I could throw a football like you I'd play for the next 20 to 25 years. You can really throw that football.' George really admired my passing."

George Blanda did go on to play 26 pro seasons, with the end of his career extended not by his arm, but by his ability to kick the football. The future Hall of Famer served as a kicker and backup quarterback during his Oakland Raiders days from 1967 to 1975.

The Bears released Thrower after the 1953 season and he went on to play in the Canadian Football League. His career ended with a shoulder injury at age 27.

After Thrower, there was not another black quarterback in the AFL until 1968 (and the NFL until 1970 with the merger). Marlin Briscoe (1968, Denver Broncos) and James Harris (1969, Buffalo Bills) began their careers in the AFL. Briscoe was released by Denver after one year and converted to wide receiver once he was claimed by Buffalo in 1969. Harris remained a quarterback throughout his playing days with the Bills (1969-72), Los Angeles Rams (1973-76), and San Diego Chargers (1977-81). In 1974, he became the first black quarterback to start a playoff game as well as the first black quarterback named to the Pro Bowl.

After Thrower, the NFL's early black quarterbacks came from historically black schools or smaller colleges. Briscoe was from the University of Nebraska at Omaha and Harris from Grambling State University.

Grambling also produced Doug Williams, the first black quarterback taken in the NFLs draft's first round. The Tampa Bay Buccaneers selected Williams 17th overall in 1979.

Just one year before Williams was drafted, Warren Moon went

undrafted after he led the University of Washington to a Pac-8 Conference title and Rose Bowl upset of Michigan. Moon played six years in the CFL before starting his NFL career with the Houston Oilers in 1984.

The first two black quarterbacks to win the Heisman Trophy were the University of Houston's Andre Ware in 1989 and Florida State University's Charlie Ward in 1993. Ware was taken seventh overall by the Detroit Lions, but had difficulty transitioning from his college-style run-and-shoot offense to the NFL's pro-style schemes. Ward opted to play in the National Basketball Association with the New York Knicks after speculation mounted he would be a low draft pick or undrafted in the NFL.

Other black quarterbacks, such as second-round pick Randall Cunningham, a product of the University of Nevada at Las Vegas, and first-round pick Steve McNair, from Alcorn State University, enjoyed more success than Ware. The 1999 NFL draft was a milestone draft, with three black quarterbacks selected among the first round's top 11 picks. Philadelphia chose Syracuse University's Donovan McNabb second overall, Cincinnati took the University of Oregon's Akili Smith third overall, and Minnesota tabbed Central Florida University's Daunte Culpepper 11th overall.

The number of black quarterbacks starting at major colleges and in the NFL has changed dramatically in the 21st century. Quarterbacks who happen to be black are no longer a novelty. Auburn University's Cam Newton of the Carolina Panthers and Baylor University's Robert Griffin III of the Washington Redskins are called Heisman Trophy winners before they're referred to as black quarterbacks.

By the start of the 2012 season, Jimmy Raye's 35th NFL season, the league's active rosters included six starting black quarterbacks and 16 overall in the 32-team league. Tampa Bay's 2012 season opener against Carolina matched two starting quarterbacks who happened to be black, the Bucs' Josh Freeman and the Panthers' Newton. Raye, a coach at the contest, said he was unaware until it was pointed out to him that two black starting quarterbacks were squaring off in that game.

By the end of the 2013 NFL season, the black quarterback numbers had increased to eight starters and 18 overall. Four teams had two black quarterbacks on their roster. One of those teams was the Super Bowl champion Seattle Seahawks, with starter Russell Wilson and backup

Tarvaris Jackson, an eighth-year veteran and former starter at Minnesota who played his college ball at historically black Alabama State.

And among the multitude of story lines churned out at Super Bowl XLVIII, the most noted prejudice Wilson overcame was for under-6-foot-tall quarterbacks. His race, and the fact that both quarterbacks on the Seahawks' roster were black, was reduced to a footnote.

Notes

1. Madison Kuhn, *Michigan State–The First Hundred Years*, 1955.

2. Cassette tape owned by granddaughter Kim Winkel.

3. Audio interview, *williethepro.com*.

4. *Third and a Mile*.

5. *Ibid*.

6

DUFFY AND HIS LEGACY

"Time is neutral, and the time is always right to do right."—Martin Luther King Jr.

Martin Luther King Jr. visited Michigan State University's campus in East Lansing on February 11, 1965, and spoke to a full house of 4,000, who greeted him with a standing ovation at The Auditorium. Only two months earlier King had accepted the Nobel Peace Prize in Oslo, Norway.

His East Lansing speech praised Michigan State president John Hannah, whom President Dwight Eisenhower had appointed in 1957 as Chairman of the Civil Rights Commission. King urged the government to adopt Hannah's recommendation to use federal registrars to overcome widespread discriminatory voting practices in the South.[1]

Less than a month after King's trip to East Lansing, "Bloody Sunday" took place in Alabama when 600 Civil Rights protesters attempted to march from Selma to Montgomery. In another six months, the Voting Rights Act of 1965 would be signed on August 6 by President Lyndon B. Johnson.

When King finished his Michigan State speech, the students rose again with a second standing ovation.

There was no mention from King of the trails blazed by Michigan State's Underground Railroad, head coach Duffy Daugherty, or the Spartans' fully integrated roster that would start its remarkable two-year run in the fall with back-to-back Big Ten and national championships. But a portion of King's speech was about Daugherty more than any other college football coach in the nation. King addressed the issue of when was the "right time" to push integration despite push back from those who asked for patience—to wait for the "right time."

"Time is neutral," King told the audience, "and the time is always right to do right."

Michigan State football coach Duffy Daugherty and Ara Parseghian shake hands after their game at East Lansing that resulted in a 10-10 tie, Nov. 19, 1966. [AP Photo]

Time had been neutral for Daugherty throughout his coaching career. He did not wait for approval from the alumni to tell him when the time was right to recruit black athletes. He did not wait to defy Jim Crow and put on clinics for black high-school coaches in the South. He did not balk when his 1966 team voted in two black team captains, Clinton Jones and George Webster, believed to be the first pair of black team captains in major college football. Daugherty also knocked down the last position of white supremacy on the football field when he decided time was neutral for a black quarterback, Jimmy Raye, to be his starter. Daugherty later encouraged Raye to join in his staff in 1971 as a pioneer among black assistant coaches.

"[Daugherty] was one of the most courageous persons I've had the privilege to be associated with in my athletic career," Raye said. "I can only imagine the pressure he must have been under and received when he made the decision to make me the starting quarterback in the mid-1960s. Most of the things that happened to me in my coaching career—if not all—came as a direct result of the opportunities he gave me. I will be forever grateful for the courage he had and the kind of individual he was to give a chance to a young man who was denied a chance in the South to pursue an academic and athletic career."

A smaller legacy within Daugherty's overall legacy was the number of black players on his roster who did not turn out to be stars, starters, or even play. It is important to remember that the 1950s and 1960s was a time when professional teams only kept black athletes who were starters. Daugherty was willing to take a chance on a lightly recruited black player who may not turn out to be a star.

Michigan State All-American tight end Billy Joe DuPree was lightly recruited when Spartans assistant coach Vince Carillot found him in 1968 in West Monroe, Louisiana. In the 1972 season, DuPree was Daugherty's last All-American player among his Underground Railroad recruits. He was an NFL first-round draft pick by the Dallas Cowboys and three-time Pro Bowler in 11 seasons.

Carillot discovered DuPree as he pursued a more highly recruited Louisiana player (who eventually picked Grambling State). Carillot asked the recruit's high-school coach if he knew any other players in the area.

"You should talk to this kid Billy Joe DuPree over in West Monroe at Richardson High School," the coach told Carillot.

DuPree said he had considered either attending historically black Southern University in Baton Rouge or joining the military before Carillot invited him to take a trip to Michigan State. His college options in the South were limited when he graduated. Not only were Louisiana's high schools still segregated, Louisiana State University's football program remained all-white until 1972.

"I knew about Michigan State's great teams," DuPree said. "I knew they recruited black athletes from the South, and that was inspiring to me."

DuPree met Daugherty on his recruiting trip and came away feeling Daugherty and Grambling coach Eddie Robinson were men of similar character. DuPree had originally wanted to play at Grambling—until he met the great Robinson on a visit to Grambling's campus. When DuPree said he wanted to major in civil engineering, Robinson candidly told him Grambling lacked a civil-engineering program and he should consider another school.

"I have to give Duffy and Eddie a lot of credit," DuPree said. "Eddie showed me he was looking for more than a football player. He asked you what you wanted to do with your life. When I went to Michigan State, I had heard about big schools that offered to take care of you and your family. But Duffy said the only thing he was offering me was a chance to play football and an education. That's all I was looking for, and I committed to Michigan State."

Not all of the chances Daugherty took paid off with an All-America player, of course, but the number of lightly recruited black players offered scholarships was the reason Michigan State had more black players on the bench in the 1966 Game of the Century than the University of Southern California had black starters in their famed 1970 game at Alabama.

In 1966, Michigan State had 20 black players, with 11 starters and nine backups. In 1967, USC won a national title with only seven total black players. And in their untelevised 1970 contest at Alabama, USC started only five black players—quarterback Jimmy Jones, fullback Sam Cunningham, tailback Clarence Davis, defensive end Tody Smith (Bubba's little brother), and linebacker Charlie Weaver—though they now had 17 black players overall on the roster, presenting an evolving image of integration.

"They talk about that 1970 USC-Alabama game and how it enlightened Bear Bryant," said Steve Garvey, a white football-baseball star at Michigan State in the late 1960s from Tampa, Florida. "A lot of people want to give Bryant credit for integration, but Duffy was at the forefront."

Dan Daugherty, Duffy's son, said Duffy's father Joseph Daugherty taught his children from an early age not to judge people by the race, creed, or religion. The Daugherty ancestors were Irish Protestants who left Ireland for Scotland during the potato famine to work in coal mines that fueled the Industrial Revolution. Consequently, Duffy, even with his Irish surname, has been sometimes misidentified as Scottish. In both Ireland and Scotland, the Daughertys faced religious conflict. Joseph Daugherty's parents subsequently left Scotland for America to work in the central Pennsylvania coal mines.

"My grandfather taught my father it's what's in the heart and soul of people—not their skin color," Dan said. "Skin color or religion didn't matter to my father or his brothers, Jack and Joe. My father was Irish Protestant and he married an Italian Catholic."

Duffy, who grew up in Barnesboro, worked in deep-shaft coal mines after high school before he saved enough money to play football at Syracuse University. His teammate in 1937 and 1938 was Wilmeth Sidet-Singh, only the third black quarterback in college football. Sidet-Singh was light-skinned and had taken his Hindu Indian stepfather's surname, thus avoiding attention.

Daugherty served in World War II as an officer in the South Pacific before he returned to Syracuse in 1946 on the staff of new head coach Biggie Munn.

Munn's Syracuse stay was a short one. Michigan State president John Hannah viewed football as a building block toward raising the profile of a school he ultimately turned into a world-class university. Hannah sought a dynamic football coach who could quickly build a powerhouse. He tapped Munn, who brought Daugherty with him. By envisioning a powerhouse, Hannah eyed an invitation to join the Big Ten in order to fill the void created in 1946 when the University of Chicago departed the conference and the ranks of big-time football.

Hannah hired Munn for his background as a former University of Michigan assistant coach familiar with the Big Ten. Munn built national champions in 1951 and 1952 and then retired to serve as athletic director following the 1953 season and 1954 New Year's Day Rose Bowl victory over UCLA. The 1953 season was Michigan State's first Big Ten title, serving as co-champions with Illinois.

Daugherty succeeded Munn in 1954 and stayed 19 seasons, compiling a school record for most wins with a record of 109-69-5.

Daugherty and Munn eventually had a falling out in their AD/coach working relationship and argued over the direction of the football program in the late 1950s. Hannah stepped in, sitting the two men down in a room to settle matters. He told them the university was bigger than their egos and ordered them to work out their problems. Daugherty later acknowledged in his 1974 book that Munn was the man who saved him from going back down in the coal mines.

Civil Rights was more than a college football story to the Daugherty family. True, Duffy talked football at home, but the coach and his wife

Francine together discussed the nightly news with their two children, Dan and daughter Dree. Dree said she and her mother were horrified when watching television news coverage of Bull Connor and his Birmingham policemen beating Civil Rights protesters with clubs and fire hoses in 1963.

"My mother was actually more liberal than my father, but they were on same page," said Dree, an emergency-room physician. "I was very young, but I grew up watching Walter Cronkite every night. We were very upset to see the way blacks were treated and the injustice going on in our country. I used to write letters to the editor."

Doing the right thing defined Daugherty, said Father Jake Foglio, who served a half-century at St. John Church and Student Center on M.A.C. Avenue just off the Michigan State campus. Foglio long knew Daugherty and his family through his association with the football program. He often traveled with the team. Clinton Jones and Gene Washington served as altar boys at St. John during their All-American seasons for the Spartans.

"When you do the right thing only because it's the right thing to do, a lot of good comes from it," Foglio said. "The black coaches in the South wouldn't send Duffy a player if they felt he used the black players. They were sure he would treat them fairly. The players he recruited were strong people. They would not have respected Duffy if they felt he was treating them as underlings. He got the best out of them by loving them and respecting them.

"He never made a big thing of bringing players up from the South and integrating college football. That speaks for itself. St. Francis of Assisi said you preach who you are by your actions. That was Duffy."

People understood Daugherty had contacts in the South to build the Underground Railroad, but few, including Foglio, knew how he defied Jim Crow with his clinics in the South for black high-school coaches.

Daugherty and Munn both brought their progressive attitudes to Michigan State long before the Civil Rights movement gained momentum and spread awareness to Americans in the 1960s.

Tom Yewcic, Michigan State's first two-sport All-American in football (1952) and baseball (1954), played quarterback for the Spartans from 1951 to 1953 under Munn as the head coach and Daugherty as an assistant. "We never had problems with white guys and black guys on our team and I believe it was because of Biggie and Duffy," Yewcic said. "Biggie and Duffy respected people and they didn't show favorites. If you were white or black, they played whoever deserved to play. We never had a confrontation between a white guy and a black guy—never once in my four years there.

"The only time I remember a problem for black athletes at Michigan State was on the baseball team when we went South in the spring. The black players were not allowed to eat in the dining hall. They had to eat in the kitchen, so we ate in the kitchen with them."

Daugherty also invited the Southern black high-school coaches up to Michigan State's campus in the summer for a clinic. In the era of segregation, many of the coaches were forced to drive non-stop through the night to reach East Lansing since they were unable to stop and spend the night along the way.

"I remember we would be doing our conditioning in the summer and Duffy would have me run patterns with Jimmy Raye throwing passes for the coaches to watch," said College Football Hall of Famer Gene Washington. "The first time I saw all these black coaches, I was wondering where they were from. I asked some and they said they were from all these places in the South. I was surprised. Duffy never said anything about what he was doing. As I got older, I began to understand the leadership he was providing. Duffy led the way in setting aside time for black coaches. He really enjoyed those clinics."

A prominent Texas high-school coach attending the Michigan State clinics was Bubba Smith's father, Willie Ray Smith. Daugherty provided the Beaumont Pollard teacher and coach with a carload of school supplies to bring back to his segregated (and resource-lacking) school.

Once Daugherty's network was in place, he faced no recruiting competition from schools in the South and little from the North.

"You have to remember the mentality of the era," said Carillot, Michigan State's defensive backs coach. "In both the North and the South, too many coaches believed black athletes weren't that good. Duffy said blacks were as good as anyone else. He said, 'Why not recruit them?'"

Ernie Pasteur was a fullback/linebacker that Daugherty recruited out of Queen Street High in Beaufort, North Carolina, as part of his 1963 recruiting class. Pasteur took recruiting trips to Michigan State, Minnesota, Wisconsin, and Purdue, but he said only Daugherty among coaches from those four schools traveled to Beaufort to visit with the promising young Pasteur and his coach, Shadrich Barrow. Duffy Daugherty, said Ernie Pasteur, "was probably the first white person at my high school." Later Daugherty made a home visit with the teenager's parents, Joe and Mildred.

"My mother cooked fried chicken and collard greens for Duffy," Pasteur said. "My mom loved him. Duffy told my mom if I went to Michigan State, I would graduate. My mom didn't hear anything else. She didn't care about football. My mom said, 'You're going to Michigan State.' "

A shoulder injury ended Ernie Pasteur's career, but his scholarship was never in doubt. He received the All-American treatment from Daugherty as a reference in the job market. Pasteur was 26 years old, teaching school and had earned his master's degree when he asked Daugherty to write a letter of recommendation for him. He had applied for a vacant vice-principal position at Grand Rapids Union High School, 70 miles northwest of Michigan State's campus.

"Duffy called in his secretary and he dictated a letter on Michigan State letterhead," Pasteur said. "The superintendent was a Michigan State graduate and football fan. When I went in for my interview, all he did was ask questions about Duffy and players like Bubba Smith and Jimmy Raye. Then, after about 30 minutes, he said, 'When can you start?'"

Pasteur later served as Grand Rapids Union principal from 1972 to 1977. He went on to take a job as the campus director at Maxey Training Facility near Ann Arbor. There were 600 juvenile students, most of them from Detroit.

"That was one of the most rewarding jobs I had," Pasteur said. "Bubba came to speak to the kids; George Webster came too. I had always wanted to be a principal. I didn't want to be in just one classroom. I felt it was my calling to lead. That letter Duffy wrote jumpstarted my career."

The DuPree and Pasteur stories are examples of how Daugherty was at his best when he was recruiting and building men with the comfortable attraction of his personality.

Before developing the Hawaiian Pipeline and the Underground Railroad, Daugherty relied on his Pennsylvania roots for his first pipeline to talent and winning football teams.

Michigan State's 1950s teams were national powers with rosters that included center Dick Tamburo, quarterback Tom Yewcic, and guard Frank Kush, three Pennsylvania players who earned All-America honors in the 1952 season. Fullback Gerald Planutis of West Hazleton, Pennsylvania, was an All-America pick on the 1955 national championship team that won the 1956 New Year's Day Rose Bowl. Daugherty learned about the Pennsylvania prospects through childhood friend Hugo Vivadelli, whose recruiting eye he trusted. Vivadelli was a high-school principal in Spangler, Pennsylvania, and he moonlighted as a referee for Friday night high-school football games. Yewcic specifically observed that Daugherty recruited him on the advice of Vivadelli.

"It didn't matter to Duffy what color his players were, but in turn he had to take a lot of crap for it," Foglio said. "He didn't get the credit he deserved for integrating college football, but he got the crap that came with it."

Daugherty ignored the racial hate mail, the comments that he was an N-lover turning Michigan State into the Grambling of the North—a reference to historically black Grambling State in Louisiana. Dan Daugherty added, with a laugh, that only one letter from an upset fan bothered his father throughout his 19 years as head coach.

"The letter was addressed to 'Duffy the Dope,' but it got delivered to him at his office," Dan said. "It didn't say Jenison Fieldhouse, Michigan State, East Lansing—nothing else—and the post office knew where to deliver it. My father said, 'I take my job seriously, but I don't take myself seriously.' He had the ability to laugh at himself."

During the peak years of Daugherty's career, he never used job offers from Texas A&M in 1958 or Notre Dame in 1964 as leverage. (It was a trait that George Perles failed to copy during his tenure as Michigan State's head coach in the 1980s and early 1990s. Perles used NFL job offers after his 1987 success with a Big Ten title and Rose Bowl victory to leverage for the dual role of football coach and athletic director.) Dan Daugherty, Duffy's son, said Texas A&M offered his father $50,000, a house, and a car among other perks. In comparison, his father's peak salary at Michigan State was $29,000 in 1972. "He came home and talked about it and asked us what we thought," said Dan, in middle school at the time. "I told him I didn't want to move to Texas—all my friends were here. I don't know if that played a part, but he turned down a lot of money to stay at Michigan State."

The Texas A&M offer came after Michigan State's 1957 national championship season. By then Daugherty already had to his credit two national titles, one Rose Bowl victory, one American Football Coaches Association national Coach of the Year award, and one *Time* Magazine cover.

Texas A&M, of course, was still segregated in the 1950s, which raises an interesting question of how Daugherty might have influenced the integration of college football if he was at a school in the South. Texas A&M's student body was integrated in 1962—one year before Alabama and the same year Mississippi students rioted to protest the admission of black student James Meredith. The Aggies' football program was integrated in 1967.[2]

The Notre Dame opportunity began to breed rumors in the spring of 1963. On March 13, 1963, Notre Dame announced that Hugh Devore would succeed Joe Kuharich, who had resigned, on a one-year interim basis. Duffy Daugherty was asked to comment on the potential Notre Dame head coaching vacancy following the 1963 season. "You can speculate all you want—I have no comment," replied Daugherty. "Notre Dame is a fine school, but the day Kuharich quit, I had a staff meeting trying to jack up our offense for next fall."[3]

The rumors persisted, and they were not without foundation. Notre Dame president Father Theodore Hesburgh called Hannah to request permission to speak with Daugherty about the job. Hannah broached the subject with Daugherty on October 14, 1963, when the team traveled to face USC at the L.A. Coliseum. The Spartans lost 13-10, but they stayed the night at the Sheraton Hotel before traveling home the next day. Hannah invited Daugherty up to his suite after the game.

"My Dad told me this story," said Dan Daugherty. "Hannah said, 'Sit down, Duffy. Father Hesburgh called me and wants to talk to you about Notre Dame. I'm not going to let him do that. In this room are the two most important people to Michigan State University.' It was only my Dad and Hannah, and my Dad started looking around. My Dad said, 'It's just the two of us—who else are you talking about?' Hannah asked, 'What will it take to keep you?'"

According to Dan Daugherty, Hannah had previously told his father he had job security as long as he had a winning record against Michigan and Notre Dame. Entering the 1963 season, Daugherty was 7-1 against Notre Dame (he finished his career 10-7-1) and 5-2-1 against Michigan (he finished 10-7-2).

The hotel suite meeting ended with Hannah presenting Duffy Daugherty, who had worked as a tenured professor without a contract, with a five-year deal. Hannah also eased the animosity between Munn and Daugherty by agreeing that Daugherty would report to Hannah and not to Munn.

In return, Duffy was about to lift Michigan State to its greatest heights with a 19-1-1 overall record, back-to-back Big Ten titles with a 14-0 conference record, and shares of the national championship both seasons.

No Big Ten school has duplicated Michigan State's 1965-66 run. Ohio State and Michigan dominated the Big Ten throughout the 1970s, but following each unbeaten season the Buckeyes or Wolverines suffered either a loss or a tie in conference play the next year. Ohio State had back-to-back unbeaten 12-0 seasons with 8-0 Big Ten records in 2012 and 2013, but the Buckeyes were ineligible for the Big Ten title in 2012 after NCAA sanctions and were beaten by Michigan State in the 2013 conference title game.

Oddly enough, another major turning point in Daugherty's coaching career would occur in a Los Angeles hotel during a stay for a USC game. Before the third game, he called team captains Billy Joe DuPree and Brad Van Pelt and told them that 1972 would be his final season. A month later Daugherty made his decision public before the Spartans beat Purdue.

Munn was inducted into the College Football Hall of Fame in 1959 and passed away in 1975 at the age of 66. Daugherty was inducted into the College Football Hall of Fame in 1984 and passed away in 1987, at the age of 72.

Michigan State named athletic facilities on campus after both Daugherty and Munn—football's Duffy Daugherty Building and the Munn Ice Arena. But otherwise there has been a feeling among Daugherty's players that the school officials wanted a separation from the high-water marks of the Daugherty era. Michigan State waited until 2012 to add Daugherty and Munn to the Ring of Fame alongside seven players previously honored.

"I think the powers that be were determined to start with a clean slate," Raye said.

He also believes that was why former Daugherty assistants from the

1960s who had moved on weren't considered candidates to bring back to East Lansing.

Daugherty compiled impressive win-loss numbers on the field, but the opportunities the brave coach provided for his Underground Railroad passengers and the African-Americans they subsequently influenced is incalculable.

"I tell my six children the most important thing to remember about their grandfather and his legacy is he helped facilitate integration with black athletes," said Daugherty's daughter Dree. "Football opened the door to everything else that happened in that era. I teach my children—and now my grandchild named for my father—we're very proud of that. It's a wonderful legacy and the one I try to pass on."

Notes

1. *The State News*, Feb. 12, 1965.

2. *archiveexhibits.library.tamu.edu*.

3. *Lansing State Journal*, March 15, 1963.

Duffy Daugherty announcing his retirement. Photo courtesy Michigan State University.

7

BUBBA

"I think of all the black athletes of that era, Bubba did more than anyone for social change. He openly dated women of his choice. He joined fraternities of his choice. A 6-foot-8, 300-pound African-American male was not going to let a 5-8 coach tell him what he could and could not do with his college social experience. Bubba eliminated guardrails in terms of social activities with his jovial persona and great talent."—Jimmy Raye

Everyone seems to have a Bubba Smith story, though Michigan State football coach Duffy Daugherty and athletic director Biggie Munn dealt with far more than they preferred. Bubba cut a wide swath across campus with waggish tales ranging from football exploits to the Bubbacar to, of all things, a gymnastics class.

The massive Smith took the class from George Szypula, who told the story the night the 91-year-old retired coach was inducted into Michigan State Hall of Fame.

"Bubba was bouncing on the trampoline when I wasn't watching," Syzpula said. "I yelled, 'What are you doing? You're going to kill yourself and then Duffy and Biggie are going to kill me.' He made a nice jump through the air, landed on the mat and he threw his arms out like he was in the Olympics.

"I said, 'Bubba, you're nuts.' He said, 'No, I'm not. I'm great. I'm from Texas. My dad was a football coach and he also taught us trampoline.'

"Bubba liked to say he was great."

Charles Aaron "Bubba" Smith. Photo courtesy Michigan State University.

Charles Aaron "Bubba" Smith, who passed away at the age of 66 in 2011, arrived at Michigan State from segregated Beaumont, Texas. His father, Willie Ray Sr., and mother, Georgia, were both teachers. Bubba, his older brother Willie Ray Jr., and younger brother Tody all played at Pollard High for their father, a renowned Texas high-school coach who won 235 career games. The Beaumont Independent School District re-named a school in the 1990s after the family patriarch: Willie Ray Smith Middle School. Tody Smith was writing a family history when he passed away at age 50 in 1999.

On Michigan State's campus, Bubba was big enough to block out the sun. He was spotted everywhere and anywhere. He might be at the Union Building shooting pool like one of the guys rather than a leg-end. He walked through Brody Complex one spring day and took part in a water balloon fight when invited by a group of surprised white students. Another day, Smith might be at the Jewish fraternity—which he had joined.

Why would a black man from segregated Texas join a Jewish frater-nity at a Midwestern college in the mid-1960s?

"Because he could," said Jimmy Raye.

The 1965 and 1966 powerhouse Michigan State Big Ten and national championship teams are more closely identified with Smith than any of the other players, thanks to his outsized personality. How-ever, Smith's mischievous nature belied the important integration role he played among black athletes in 1960s America.

He willingly stood out on Michigan State's campus in an era when black students at a predominantly white school were inclined to keep a low profile. Black students felt the less attention they drew, the fewer misunderstandings based on racial prejudices and stereotypes they would unexpectedly encounter. Smith's aura and confidence were too big for such concerns. He wanted to enjoy college life the same as any American kid away from home for the first time.

"I think of all the black athletes of that era, Bubba did more than anyone for social change," Raye said. "He openly dated women of his choosing. He joined fraternities of his choice. A 6-foot-8, 300-pound African-American male was not going to let a 5-8 coach tell him what he could and could not do with his college social experience. Bubba elimi-nated guardrails in terms of social activities with his jovial persona and great talent.

"He was the first black athlete who enhanced opportunities for black student-athletes to enjoy the whole college experience. He transcended the stereotypical box that black athletes had been placed in."

Michigan State fans embraced him in his two All-American seasons. On Saturday afternoons at Spartan Stadium, they urged Smith on, chanting "Kill, Bubba, kill!" The cheer started with the student section and soon spread to the rest of the 76,000 fans in green and white.

During the school week, Smith stood out on campus whether on foot or driving his self-proclaimed Bubbacar, a white Riviera with "Bubba" spelled out on the driver and passenger doors. Parking was always hard to find on a campus of 40,000 students. He might park on a campus lawn or in President John Hannah's parking spot at the Administration Building at the center of campus. He wasn't trying to hide anything—except maybe his excuse for parking in the president's spot.

Years later, Richard Lewis, Michigan State Dean of the College of Business from 1974 to 1993, said Smith brought up the incident when his car was towed from Hannah's spot. Michigan State had sent Lewis to Los Angeles on behalf of the university development fund.

"You could tell after all these years it still bothered him because we didn't bring it up—he did," Lewis said. "What bothered him is it got in the newspaper and made him look like he didn't respect Hannah. He said Hannah had told him he would be out of town. He said he thought the world of Hannah."

Raye isn't buying Smith's excuse even all these years later. "He just didn't want to walk to class."

Smith's car became part of his identity. Raye's most priceless Bubbacar story took place the day before the Game of the Century. The quarterback was the lone passenger in Smith's car when an East Lansing policeman pulled Smith over on Grand River Avenue. Many Michigan State and Notre Dame fans have heard that Smith was arrested for unpaid parking tickets, but most accounts have been embellished over years.

One story tells of Biggie Munn, who came down to the police station to bail out Smith, imperiously threatening the East Lansing police chief, "Do you like your job?"

But Raye, who phoned Munn from the police station and waited for him to arrive, says that did not happen. "That was a story Bubba told later."

Raye provides an account that is more reliable—and nonetheless humorous. The Spartans' Friday routine the day before a home game required the players to report to the Kellogg Center for a 5 p.m. team dinner and spend the night at the centerpiece of Michigan State's renowned Hotel and Restaurant business school. Raye lived at Wilson Hall and Smith next door in Wonders Hall. Smith told him he would pick him up at about 3:30 p.m. to join the team.

Michigan State University is laid out upon a sprawling 5,000-acre campus, but Smith and Raye could have walked from their dorms to the Kellogg Center, crossing a bridge over the Red Cedar River behind Jenison Fieldhouse. Bubba opted for some enjoy-the-moment fun. As Raye slid into the passenger's side, Smith told the quarterback, "Come on, Raye. Let's profile."

Smith took a right turn at Shaw Lane, a main road crossing campus end to end. He turned left up Hagadorn Road toward Grand River Avenue, the main drag separating East Lansing stores and the campus. Once they reached Grand River, traffic soon slowed. Cars were backed up at intersection sidewalks jammed with foot traffic from students and out-of-town fans launching into pre-game revelry. Smith's distinctive car was spotted and fans shouted, waved, and broke into their Spartan Stadium chant.

"They're hollering, 'Kill, Bubba, kill!'" Raye remembered. "Bubba opens the sun roof and he's waving out the top. He's enjoying the whole deal."

Smith's impromptu parade down Grand River was just about finished. He planned to turn left off Grand River and head toward Harrison Road and the Kellogg Center. That's when the patrol car pulled up behind him. The police officer approached the driver's window and instructed Smith to follow him.

"We get to the police station and the guy tells Bubba, 'Mr. Smith, we have a warrant for your arrest. You have 300 outstanding parking tickets.' Bubba says, 'You don't know who I am?' He says, 'I know exactly who you are.' He takes the keys to the car and says, 'Follow me inside.'"

Smith turned back to Raye and said, "Call Biggie. Tell him they got me."

Raye placed a call to Munn at his Jenison office from a police station pay phone. He explained to Munn what happened—the arrest and the parking tickets.

"That son of a bitch!" Munn barked into the phone. Raye is still unsure whether Munn meant Bubba or the cop.

"When Biggie got there, the cops snapped to attention," Raye said.

The matter was settled quickly without the embellished conversations that Smith later attributed to Munn and himself. In fact, Smith and Raye arrived at the Kellogg Center with 15 minutes to spare.

The arrest was just a funny story to Smith and did nothing to distract his play in the Game of the Century. On Notre Dame's second offensive series, Smith tackled Notre Dame quarterback Terry Hanratty, separating Hanratty's shoulder and knocking him out of the game. By the end of the afternoon, as the clock ticked down on Notre Dame's final possession, Smith engaged Notre Dame coach Ara Parseghian and the Irish offensive players, screaming at them for settling for a tie.

There were newspaper accounts of Bubba yelling at Parseghian and the Irish players that they were afraid to try to win. In a 1983 *Playboy* interview, Bubba was more descriptive, repeating the X-rated words he directed at Parseghian and the players.

Despite the many dimensions to Smith, his teammates said in reality he was a gentle giant. "Bubba wouldn't kill a gnat," opined Raye. "If he would have played with the ferocity of Deacon Jones, he would have been out of control. But he wasn't trying to be Dick Butkus."

Even though he had size and talent, Smith was not Michigan State's most promising player coming out of freshman football as fall camp opened for his first varsity season in 1964. Duffy Daugherty grew frustrated trying to motivate the gifted athlete with unusual size and quickness. At one point Daugherty dropped Bubba to the scout team. Smith went to the coach's office to ask why.

"I told him, 'Bubba, you're either going to be a great All-American for Michigan State, or you're not going to play a single minute of varsity football,'" Daugherty said later. "It's as simple as that. If you refuse to go all out, and you don't give 100 percent, you don't play for me."[1]

Smith had yet to make his varsity debut as a sophomore in the days of NCAA freshman ineligibility when the Spartans prepared for their 1964 opener against North Carolina. Yet Ken Willard, the Tar Heels' senior fullback, said Smith's mammoth size that was rare for those days had their attention.

"I don't know how we knew about him, but we did," said Willard, who went on to play 10 NFL seasons. "I think Bubba batted down more passes than our sophomore quarterback completed."

Despite Smith's strong debut, his 1964 season was an overall disappointment. The light eventually stayed on for Smith in his 1965 and 1966 All-American seasons, but his reputation for turning up and down his intensity remained a lightning rod for critiques—some fair, some embarrassingly exaggerated. During his senior year, Michigan State played at Northwestern University three weeks before the Game of the Century. The sports page of the *Chicago Daily News* on Friday, October 28, featured a story bannered across the top with this headline: "Bubba Smith ... 285 Pounds of Myth."

The writer, Tom Fitzgerald, mocked Daugherty for saying he considered Smith a Heisman Trophy candidate. He cited anonymous players from Michigan State's first four Big Ten opponents, Illinois, Michigan, Ohio State, and Purdue. They claimed they "nullified" Smith with one-on-one blocking.

However, following Michigan State's 20-7 win over Michigan, the *Detroit Free Press* game story noted Michigan often used three players to block Smith.[2]

"I don't like it, but it leaves somebody else free and that's good," Smith said.

Fitzgerald also wrote, "It is a colorful anecdote, the one about Michigan State students cheering each Saturday, 'Bubba, kill!' but his actual mortality rate has been far less frightening than that of the common cold." Another reason Fitzgerald said Smith was overrated was that he ranked only eighth on the team in tackles.

"Teams ran away from Bubba," said Hank Bullough, Michigan State's defensive coordinator. "It isn't always the tackles you make—it's the attention you draw."

Someone on the sports desk at the *Chicago Daily News* apparently took exception to the Fitzgerald story, and in Saturday's edition printed a syndicated column from Milton Gross, a New York sportswriter. Gross's story quoted former New York Giants head coach Jim Lee Howell, who evaluated Smith in his role as a scout.

"He is so big and so strong that he scares you," Howell said. "I've seen him go through a pair of blockers, knocking one this way and one that way, as though they were a couple of swinging doors."

The next week when Smith was back on campus, students asked about the game and the *Chicago Daily News* story.

"Yes, it's true I only had two tackles," he said. "But those were the only two plays they ran to my side."

Another criticism Smith heard was that he lingered in the backfield after a play rather than hustling back to the defensive huddle.

"Yes, I'm sometimes slow to go back to the huddle," Smith explained. "That's my way of telling the offensive linemen, 'I got through again.' "

The opponents that ran away from Smith were swept up and tackled by two-time All-American roverback George Webster on his side of the field or All-Big Ten linebacker Charlie Thornhill in the middle.

"The debate always raged about who was better, Bubba or George," Raye said. "They had their own special gifts that made them both great players."

There was an indication of separation in the minds of Michigan State's coaches and athletic officials when off-the-field reputations were factored in. Bubba was a maverick and constant source of consternation. George was the ultimate team player, a team co-captain and the leader the coaches went to when they had a problem on the team. Webster's No. 90 was retired in 1967, one year after his senior season. Bubba had to wait 40 more years—his number wasn't retired until the 2006 season.

Schools also drive nominations into the College Football Hall of Fame, and Webster was inducted in 1987 and Smith in 1988. Both players were inducted into Michigan State's inaugural Hall of Fame class in 1992.

There was certainly no debate over Smith's value among scouts in the first combined NFL draft in 1967 when he was the No. 1 overall pick. But before the merger agreement put an end to bidding wars between the AFL and NFL teams, pro teams had asked to meet with Smith.

"They wanted to establish a relationship with him if there was no merger so they would be in a friendlier negotiation position," Raye said. "They were willing to pay an astronomical amount of money. Bubba was setting an economic structure for pro athletes of that era."

In Smith's second year with the Colts, he was a key to one of the most dominant defenses in NFL history. Baltimore won the 1968 NFL title, but two weeks later the Colts were relegated to a place in pro-football ignominy. They lost to the New York Jets and Joe Namath in Super Bowl III, the first NFL team to lose to an AFL club.

The Colts returned to the Super Bowl two years later and this time downed the Dallas Cowboys in Super Bowl V. Smith was named to the Pro Bowl in the 1970 and 1971 seasons and was voted first-team All-Pro in 1971 in an era when players coveted the recognition and the payday that came with Pro Bowl honors.

Smith was on a path for the Pro Football Hall of Fame until he suffered a devastating knee injury in the 1972 preseason. He was chasing a play toward the sideline when his knee became entangled with the metal sideline marker. In those days, the chain crew retreated when a play came their way but left the markers in place. As a result of Smith's injury, chain crews have forever since pulled the markers out of the way with them. The poles also are now made of a flexible plastic.

Baltimore's team doctors said Smith's knee injury was one of the worst they had ever seen. His rehab in the 1972 season included watching the Colts play from the sideline in a wheelchair.

"Bubba would be in the Pro Football Hall of Fame if he wasn't injured," said Bullough, later a longtime NFL coach, including with the Colts and Smith.

At both Michigan State and with the Colts, Bullough recognized Smith had rare ability for a man his height to play nose tackle in addition to his defensive-end role. At defensive end, Smith could beat an offensive tackle with a bullrush as well as with a quick step to get inside or outside of the blocker. Opponents were forced to put a tight end on Smith's side and leave a fullback in for protection. At nose tackle he could tie up two or three blockers or still penetrate the line.

Bullough first moved Smith to nose tackle in certain situations during Michigan State's 1966 season.

"We had three good defensive ends," said Bullough, referring to Smith, Phil Hoag, and backup George Chatlos. "Moving Bubba to nose tackle was a way to get all three on the field. One of the reasons for our success that year was we had a very unselfish team." Bullough later used the same strategy with the Colts when Smith enjoyed his best seasons.

Before the 1973 season, Baltimore, where management understood the severity of Smith's 1972 injury, traded him to Oakland. No longer dominant, he played two years with the Raiders and two more with the Houston Oilers in 1975 and 1976 before he retired.

"Bubba had the rare gift of size and personality," Raye said. "His gregarious personality lent itself to his transition from football into TV and the movies. All of that was part of him when he was expanding and experiencing life as a student-athlete at Michigan State. His athleticism and personality gave him choices."

By 1977, Smith enjoyed success as a pitchman in Miller Lite beer commercials. The low-calorie beer was a new product, and Smith's popular commercials helped Miller rapidly increase sales. In Smith's first Miller Lite commercial, he stood at a bar and dwarfed people as he spoke into the camera: "I had my own way of tackling. I used to grab the whole backfield. Then I threw guys out until I found the one with the ball. When I started drinking beer, I did the same thing. And this is the one I'm holding on to—Lite beer from Miller. It has a third less calories than a regular beer. It's less filling and it tastes terrific, too."

Then Smith's hands swallowed the beer can as he ripped off the top third: "I also love the easy opening can," he deadpanned.

Bubba also teamed with NFL legend Dick Butkus in a series that depicted Smith and Butkus in various skits. In one scenario, they dressed in polo outfits and retired to an elite country club bar. In another, they were bowlers.

Smith enjoyed the commercials and was rewarded financially. He and Butkus made appearances around the nation. Smith didn't drink, but the Miller competition with beer giant Anheuser-Busch drove him to push sales anyway.

Despite the success, however, Smith grew to regret the popularity of the beer commercials by the mid-1980s. His second thoughts began when he returned to Michigan State and served as grand marshal of the homecoming parade. He was disturbed by the number of drunken college students and their reaction to his appearance.

"The people were yelling, but they weren't saying, 'Go, State, go!' One side of the street was yelling, 'Tastes great!' and the other side was yelling 'Less filling!'

"Then we go to the stadium. The older folks are yelling, 'Kill, Bubba, kill!' But the students are yelling 'Tastes great! Less filling!' Everyone in the stands is drunk. It was like I was contributing to alcohol, and I didn't drink. It made me realize I was doing something I didn't want to do."[3]

Smith, who was in the process of negotiating a contract renewal, walked away from significant money when he decided to end his affiliation with Miller Lite. It was not until a year later that people realized Smith chose to discontinue his Miller Lite commercials—not the other way around.

His decision revealed his integrity, a part of him overshadowed by his many antics and the oafish characters he played in the movies. It was several years after Smith quit the commercials when Lewis visited him in Los Angeles.

"We were in a restaurant and people recognized him," Lewis said. "He had at least five or six people come and offer to buy him a drink. He politely thanked them all and said, 'I don't drink.' They were all surprised."

Smith's integrity still resonated 20 years later with Pat Gallinagh, a starting defensive tackle on Michigan State's 1966 defensive line. The old Spartans gathered for the 2006 Notre Dame-Michigan State game at Spartan Stadium when Smith's No. 95 was finally retired.

"The last time I saw Bubba was at that 40th reunion," Gallinagh said. "I told him how proud I was of him for dropping out of those Miller Lite commercials."

After Smith's death, Michigan State athletic director Mark Hollis recalled the times he spent with Smith. He knew Smith was much deeper person than the characters he played. "Years ago, I had the opportunity to spend some time with him when he served as the grand marshal for the homecoming parade and again when he returned to campus for the retirement of his jersey number, and he had a great presence wherever he went. Despite his stature and notoriety, you felt comfortable around him because he had an engaging personality. As both a football player and later as an actor, Bubba was a great ambassador for the university."

In the 1979 NFL season, a former sports editor at *The State News*, Michigan State's student paper, spotted the retired Smith standing with a friend on the sideline at the end of an NFL game between the San Diego Chargers and Los Angeles Rams at the Coliseum. The young sportswriter apprehensively introduced himself as a fellow Michigan State alumnus, not knowing if he would be greeted by a gracious and legendary Spartan or by an arrogant Hollywood celebrity who didn't care to be bothered.

Bubba Smith turned his attention from the game and extended his giant paw with a friendly smile. "It's my pleasure," he said.

Smith later became best known to a new generation for his role as Moses Hightower in the *Police Academy* series, playing the character in six movies in the 1980s and 1990s.

For all of his fun and games, Smith's serious side was the reason two-year starting cornerback Jimmy Summers was in the Michigan State lineup for the Game of the Century.

Summers arrived at Michigan State as a high-school running back, but the backfield was crowded with Clinton Jones, Gene Washington, Charlie Thornhill, and others in a talented class. After a fall season of practicing together on the freshman team, Summers and Jones ranked as the top two backs among the freshmen. Washington was later converted to wide receiver and Thornhill to linebacker.

By the end of spring drills, Daugherty implemented a philosophical change to his offense. New rules in college football allowed for two-platoon football. Daugherty switched to bigger backs. (In one-platoon football, coaches tended to use smaller players who could play 60 minutes with better endurance than larger men. That was less of a concern with two-platoon football.)

In the 1964 spring practices, Jimmy Summers felt he was playing well, but he measured 5-10, 175. Jones, in contrast, was a 6-1, 215-pounder.

"The third week of spring ball, Clinton exploded," Summers said. "That's when it changed. They said, 'Okay, Clint is going to be our big guy.' In 1964, we also had Dick Gordon, who was 6-0, 210 and Eddie Cotton (6-1, 225), another big guy."

The coaches later told Summers they wanted to switch him to cornerback. His first thought was to transfer, but Bubba Smith convinced him to stay.

"Bubba said, 'We need you, man,'" recalls Summers, shifting into an exaggerated deep voice.

Smith empathized with Summers. He knew what it meant for a running back to see his dreams end. His older brother, Willie Ray Smith, Jr., had his career derailed by a knee injury after initial success at Iowa.

"Bubba dealt deep in terms of understanding what was happening to me," Summers said. "We talked about his older brother. He said, 'If you're so convinced you're the best, then go back and ask for another shot at running back.' But he also said, 'If you get the shot and it doesn't work out, then come back to defense—and let's have some fun.'

"It was the right decision. I'm glad we had that conversation and the switch was made. In the long run, it was the right move."

That was the side of the gentle giant that Smith's teammates knew.

Bubba Smith always meant to be playful, but later in life he told Duffy Daugherty he realized the conflicts he created. The two men had a falling out when Bubba's younger brother Tody, who was on the Spartans' freshman team in 1966, was injured and transferred from Michigan State to USC in 1968. Daugherty said they patched things up in 1973 when they met unexpectedly at ABC-TV's studios in Los Angeles. Daugherty, who retired after the 1972 season, taped a film in his new role as an ABC college-football analyst. Smith was still playing in the NFL with the Oakland Raiders.

"We had a good long chat and Bubba said, 'Coach, I don't know how you ever put up with me," Daugherty said.

Duffy, who once described Smith as "a charming con man," replied he didn't know either, but he was glad he did.[4]

Notes

1. *Duffy*, Doubleday, 1974, p. 131.

2. *Detroit Free Press*, Oct. 9, 1966.

3. Scott Ostler, *Los Angeles Times*, Sept. 9, 1986.

4. *Duffy*, p. 132.

8

THE MISSING HEISMAN

"He stepped out of the car and unfolded like a panther. I knew immediately it was him. He assumed his 6-5 frame and I thought, 'This h-a-a-s to be George Webster.' You could instantly see the physicality that he exuded."—Jimmy Summers, upon meeting George Webster as high-school seniors

Michigan State two-time All-American roverback George Webster might have been the first defensive player slighted by the Heisman Trophy's dubious history of being awarded virtually always to offensive players.

No less a Michigan State rival than Notre Dame All-American linebacker Jim Lynch said he would have voted for Webster if he had a 1966 Heisman ballot. Lynch, who faced the Spartans in the Game of the Century, won the 1966 Maxwell Trophy as the nation's finest player. He joined Webster in the College Football Hall of Fame as a 1992 inductee. He also played 11 years in the National Football League.

"George Webster should have won the Heisman that year," Lynch said.[1]

Notre Dame quarterback Coley O'Brien, who was thrust into the game early in the first quarter when starter Terry Hanratty suffered a broken collarbone on a Bubba Smith sack, remembered watching game film of Michigan State's defense with trepidation.

"George Webster was the guy we feared the most," O'Brien said. "He was tall, rangy and could deliver a blow. We watched their film and said,

'*Th-a-a-t's* George Webster?' Bubba Smith was a great defensive end, but George Webster was the guy I worried about."

The Heisman Trust's mission statement declares that the award "annually recognizes the outstanding college football player whose performance best exhibits the pursuit of excellence with integrity." Nowhere is "offensive player" mentioned, and Webster's coaches and teammates knew of no athlete with more excellence and integrity than the Spartans' College Football Hall of Famer.

The 1966 Heisman Trophy went to University of Florida senior quarterback Steve Spurrier in a landslide decision over Purdue senior quarterback Bob Griese. The Game of the Century was represented in the Heisman Top 10 voting by three players—Notre Dame senior fullback Nick Eddy, third; Michigan State senior halfback Clinton Jones, sixth; and Notre Dame sophomore quarterback Terry Hanratty, eighth.

Only two defensive players received enough votes to finish in the Top 10—and neither one was George Webster or Bubba Smith. University of Arkansas tackle Lloyd Phillips was ninth and University of Georgia tackle George Patton was tenth.

Webster, who passed away in 2007 at age 61, combined rare size, power, and speed. In the mid-1960s, roverback was still considered an innovative position, but head coach Duffy Daugherty first devised it in 1959. A roverback was part safety, part linebacker in an era where teams lined up only one safety in the secondary rather than two in today's schemes with a free safety and a strong safety.

Prior to Webster, other Michigan State roverbacks had excelled. In 1964, when the Spartans positioned Webster at defensive end, Charlie Migyanka was a senior roverback who earned first-team All-Big Ten honors.

When the Michigan State roster assembled for the 1965 season, Daugherty moved Webster to roverback. The 6-foot-4, 220-pound Webster raised roverback innovation to another level. Daugherty saw Webster as part safety, part linebacker—and part defensive end. The move also put Webster at a position that defied the stereotypes of the era that blacks could not play a position that required intelligence and leadership.

"George brought a new kind of national attention to the roverback

George Webster. Photo courtesy Michigan State University.

position in the 1965 and 1966 seasons," said Hank Bullough, Michigan State's defensive coordinator on Daugherty's staff.

The Spartans would place Webster on the wide side of the field, where he had the agility to patrol from the hash marks to the far sideline. On the short side, the 6-8, 285-pound Bubba Smith was a roadblock. Pick your poison, opposing quarterback.

Michigan State's 1965 defensive unit established a still-standing Big Ten record of just 34.6 rushing yards allowed per conference contest. The 1966 defense held opponents to a mere 51.4 yards rushing a game. As a senior, Webster finished with 93 tackles and 10 tackles for a loss—prodigious numbers for a 10-game season.

After Webster's college career, Daugherty and Biggie Munn, the Spartans' athletic director and previous head coach, waited only one year to retire Webster's No. 90 jersey in 1967, an unusually short time for the era. Webster's number was only the second one retired, joining the No. 78 worn by Don Coleman (1949-51).

"George Webster is not only the finest player I have ever seen, but he symbolizes our 1965 and 1966 teams," Daugherty said at the retirement ceremony.

Jimmy Raye says he's never been around a better football player than Webster—at any level. Other players might be the best at a specific skill, but Webster was nearly equal to their best skill in addition to possessing superior all-around ability.

"I've been around guys who were great at a skill set," Raye said. "I was at Kansas City when Derrick Thomas was rushing the quarterback. But in terms of changing the outcome of a game, George was the total package. He had the best combination of all attributes that I've ever had the experience to be around."

Raye added Webster would have been just as dominant an offensive player, perhaps at tight end, as he was on defense.

"He had the size, the speed, and the first-step quickness for football," Raye said. "He had explosiveness at impact. He had the ability to defend the run, the pass or rush the quarterback. He had defensive-back ability with defensive-line capability."

The Heisman Trophy voting might be the only time in George Webster's career that he didn't show up. Even in an era when most of the Southern black stars Michigan State recruited played in the relative anonymity of segregation, Webster stood out. Daugherty began recruiting Webster the summer before his senior year at Westside High School in Anderson, South Carolina. That summer of 1962 was one of the years Daugherty flouted Jim Crow at a clinic he staged for black coaches in segregated Atlanta. Bullough, who was at the clinic, tells of a high-school coach approaching Daugherty.

"The guy told Duffy, 'I know a great football player and I want him to play for you,'" said Bullough.

That player turned out to be George Webster. The popular Daugherty, with friends everywhere, instructed Bullough to contact Clemson University head coach Frank Howard for a scouting report.

Clemson was located near Webster's hometown of Anderson, but the Atlantic Coast Conference school was all-white until 1971. The 1960s was a time when prominent southern college coaches had little to no knowledge of black talent in their segregated states. But Howard was well aware of Webster, whose high-school legend in South Carolina transcended segregation.

"Frank Howard told me if he could take one black player, he would take George Webster," Bullough said.

That was all Daugherty needed to hear. A player destined to be labeled "The Greatest Spartan of Them All" was about to board the Underground Railroad, but not before Daugherty won a recruiting battle with Minnesota, Ohio State, and other Big Ten schools who learned about him.

The first Michigan State player to understand George Webster's athletic aura was Jimmy Summers. They were high-school standouts in South Carolina as seniors in the 1962-63 school year.

Summers played football and ran track at Orangeburg Wilkinson, but his star paled compared to Webster's legend. Webster was a football/ basketball/track star at Westside. When Summers' high school hosted a Christmas basketball tournament that included Webster's school, he looked forward to meeting him.

"I was wondering, 'Who is this great high-school player that I have been hearing about?'" Summers said. "I went looking for him and was told he was in the parking lot."

Summers found a group of young men hanging out around a car and told them he was looking for George Webster. One of the young men said he was Webster, but Jimmy knew better than to believe him. The stranger was no bigger than the 5-9, 175-pound Summers.

"I said, 'Come on, guys,' and then another guy in the back seat said something," Summers recalled. "He stepped out of the car and unfolded like a panther. I knew immediately it was him. He assumed his 6-5 frame and I thought, 'This *h-a-a-s* to be George Webster.' You could instantly see the physicality that he exuded."

Webster, true to his nature, was happy to meet Summers. They struck up a lifelong friendship that winter night in the school parking lot. In fact, without Webster encouraging Michigan State to recruit Summers, the fleet Orangeburg prospect planned to attend Morehouse College in Atlanta.

Summers' predicament, despite his talent, was that he lived in segregated South Carolina. There were a limited number of options to play major college football. No major school in the South, of course, would recruit him. Only three integrated Big Ten teams knew about him in an era when schools generally recruited regionally rather than on a national scope.

Webster and Summers met up again in the spring and discussed college recruiting when they sat together during weekend high-school invitational track meets.

"George had visited Michigan State and told me he really liked it," Summers said. "He said, 'Why don't you give Michigan State some consideration?'"

Actually, Michigan State *had* contacted Jimmy Summers, along with Minnesota and Ohio State. He had received early information from the three schools, but then the contacts stopped. He confided in Webster, expressing his disappointment and confusion over the sudden silence.

Webster told his high-school coach, and Westside's coach also thought it odd Michigan State stopped recruiting someone with Summers' talent. Summers says he later pieced together what happened—why he had stopped hearing from the three Big Ten schools. "My principal wanted me to go to his school, South Carolina State," a historically black school located in Orangeburg. "He was telling recruiters that's where I was going when they called about me."

So went the recruiting process back then, with college coaches having to go through both principal and coach to contact an athlete. Recruiting therefore routinely stretched into the spring before a February national letter-of-intent signing day was established. Now, high-school athletes routinely commit a year or more before they graduate from high school. The athletes deal directly with the college coach from start to finish through phone calls, social media, and frequent unofficial campus visits. There is unlimited information on athletes, thanks to the Internet and subscription recruiting services.

Fate intervened on Summers' behalf when Michigan State assistant coach Cal Stoll, who recruited the Carolinas, spoke with Webster's coach. The Westside coach conveyed to Stoll what Summers had told Webster. Acting on the tip, Stoll picked up the telephone.

"Cal tried my high school one last time," Summers said. "The principal wasn't at school when he called. Cal was put through to my vice-principal. I had already graduated and was visiting my sister in New York. I was planning to go to Morehouse. So the vice-principal asked Cal if he wanted to call my mother. Cal called and asked my mother if I could come up to Michigan State for a visit. She said, 'Absolutely!'"

Summers recalled his mother's only concern: academics. It did not take much for Stoll to assure Jessie Summers that her son would receive a quality education. Michigan State was a growing Big Ten school and about to become a member of the Association of American Universities, a prestigious group of research universities.

"Cal caught my vice-principal and my mom at the right time, and my mother made the decision for me," Summers said. "My mom was very excited. She knew how badly I wanted to go to a Big Ten school. That's where the best football was being played."

Without Summers, a two-year starting cornerback and one of the top sprinters in the Big Ten track season, perhaps Michigan State loses its 1965 Big Ten opener against Illinois. In the third game of the 1965 season, the Spartans trailed Illinois 12-9 when Summers tracked down All-American running back Jim Grabowski to prevent a touchdown. Illinois failed to score and Michigan State won 22-12, improving to 3-0 and 1-0 in Big Ten play before 71,237 at Spartan Stadium.

In the 1966 season at Ohio State, Summers picked off a pass to end the Buckeyes' comeback attempt. The interception occurred at the Michigan State nine-yard line with 3:37 to play, protecting an 11-8 lead. That lead turned into the final score as the Spartans improved to 5-0 overall and 3-0 in the Big Ten.

Years later at a team reunion, Vince Carillot, who coached the Spartans' defensive backs, and Summers recalled old times and the decision to switch Summers from halfback to defense.

"Vince said, 'Speed was the one thing that we could not coach and you had it. You made a difference for us. We needed your speed back there.'"

Not a bad way to be remembered, as part of one of the greatest defenses in college football history.

For Webster, nicknamed Mickey, acting with genuine concern for a new friend's future was typical of him throughout his life. At Michigan State, he was as influential to the Spartans' success off the field as he was on it.

"We could go to Mickey if we were having trouble with any of the players—black or white," Carillot said. "If I told him a player was causing a problem he'd have a talk with him. We had no more problems. Mickey had the absolute respect of everyone—no question about it—as an individual and as a player. They respected him, they loved him and they feared him."

That included the Spartans' independent gentle giant, Bubba Smith. Carillot said Smith had a tendency to practice harder the week of a television game than other weeks. During one non-TV week of practice, Carillot grew frustrated with Smith.

"I got so mad I walked up to George Webster," Carillot recalled. "I said, 'Mickey, Bubba isn't practicing the way we want him to practice. I'm getting so mad, one of us is going to get canned—and it will probably be me.'

"Mickey said, 'Coach, don't worry. I'll take care of it.' He walked up to Bubba, and to this day I don't know what he said to Bubba, but I never had a bit of trouble with Bubba from that day on."

Dan Daugherty spent time around his father and the team on the practice field and sidelines during games as a high-school student in East Lansing and a Michigan State student. "There wasn't a player on the team who didn't fear George Webster," he said.

Webster, as much as Duffy Daugherty, solved a potential NCAA problem when Bubba showed up with a new Oldsmobile in 1966. The car raised eyebrows and a national magazine article suggested an alumnus had purchased it. Duffy had his own suspicions. The AFL and NFL were still battling for players before the merger resulted in the first combined draft in 1967; the car marked a headstart in the negotiation process.

"The Houston Oilers bought the car for Bubba," said Dan Daugherty.

"When George Webster heard about it, he was mad. He threatened to take Bubba out behind Jenison and beat that crap out of him. They were worried the NCAA would take away their wins in the 1965 season."

Smith got rid of the Oldsmobile, but then his father financed a Buick Riveria through a bank in Houston. Duffy checked with the bank and was satisfied. The irony of the story is that in 1967's first combined AFL-NFL draft, Webster was the player the Oilers drafted with the No. 5 overall pick. Smith was taken No. 1 overall pick by the Baltimore Colts.

Webster also was voted a team captain along with two-time All-American halfback Clinton Jones as seniors in 1966. Their stature as co-captains represented more groundbreaking barriers traversed by the Underground Railroad.

A black team captain at Michigan State was nothing new by 1966, but the Spartans' previous black co-captains shared the role with a white teammate. Leroy Bolden, a black halfback from Flint, Michigan, who was an All-American, was a team captain in 1954 with Don Kauth. Herb Adderley, a halfback from Philadelphia who went on to the Pro Football Hall of Fame, was a team captain in 1960 with Fred Arbanas and Fred Boylen. Sherman Lewis, an All-American halfback from Louisville preceding a long coaching career in college and the NFL, was a team captain in 1963 with Dan Underwood.

Clinton Jones and George Webster were Michigan State's first two black team captains without a white teammate also shouldering the role. With Jones and Webster as captains and Raye as the quarterback, the 1966 Spartans debunked the prejudiced belief of the era that blacks could not lead whites.

Webster's teammates also respected his command of the defensive huddle. He merely had to say in an even-toned voice, "Come on, y'all." The players responded as if he had emotionally implored them.

"He raised the level of play on the team like no other player I've been around," said Raye, whose assessment includes his coaching career in the NFL. "He said little, but when he spoke everyone listened."

When Raye moved from the college ranks to the NFL as an assistant coach with the San Francisco 49ers in 1977, he better understood how hard Webster played. In the NFL, coaches routinely rest their heavy hitters early in the week, but it was rare to rest a college player in the 1960s.

"George played so hard on Saturday, his body didn't recover and he didn't practice until Wednesday," Raye said. "He hit with his body with a violent impact. He was a dominant force, a game-changer. He could change the scope of a game with a play or a hit."

George Webster and Illinois linebacker Dick Butkus, a College and Pro Football Hall of Famer, were giants of their time. Many in the Big Ten argue, too, that they were the conference's two greatest defensive players. They played at a time when the Big Ten dominated college football. When the subject of Butkus or Webster as No. 1 came up, Webster refused to be drawn into the debate.

"It was never about me," Webster once said. "That's what people didn't understand. We had so many guys—(Robert) Viney, Mad Dog (Charlie Thornhill), Bubba (Smith), and the rest. We were a team and we still are."[2]

Curiously, Webster's name was left off the list of football awards the Big Ten established in 2011 when the conference added the University of Nebraska to expand to 12 teams. The idea was to honor positions with trophies in the name of two all-time legends. The Defensive Player of the Year was christened the Nagurski-Woodson Award, named for the University of Minnesota's Bronco Nagurski (1927-29) and the University Michigan's Charles Woodson (1994-97). In all, there are 22 Big Ten legendary names attached to 12 player awards. The only Michigan State player honored was Bubba Smith for Defensive Lineman of the Year along with Penn State's Courtney Brown (1996-99). As a rover-back, Webster fits for a defensive back or a linebacker award. The defensive back award was named for Ohio State's Jack Tatum (1968-70) and Purdue's Rod Woodson (1983-86). The linebacker award was named for Butkus and Northwestern's Pat Fitzgerald (1993-96).

In Webster's pro career, injuries robbed him of his due. Webster was the 1967 AFL Rookie of the Year and was a three-time Pro Bowler in a 10-year career. But that list of pro accomplishments fails to do Webster justice, according to Hank Bullough.

Bullough was Michigan State's defensive coordinator when Webster played, but when he left Michigan State for the NFL he followed Webster closely as a longtime NFL coach. He was an NFL defensive coordinator and later a head coach for two years with the Buffalo Bills. Bullough contends Webster would be in the Pro Football Hall of Fame in addition to the College Football Hall of Fame if not for knee injuries.

Webster first hurt his knee in high school and then was plagued by more injuries as a professional.

"I coached George when he came to New England," said Bullough of Webster's final NFL seasons from 1974 to 1976. "George was only a shadow of himself."

In the offseason of Webster's NFL career, he returned to Michigan State to complete work toward his degree. He had made a promise to his mother he would graduate when he left the segregated South for a chance at education and an opportunity to play football in the Big Ten. As a student at Michigan State, Webster wrote a paper about how much he enjoyed living in the North. He had never known an environment where whites and blacks attended classes together and interacted without strife or tension. He said he wanted to live in the North after graduation, but Houston became his home once the Oilers drafted him.

"Being at Michigan State were the best years of my life," Webster once said.[3]

Webster's battered body suffered disabilities from his NFL injuries and he was in failing health in the years before he died, but he left a final and enduring mark on Michigan State, working to establish the George Webster Scholarship Fund up to his death. The scholarship is designed to help former Michigan State student-athletes return to school to complete their degree. Each semester, a scholarship is provided to two former student-athletes.

Webster enlisted the help of Clarence Underwood, a longtime Michigan State athletic administrator and Spartans' athletic director from 1999 to 2002; Ernie Pasteur, a Michigan State teammate from North Carolina who remained in the Lansing area; and Jim Nelson, a Michigan State alumnus from Ada, Michigan. Nelson was the key to funding the endowment for the scholarship.

"I am very excited and feel honored to be the person to start this scholarship fund in George's name," Nelson said when the trust was announced.[4]

The endowment was established by November 2006. Webster was able to meet and inspire the first two athletes to take advantage of the scholarship before he passed away on April 19, 2007—former football player Richard Newsome and former basketball player Antonio Smith. The number of former athletes who had returned to school and earned their degrees through the George Webster Scholarship Fund was soon at a dozen and counting.

"George Webster was a man who exemplified the word 'Spartan,'" Pasteur said. "He was a true Spartan warrior. George loved Michigan State more than anything in the world, and he stood ready to do whatever he could for his alma mater.

"The biggest thrill of George's life came when a scholarship fund was established in his honor. That meant more to him than any football recognition he ever received, including the All-America and All-Pro honors. George firmly believed that everyone should further his or her education to the fullest. He felt that a strong educational background provided the key to a successful professional career as well as enhanced quality of life.

"When George was being recruited by Michigan State, his mother told him that he had to earn his undergraduate degree. After the NFL season, I remember George returning to campus during the summers to finish his degree. Graduating from Michigan State was that important to him."[5]

Webster died from heart failure, but he had battled throat cancer and prostate cancer. He also had both legs amputated due to circulation problems.

The first health problem that threatened Webster's future was a high-school football knee injury his junior season in 1961. Any knee injury was considered career-threatening in 1961 when athletic medicine was primitive compared to what it is now. In segregated South Carolina, Webster's likelihood of receiving proper athletic medical care even by 1961 standards was unlikely.

When Clemson coach Frank Howard heard about Webster's injury, he arranged to have the surgery performed on campus by Clemson doctors he entrusted with the care of his own injured players.

"Frank Howard made sure that operation took place at Clemson University's medical facility," Summers said. "George was probably the first black person who spent any sustained time on that campus. If it wasn't for segregation, George probably would have gone to Clemson because Frank treated him so well."

Clemson in 1961 was a particularly hostile place to confront integration issues. The University of Maryland's Darryl Hill, who broke the Atlantic Coast Conference's football color line in 1963, said one of the ACC road trips where he felt most threatened by fans and abused with cheap shots by opponents was Clemson—the players coached by Howard. Before the Maryland-Clemson game on November 16 at Clemson's Memorial Stadium, Hill's mother was denied entrance. Clemson president Robert C. Edwards intervened and allowed her to sit in the president's box with him.

The Frank Howard-George Webster relationship is another example of how southern coaches were conflicted by maintaining their all-white teams in the segregated South. They dealt better with individual black players than the overall idea of integration.

Howard, an Alabama alumnus and close friend of Alabama coach Bear Bryant, never challenged segregation in the South. His defenders say he was not a racist. His critics say he retired following the 1969 season because Clemson's president had pushed for integration. Clemson's first black student was admitted in 1963. In 1967, Clemson's president, Edwards, began to encourage his coaches to integrate the school's athletic teams.[6]

Howard's successor was Hootie Ingram, and in his first season in 1970 he signed Marion Reeves as Clemson's first black football player. Reeves sat out 1970 due to NCAA freshman rules and lettered for the Tigers from 1971 to 1973. Those years corresponded with Alabama football and Bear Bryant finally giving in as the sixth school to integrate in the Southeastern Conference.

That was the racial climate surrounding Clemson in 1961 when Frank Howard extended George Webster, an extraordinarily caring man, a remarkable act of kindness. It may well have saved the career of one of college football's all-time greatest defensive players.

Notes

1. Mike Celizic, *The Biggest Game of the Them All*, p. 290.

2. *websterfund.org*.

3. *Ibid*.

4. *Ibid*.

5. *MSU.com.*

6. *Post Courier,* Nov. 10, 2010.

9

THE HURDLER

"When the race was over, nobody knew who I was. I've got all these people asking me what school I'm from and I tell them George Washington Carver. Then they asked me what college I was going to. I'll never forget because there were coaches from Purdue and Ohio State there, but no one from Michigan State. I said Michigan State, and they asked me how Michigan State heard about me. I'm beating college guys and no one had heard of me."—Gene Washington

Gene Washington tasted college competition for the first time in the spring of 1963 as a high-school senior at Carver High in Baytown, Texas. Running the 120-yard high hurdles in American track and field's pre-metric age, he placed second in a dead heat in a Houston-area collegiate meet. The field was motivated with athletes from across the country seeking a qualifying mark for the upcoming NCAA championships.

Washington almost won despite significant handicaps. He was younger than his competition. It was his first time dealing with the 42-inch collegiate/international height hurdles rather than the 39-inch high-school hurdles. And he was lined up against white athletes for the first time in his life, an unnerving proposition for a high-school athlete growing up in segregated America.

He would have beaten the whole field but for a fraction of a second—an edge he might have gained with a lean properly schooled at the college level. Yet the story of Washington's remarkable performance remains fresh material when he tells it, even a half-century later.

"When the race was over, nobody knew who I was," recalled Washington, who had committed to a Michigan State football scholarship only weeks earlier. "I've got all these people asking me what school I'm from and I tell them George Washington Carver. Then they asked me what college I was going to. I'll never forget because there were coaches from Purdue and Ohio State there but no one from Michigan State. I said Michigan State, and they asked me how Michigan State had heard about me. I'm beating college guys and no one had heard of me."

For most retired athletes with Washington's body of work in college and the National Football League, as well as off the field in the business world, such a feat would be a well-known side story. It would have been retold many times as an anecdote in recounting the feats of a two-time All-American in football, three-time All-American in track, College Football Hall of Famer, NFL first-round draft pick, two-time Pro Bowler and a veteran of Super Bowl IV.

For example, a similar story is frequently retold about Alabama schoolboy legend Richmond Flowers Jr.

Two years after Washington's Texas feat, Flowers competed in the high hurdles at the 1965 Modesto (California) Relays. He was a high-school senior at Birmingham Lanier when he beat 1964 Olympic silver medalist Blaine Lindgren. Flowers competed at 42-inch hurdles for the sixth time in competition.

"That was unbelievable for a kid coming off high-school hurdles," said Chuck Rohe, who would coach Flowers at the University of Tennessee. "It usually takes a kid a year to adjust to the college hurdles. Sensational."[1]

In 1965, news of Flowers' victory spread for the era with the equivalency of going viral in the Internet age. He was immediately projected as a future Olympian as he began his collegiate football and track careers at Tennessee. Though there would be no Olympics in his future, similar to Washington, Flowers went on to play pro football as a wide receiver and appear in a Super Bowl (Super Bowl V with Dallas), and the Modesto Relays feat is still fondly re-told in track and field circles.

There is more magnitude to Flowers' feat of beating an Olympic medalist, but the real difference between Flowers' legendary feat and Washington's long-lost story is explained as simply as black and white in 1960s segregated America.

Flowers competed in segregated Alabama, but he was white. His performances were dutifully reported in newspapers and picked up by track magazines that listed season bests throughout the nation event by event. Modesto Relays officials knew about Flowers when he entered the meet and welcomed him.

Washington competed in relative anonymity as a black athlete in segregated Texas. Houston's mainstream newspapers mostly ignored black high-school sports. Houston's black newspaper focused coverage on the black schools in its circulation area, reporting very little if anything on outlying Baytown Carver. Not even officials of the local college meet knew about Washington until his high-school coach entered him.

"Until then I had no idea how good I was compared to anyone else because of segregation," Washington said. "I was running times as good as anybody in the country, but it was never recorded anywhere."

Michigan State assistant track coach Jim Gibbard, who coached the sprinters and hurdlers, had no idea of his good fortune—an All-American hurdler was about to land on his doorstep. Joining Washington as football/track athletes in the same class were Clinton Jones and Jimmy Summers. All three were late-spring/early-summer commitments once football coach Duffy Daugherty learned they were available just a couple of months before they enrolled at Michigan State.

Washington, Jones, and Summers all contributed as sophomores to the Spartans winning the school's first Big Ten Outdoor championship in 1965. (Freshmen were ineligible for varsity competition by NCAA rules.) Washington won the high hurdles and was second in the intermediates, Jones finished third in the high hurdles, and Summers was third in the 100 yards and fourth in the 220.

In 1966 as juniors, they went one better. Washington, Jones, and Summers helped the Spartans sweep the Big Ten Indoor *and* Outdoor track and field championships.

Years later, Washington visited with his old coach before Gibbard died in 2011. Gibbard revealed to Washington a story he'd never known about the football/track trio's scholarships.

"He told me Duffy was out of football scholarships and used track scholarships for us," Washington said. "Gibbard had no idea what we could do when we got to Michigan State. But he said after we made our contributions in track, he told Duffy he wasn't going to recruit anymore. He was just going to let Duffy recruit for him."

Actually, Daugherty was willing to share scholarships, too. When retired gymnastics coach George Szypula was inducted into MSU's Hall of Fame in September 2012, he told a story of how he was upset with athletic director Biggie Munn for giving away one of his scholarships to the swimming coach, Charles McCaffree.

"I told him I found this recruit I thought could help us win a Big Ten title," Szypula said. "Duffy was outside talking to the secretary and heard me. He said, 'George seems upset—can I come in?' Biggie told Duffy what happened and he said, 'Is that all he wants? Give him one of mine.'"

Track was Washington's first love in high school, and as late as the spring of his senior year he was likely bound for Texas Southern, a historically black college in Houston with a world-class track reputation. His teammates would have been Jim Hines and Homer Jones. Hines was the 1968 Olympic 100-meter gold medalist with a world-record time of 9.95 seconds—a record that stood for 15 years. Jones ran track at Texas Southern and later played football for the New York Giants.

But Washington's life path changed from track to football thanks to Willie Ray Smith Sr., the father of Michigan State football recruit Bubba Smith. Willie Ray Smith coached at a Carver rival, Beaumont Pollard. He informed Daugherty he should recruit Gene Washington as well as his son.

Daugherty sent Danny Boisture, an assistant on Daugherty's staff from 1959 to 1966, to Washington's home in La Porte, Texas, to gain a commitment.

"Danny Boisture came to our house, and because of segregation, it was the first time a white person had been in our home," Washington said. "I remember my parents were looking at each other because they had never had white person in their house. We were trying to figure out where Michigan State was and Danny started telling us all about Michigan State. But my Dad only wanted to know one thing, and he asked, 'Sir, is all of this free? Will we have to pay anything?'"

Gene Washington still laughs at the memory a half-century later. No, his family would not have to pay for anything but a bus ticket. When Washington left home in 1963, he traveled by bus for two days before reaching East Lansing.

"I'll always remember that bus trip," Washington said. "I think we stopped in every town in Texas and Oklahoma on the way up. With segregation, I couldn't sleep anywhere and stayed on the bus. In those days, if you had a trip of more than 100 miles, you had to make sure you had relatives to stay with on the way. You had to have a place to stay and a place to use the restroom. If there wasn't a black part of the town, you were on your own and probably in big trouble."

Once Washington reached Michigan State's campus, there was no looking back. He was an ideal athlete for the rigors of competing year-round in three seasons—football, indoor track, and outdoor track. He remained on campus in the summer to train and work toward his degree. Washington graduated in four years and earned Academic All-America honors in football and track.

"It was so much nicer at Michigan State than in the segregated South," Washington said. "You knew when you went home what it would be like and it wasn't like Michigan State. After my freshman year, I didn't go home often. There was no way I wanted to go back to Texas. It was really bad the way they treated you in Texas. We didn't really talk about it that much when we got to Michigan State because you knew that's the way it was in the segregated South. As I got older and looked back on it, though, it was disgraceful."

As a fully integrated team, Michigan State's black players avoided the abuse black athletes say they experienced at other schools just beginning to integrate.

"We didn't have that," Washington said. "We would go to class, to football practice, and we supported each other. We didn't get into racial discussions. We didn't say you're black or you're white. We were a family. Duffy never had to say anything to anyone."

Washington was inducted into the Michigan State Hall of Fame in 1992 and the College Football Hall of Fame in 2011. His name was added to Michigan State's Ring of Fame at Spartan Stadium during the 2011 season following his College Football Hall of Fame induction. He was an NFL first-round draft pick in 1967, the eighth overall player taken, selected by the Minnesota Vikings. He was a two-time Pro Bowler and played in Super Bowl IV, targeted by the legendary wobbling spirals tossed by quarterback Joe Kapp.

Though Duffy Daugherty was a run-oriented coach, Washington rewrote Michigan State's receiving record book. His marks stood for years until freshman eligibility, new rules favoring the passing game, and 11-game seasons (now 12) helped players surpass his totals. In Washington's time, Michigan State's regular seasons lasted nine games his sophomore year and 10 games during his junior and senior seasons. The NCAA permitted an 11-game season in 1971, expanding to 12 games in 2002. When comparing statistics, football is a far more wide-open game now.

"My pass routes were simple," Washington said. "I just ran downfield as fast as I could. What helped with the long passes is with our great defense we always got the ball in great field position. The other part that helped was the defense had to be scared of Clint—he could break it and go 80 or 90 yards—so every once in a while we would slip in a long pass. Most of the time I was blocking, but all of the sudden I would take off down field. There was not a lot you could do against that."

Washington stood 6-foot-3, weighed 218 pounds, and flashed game-breaking speed. He would still be considered a big and fast wide receiver in today's NFL. In college football in the mid-1960s, he was a moose with the quickness of a deer.

Washington's Michigan State season record of 25.1 yards per catch as a senior in 1966 still stands. His career average of 18.2 yards a catch ranks ninth on the all-time list, and his 16 career touchdown receptions is seventh. At the time he finished his career, he was the all-time leader in receptions (102), receiving yards (1,857), and touchdown catches (16).

Washington's 102 career catches and 1,857 career yards receiving records stood more than a decade until Kirk Gibson played from 1975-78. Gibson benefitted from playing in more games and from head coach Darryl Rogers, who arrived from the West Coast with a passing game that was ahead of its time in the Big Ten.

Washington led the Spartans in receiving three straight years; he caught 35 balls for 542 yards and five touchdowns as a sophomore in 1964, 40 for 638 and four touchdowns as a junior in 1965, and 27 for 677 and seven touchdowns as a senior in 1966. He was perpetually a deep threat.

"If I only caught one or two passes, the most important thing is we won the game," Washington said. "I never complained to Duffy or Jimmy, never even thought about it. I was the fastest guy on the team and I might have two or three passes thrown to me. I look at these guys playing today who catch so many passes, and I believe I was as good as any of them. But it depends on the system you're in. A lot of those guys who catch a lot of passes didn't win a national championship and they're not in the Hall of Fame."

Washington had six career 100-yard games when 100-yard games were a rarity. He had two as a sophomore, with seven catches for 104 against Wisconsin and nine for 150 against Notre Dame. During his junior year, he caught eight balls for 112 yards against Indiana. As a senior, he broke out: four catches for 143 yards against Penn State; four for 114 against Indiana, and five for 123 against Notre Dame in the iconic 10-10 tie. Amidst the defensive struggle that was Notre Dame-Michigan State Game of the Century, Washington's 123 yards receiving is astounding.

"Gene was the best deep threat in college football at the time," Raye said. "He possessed great size, speed, and the ability to track the ball. He was the consummate teammate that never complained about lack of catches or pass plays. His presence brought fear to the defense and created the run environment that existed at Michigan State."

He was also a big-game player, as evidenced by his Notre Dame performance. The Spartans turned to him when they needed big plays. His blocking contributed to a run-oriented offense that averaged 230.5 yards rushing a game his senior year and 215.3 as a junior.

"We really didn't need a passing game," Washington said. "With Clint Jones, Bob Apisa, Jimmy Raye, and everybody else in the backfield, we could go all the way. Jimmy could fake to Clint or he could go back to pass or he could take off. It was hard for a defense to stop us."

Despite the limitations to the passing games Washington played under at Michigan State and later with the Vikings in the NFL, Washington was named in 1970 to the all-time Michigan State football team and the all-time Big Ten team. In 2010, he was named as one of the 50 greatest Vikings when the team marked its 50th season.

During track season, though, there was no ball to limit Washington's numbers—only the clock. He reigned as NCAA indoor champion and All-American at the indoor 60-yard high hurdles. In all, he was a six-time Big Ten hurdles champion, three indoors and three outdoors.

Gene Washington competed in an era of yards rather than meters, but the high hurdles is the one race that is the same distance at 120 yards or 110 meters. Thus, Washington's Michigan State outdoor 120-yard high-hurdles record of 13.82 seconds remains tied for the school mark. His 13.82 stood alone for 15 years until Tony Gilbert tied it in 1981, although it should be noted that Washington competed before the modern-day fast synthetic surfaces.

Washington and Jones teamed up as juniors in 1966 with Bob Steele and Fred McKoy as part of a national record set in the shuttles hurdles at the Drake Relays. Steele was a two-time NCAA champion in the 440-yard intermediate hurdles in 1966 and 1967.

Yet another school record fell for Washington's 440-yard relay team that also earned All-America honors. The foursome of sprinter Daswell Campbell and football teammates Washington, Jones, and Summers placed third at the 1965 NCAA finals.

Campbell, who is white, was from Hazel Park near Detroit. With Michigan State's reputation for integrated teams and the recognition the relay team gained as an NCAA third-place team, Campbell related that many track fans as well as track athletes assumed from his southern first name he was black. "People would come up to me at track meets and ask, 'Hey, where's Daswell Campbell?' I'd tell them, 'I don't know where that guy went.'"

Washington's white track and field teammates received an ugly view of the shameful segregation and discrimination southern blacks grew up with when the Spartans traveled to other cities—and not necessarily only in the South.

Steele, who is white and from Plymouth (near Detroit), arrived at Michigan State in the same freshman class with Washington, Jones, and Summers. He said his eyes were rudely opened to segregation when a group of Michigan State freshmen attended the 1964 Ohio State Relays. The meet had open events, providing freshmen a chance to compete in the era of NCAA freshman ineligibility. Daugherty allowed Washington to travel to the Ohio State Relays, but he wanted Jones and Summers, as halfbacks, to stay behind on campus for spring football practice.

"We went out to eat for lunch in downtown Columbus," Steele said of the group of freshmen, white and black alike. "We went to this place and Gene turned to me and said, 'Do you think they'll let me in?'"

Steele said the possibility of his black teammates not being served because of skin color caught him off guard. He sensed Washington was embarrassed by the predicament. After all, this was *the* Ohio State University—the alma mater of Jesse Owens, the four-time 1936 gold medalist at the Nazi Olympics in Berlin. Owens brought international fame to the Buckeyes as a black athlete. He set world records and debunked Hitler's white supremacy theories as the fascist dictator watched from the Olympic Stadium stands.

"There were 18 of us, and we were all in our track blazers," Steele said. "The manager in the restaurant looked at us and didn't want to let us in. I told him, 'It is all 18 or nothing.' He left and sent a waitress over to serve us. These kinds of things would happen in Columbus and Iowa City, but they never happened in East Lansing."

Aside from embarrassing moments of discrimination on the road, Washington appreciated pursuing his first love of track over spring football. Daugherty and receivers coach Cal Stoll could trust Washington to be ready in the fall if he missed some spring football practices.

In the spring of 1966, Washington doubled up. He ran in a dual meet against Ohio State at Michigan State's track and played in the Michigan State spring football game the same day at Spartan Stadium. In track, he won three events—100 yards, 120 high hurdles, and a leg on the 440-yard relay team. Then he trotted from Ralph Young Track and Field complex next door to Spartan Stadium for the spring game and caught a touchdown pass.

"I'm thankful that Duffy allowed me to compete in track because I certainly didn't have a great interest in participating in spring practice," Washington said. "Duffy said I could run track if I could contribute. Like Duffy and my position coach, Cal Stoll, Jim Gibbard played an important role in my personal development. I learned a ton from Jim—not only as an athlete but as a person and leader. With different drills, he actually helped me run better pass routes as well as improve my speed in the open field. Jim also helped me to remain humble and hungry."[2]

When Washington was inducted into the College Football Hall of Fame, he reflected on how fortunate he was that Willie Ray Smith not only recommended him to Daugherty, but also that Daugherty trusted Willie Ray Smith's football knowledge and recruiting eye.

"I only had a chance to be inducted into the College Football Hall of Fame because I went to Michigan State," Washington mused. "A lot of people in the College Hall of Fame from states like Alabama, Florida, and the segregated South never played against a black athlete. When I was elected to the Hall of Fame, I thought, 'Now I'm with everybody else.' That's the way it should have been.

"A whole lot of black athletes never had a chance to be in the College Hall of Fame; they never had an opportunity. That part troubles me when I think about my accomplishments. I owe a lot to Bubba and his father. On the other hand, I look at all the excellent players that didn't get a chance."

On Michigan State's campus, Washington didn't see "whites only" drinking fountains or fear interactions with white people. He immediately knew he was in a better place.

"Some people in the South were evil," Washington said. "My brother served in the military and when he came home people treated him badly. I have issues when people talk about states' rights. That's why we had the Civil Rights movement—because of states' rights."

Washington's life at Michigan State was an adjustment in many ways, but academically he found he was well prepared and motivated to succeed by his teachers at Carver.

"The teachers at Carver were great at preparing us academically and athletically," Washington said. "With segregation, we were taught you had to do your best in the classroom because we were treated as second-class citiens. We had to be better than the white students. We really worked hard and we were motivated to do well."

As a senior at Michigan State, Washington won the Big Ten Medal, which is presented to the top student-athlete at each conference school. He earned his bachelor's degree in four years and returned to campus in the off-season from his NFL career to earn his master's degree. In 2013, the Big Ten honored him with the Ford-Kinnick Leadership Award named for President Gerald Ford, a Michigan football player, and 1939 Iowa Heisman Trophy winner Nile Kinnick. Washington was honored at the Big Ten Championship game when Michigan State defeated Ohio State at Lucas Oil Stadium in Indianapolis.

He worked for 43 years following graduation, including during his NFL playing days, as an executive in Minnesota primarily with Dayton-Hudson Corp. and the 3M Company. He worked at Michigan State's Student Placement Services during five off-seasons with the Vikings, including establishing a Diversity Career Fair Program that was the first of its kind in the nation. He also established diversity programs at Dayton-Hudson and 3M.

"My teachers and counselors, after so many years of what they went through, saw the opportunities that we could do something they couldn't enjoy," Washington said. "It was the same for Jimmy Raye, George Webster, Bubba Smith, and others. They saw athletics as our way out. We had a lot of people pulling for us to make it. Our joy wasn't just being egotistical about ourselves. I wanted to do it for my parents and all the teachers I had who had invested in me."

Gene Washington was invited home to Baytown in 2010 to speak when George Washington Carver High School established a historical marker from the state of Texas. At the Baytown historical marker ceremony, he repeated a thought that his teachers had instilled in him: "We were taught that you can have an education and not be free, but you cannot be free if you don't have an education."

The failure of many inner-city schools in contemporary America to properly educate youths and protect them from violence saddens Washington when he reflects on his youth. The decline of inner-city schools also means that these schools are no longer the fertile recruiting turf they were 10 or 20 years ago.

"When I was growing up, everybody was off the street by nightfall," Washington says. "If you weren't off the street, Mrs. Jones or Mr. Lewis would take you back home. If you were out on the streets, they knew you didn't have anybody on your side. The law officials weren't on your side. It was your word against their word, and your word wasn't worth anything. It was tough times. We didn't have people on the streets and everybody knew where everybody was. Now you have all this freedom. You can enjoy the freedom, but some kids have too much freedom."

For Washington, school segregation meant he was bused 15 miles to Carver, the nearest black high school in Baytown. The white high school in his hometown of La Porte was 10 blocks from his family's home, but he had to get on a bus every morning. The bus returned to Baytown after school's final classes, so Washington relied on his dedicated coaches for rides home after football, basketball, and track.

But Washington is unequivocal that there was one great moment in his life that came about thanks to segregation—he met his future wife, Claudith, at Carver.

Claudith is a Michigan State graduate with a master's degree from St. Thomas University in St. Paul, Minnesota. All three of their daughters, Lisa, Gina, and Maya, have graduate degrees, with Gina earning a law degree at the University of Minnesota.

"My wife lived in Highlands and for the same reason I was bused to Baytown she was bused," Washington said. "If the schools in La Porte and Highlands had been integrated, we would have never met. We met as ninth-graders and have been together ever since then."

Notes

1. *Sports Illustrated*, July 7, 1997.

2. *MSU.com*, May 17, 2011.

10

MAD DOG, THE
SPORTSWRITER, AND THE
MYTH

"I listened and he said, 'Charlie was picked as Back of the Year.' He said, 'Remember, he's black. He's the first black player ever picked for this award.'"—Vince Carillot

Charlie "Mad Dog" Thornhill might be the first—and only—All-Big Ten linebacker successfully recruited on the advice of a sportswriter. Black high-school coaches in the South had company in offering unsolicited tips to Michigan State coach Duffy Daugherty and his staff as the Spartans' reputation grew for recruiting southern black talent. In early December 1962, a sportswriter in segregated Roanoke, Virginia, called the Jenison Fieldhouse football office.

Michigan State assistant coach Vince Carillot took the call from Bob McLelland, a sportswriter at the Roanoke (Va.) *Times and World News.* He told Carillot about Thornhill, a fullback/linebacker from Roanoke Addison, a black high school in the city.

"The sportswriter liked Michigan State, and when he called the office, they gave me the phone," Carillot said. "He said, 'I want to tell you something about Charlie—you really want to recruit him.'"

Carillot, of course, was justified in being skeptical of a sportswriter offering recruiting advice. Coaches do not typically trust the scouting eye of a sportswriter—especially one they do not know. But Carillot was patient and realized this was no ordinary tip being proffered.

"I listened and he said, 'Charlie was picked as Back of the Year.' He said, 'Remember, he's black. He's the first black player ever picked for this award.' In those days we watched 8mm film and if we liked him we invited him for a recruiting trip. We sent for some film and decided to recruit him. We brought him up for a visit."

The coaches asked Clifton Roaf, a senior lineman from Arkansas, about to graduate despite an injury ending his career, to serve as their ambassador and Thornhill's recruiting host. Thornhill had grown up a Notre Dame fan and was leaning toward the Irish before Michigan State discovered him.

"I showed Charlie and his high-school coach around," Roaf said. "He liked the campus. The one parting message I gave him was, 'Get your degree.' This game can end with one block—as I discovered."

Thornhill, who died in 2006 at age 61, turned out to be a key member of Michigan State's vaunted defenses on their back-to-back Big Ten and national championship teams in 1965 and 1966.

"Charlie was the most intense and inspirational player I ever encountered," Raye said. "He had natural strength and a great feel for the football. He was the catalyst of the defense. His inspired play forced everyone to play at a higher level."

Thornhill announced his commitment to Michigan State the day he received his 1962 high-school season award at the Roanoke Touchdown Club's banquet on January 14, 1963, at the Hotel Roanoke.

"Football has been good to me," Thornhill was quoted as saying that night. "I have learned sportsmanship and a sense of responsibility. I know that I have received more than my deserved amount of publicity and I am thrilled and humble to be the first player of my race to be honored by the Touchdown Club."[1]

Thornhill compiled three straight 1,000-yard seasons, three straight league titles, and a 25-game winning streak, also leading the city and county high schools in scoring as a junior and senior. White fans began to attend Addison's games at Victory Stadium, which was used for white games on Fridays and black games on Saturdays. At the Saturday Addison games, the white fans sat on the stadium's west side and the black fans sat on the east side.

At the Touchdown Club banquet, Thornhill was pictured with four white players also receiving their awards—two each from the Virginia Military Academy and The College of William and Mary.

Bernard Brown, Thornhill's high-school coach, arrived at the banquet to announce that Thornhill had commited to Michigan State. A story about Thornhill's scholarship was published the next morning, accompanying the article about the Touchdown Club's keynote speaker, Alabama Crimson Tide head coach Paul "Bear" Bryant.

At the time, Roanoke was a thriving railroad hub and the Touchdown Club likely had the wherewithal to fund a Bryant appearance. He was introduced by former Virginia Tech University coach Frank Moseley, a Bryant teammate at Alabama in 1933.

As time passed, somehow a myth developed that Bryant had met Thornhill at the banquet, informed Daugherty about Thornhill, and steered Thornhill to Michigan State. But Carillot and the Michigan State staff knew about Thornhill more than a month before the banquet.

Thornhill's younger brother, William, attended the dinner as a wide-eyed nine-year-old who says he'll never forget seeing Bryant in his red hat (Bryant later switched to his distinctive houndstooth style). The then-segregated Hotel Roanoke made an exception to allow the Thornhill family to attend. "Charlie had been interested in Notre Dame, but he had already committed to Michigan State by the time he met Bryant," William said. "Bryant told Charlie Duffy was a good man and he made a good decision."

William explained McLelland had advocated black athletes deserved to be eligible for such awards until Charlie was finally the breakthrough recipient. "The man stuck his neck out pushing for black causes, "Bob could have lost his job in those days. He said it wasn't right that black kids weren't being considered."

Brown, Thornhill's coach, is quoted in the separate story about Thornhill's Michigan State commitment, saying that Thornhill was "one of the greatest athletes in Addison history." Nowhere is there a mention that Bryant played a role, as the myth purports.[2]

One of several other holes to punch in the Bryant-Daugherty-Thornhill myth is the tale that suggests Daugherty answered Bryant's phone call and accepted Thornhill sight unseen as a major college recruit. However, Carillot said during the recruiting process that he and others on the staff had to convince Daugherty they had studied Thornhill's game film and believed he could play for the Spartans.

"Duffy wasn't sure about him because he was small—only 5-9," Carillot said. "But he was so well-built. He never lifted weights, but he was so strong he looked like he lifted weights his whole life."

Fortunately for the Spartans, Daugherty was the type of head coach who accepted opinions of his assistant coaches and took a chance on Thornhill and other players who evolved into stars. Quarterback Jimmy Raye, so key to the 1966 team's success, was another example of a prospect that assistants encouraged Daugherty to offer a scholarship.

Thornhill arrived at Michigan State for his freshman year in the late summer of 1963, traveling by bus. He arrived at the East Lansing bus terminal at 5:15 a.m.

"He called me and said, 'Coach, this is Dog. I'm at the bus station,'" Carillot said. "I went down and picked him up and he was sitting on the curb with a suitcase. I took him home for breakfast and then to the dorm to get him set up with the guys. Charlie was one my favorites."

Thornhill gained "Big Dog" as a nickname when he was 12 years old. The tag morphed into "Mad Dog" at Michigan State for his intensity, but his transition from the freshman team to a starring role on the 1965-66 powerhouses was a rocky road. On the freshman team, he suffered a hamstring injury that dogged him all year. He also wasn't friendly—especially with white people. He explained years later that living in the segregated South gave him a surly countenance.

"He told me once he never met a white person he could trust until he went to Michigan State," said Kaleb Thornhill, now the director of player development for the Miami Dolphins. "He was able to let his guard down. That was part of his assimilation. He became an extrovert, and his experiences at Michigan State played a big part in that."

Kaleb and his older brother Josh both followed their father to Michigan State as starting linebackers—Josh (1998 to 2000) and Kaleb (2004 to 2007). Josh was named first-team All-Big Ten in 2000.

One consequence of Charlie's true personality emerging was Kaleb and Josh now dreaded going to the grocery store with their father for fear of being stuck inside for an hour if Charlie ran into someone. Once they went to the concession stand at halftime of a Michigan State game and missed the third quarter.

"My dad was all about relationships and taking the time out of his day to talk about football, life or anything in between," said Kaleb. "He had an engaging personality and he passed that on to my brother and me in terms of how to treat people."

Charlie Thornhill's personality transformation began on the football field midway through his sophomore season in 1964. Bubba Smith's free-spirit personality may have frustrated Daugherty, but Thornhill's surly attitude truly angered the jovial coach. Mad Dog was buried as deep as the No. 5 fullback on Michigan State's depth chart and he was deep in Daugherty's doghouse.

Thornhill's career changed with an opportunity that arose when a linebacker went down in practice and the coaches hollered to the sidelines for a new linebacker. Mad Dog ran onto the field before anyone else responded.

Carillot saw what happened, but he allowed play to continue. Defensive coordinator Hank Bullough had recently suggested Thornhill be switched to linebacker. Offensive guard was another option discussed. Fullback almost certainly was no longer viable with promising freshman Bob Apisa eligible for the varsity as a sophomore in 1965.

Practice resumed, and Thornhill made the tackle on the first play. He made the next four tackles, too. From that point various accounts are told on how many tackles he made, but there is no debate among Michigan State players about what happened on the last tackle. When Daugherty instructed his offensive linemen to punish Thornhill on the next play, Thornhill leaped over the line as the ball was snapped and tackled the quarterback.

Daugherty immediately moved Thornhill into the starting lineup, and the Spartans beat Wisconsin and Purdue the next two weeks for a 4-3 overall record and 3-2 Big Ten mark. It was the first time during that disappointing season that the Spartans climbed above .500, but they lost their final two games at Notre Dame and Illinois and finished with a 4-5 record.

The next two years, Daugherty moved George Webster from defensive end to roverback and Bubba Smith began to play up to his potential at defensive end. Charlie Thornhill flourished between the pair of two-time All-Americans, gobbling up ball carriers trying to run away from Webster and Smith. Thornhill was first-team All-Big Ten as a senior in 1966.

Mad Dog was a fitting sobriquet for the intensity with which he fueled the Spartans. In the 1965 regular season finale at Notre Dame, the

No. 1-ranked Spartans trailed No. 4 Notre Dame 3-0 at halftime. The Big Ten title and Rose Bowl trip already had been clinched, but Daugherty worried the Spartans would not score enough points to preserve the unbeaten season and No. 1 national ranking.

"They aren't scoring on us again, Coach," Thornhill told Daugherty. "We only need one touchdown."

Michigan State won 12-3, as the Spartans held Notre Dame to minus-12 yards total offense for the day. Thornhill also supplied an interception. The Spartans celebrated their 10-0 regular season on the train ride home, where they were greeted by 4,000 fans at the Lansing train station.

Charlie Thornhill led the 1966 all-star defensive unit with 102 tackles. That's a lot of tackles for a team forcing three-and-out punts, in an era when there were fewer passes to stop the clock and no TV timeouts to slow down games.

Thornhill, who finished his high-school career winning 25 straight games, tagged on a 19-1-1 college record his junior and senior years as the starting middle linebacker for the Michigan State's vaunted back-to-back Big Ten champion defenses. He was drafted in the ninth round by the AFL's Boston Patriots in 1967, but an injury in fall camp ended his career before he could play professionally. He remained in the Lansing area, working at the State Capitol as the sergeant at arms for the Michigan State Senate before passing away from heart failure in 2006 at the age of 62.

Despite the Bryant-Daugherty-Thornhill myth, Kaleb Thornhill said his father only spoke of Bryant encouraging him to play for Michigan State and Daugherty. His father never told him he owed his scholarship to Bryant rather than Michigan State's coaches.

The Bryant-Daugherty-Thornhill myth might have been an example of an account loosely reported in a newspaper at some time and then in the future picked up over and over in other publications throughout the years until it became accepted as fact. But a lawsuit filed on July 2, 1969 by the Alabama Afro-American Student Association damaged the myth even further, showing that Bear Bryant had little to no knowledge of Alabama black-high school athletes and little to no interaction with black high-school coaches.

The Afro-American Student Association's lawsuit attempted to force Bryant to begin recruiting black football players at a school with a student body that had been integrated since 1963. The association was represented by Birmingham Civil Rights attorney U.W. Clemon, who in 1980 was appointed the first black federal judge in Alabama by President Jimmy Carter.

"We did quite a bit of discovery," Clemon said of the 1969 case. "We talked with a fair amount of black coaches who told us that Bryant was not serious in the recruitment of black athletes. We took his deposition. He was a very gracious guy ... he equivocated a lot in his deposition. We were prepared to show that the contacts with the black coaches were superficial and they were convinced he was not really serious."[3]

"I actually met with Bear Bryant to suggest to him that he should spend more effort in trying to recruit black players," Clemon said later in an HBO documentary. "His initial response was that he couldn't find any."[4]

"We haven't so far had many, if any, that qualified academically and athletically both," Bryant claimed in the same HBO documentary.[5]

Bryant, of course, had met Michigan State-bound Thornhill in January 1963. Thornhill was joined in the 1963 recruiting class by other qualified black athletes from throughout the South, including Bubba Smith, George Webster, and Gene Washington.

In fact, five Southeastern Conference schools found qualified black athletes and desegregated ahead of the Crimson Tide's first integrated team in 1971. One of the five was Alabama's bitter instate rival, Auburn, in 1969.

Another part of the Bryant-Daugherty-Thornhill myth often told is that Bryant sent Thornhill to Daugherty as repayment for Daugherty sending quarterback Joe Namath to Bryant two years earlier. However, in Bryant's 1974 book, he says Maryland's coaching staff informed him of Namath's availability after Namath had failed to meet Maryland's college-qualifying scores. Bryant makes no mention in his book of Thornhill or of Daugherty and Michigan State as part of the Namath equation.[6]

Namath also says Maryland steered him to Alabama: "The coach at Maryland, Tom Nugent, called Coach Bryant at Alabama and said, 'Look, Namath is still out there.'"[7]

Namath makes no mention of Michigan State, although it is true that Duffy Daugherty tried to recruit the talented young quarterback in 1961. Namath and Tom Krzemienski, teammates at Beaver Falls High in

Pennsylvania, visited Michigan State University together on a recruiting trip. Michigan State's admissions office informed Daugherty that Namath would not be admitted, but Namath was apparently more interested in Maryland by then. Krzemienski committed and was the Spartans' second-leading receiver as a junior behind Sherman Lewis in 1963 and again as a senior behind Gene Washington in 1964.

Left unexplained by the myth is how Bryant and Alabama accepted a white quarterback denied admission by Michigan State, the same school with 20 black athletes on its 1965 and 1966 national championship rosters, including Thornhill, at a time when Bryant said there were no qualified black athletes available to him.

Duffy Daugherty recruited 44 Underground Railroad passengers from the South between 1959 and 1972, but none came from Alabama. That's not a track record that supports the myth Bryant benevolently fed Daugherty recruits. In fact, Daugherty landed black players from 10 of the 13 segregated states represented by the Atlantic Coast Conference, Southeastern Conference, and Southwestern Conference.

It's unlikely Bryant knew about Thornhill in Virginia, 874 miles away from his Tuscaloosa campus, when he was unaware of black players in his own back yard. The only southern states Daugherty never tapped were Alabama, Tennessee, and Maryland. If there was an unexplained connection between Bryant and Virginia talent, Bryant could have been expected to have known about Willie Lanier, a linebacker in that same recruiting 1963 class as Thornhill from Richmond, Virginia. Lanier played at Maggie Walker High, a black high-school power, but he says the only major college or coach he heard from other than historically black schools was Dan Devine at Missouri. Lanier became a small college All-America player at Morgan State and blossomed into one of the all-time NFL greats with the Kansas City Chiefs as an eight-time All-Pro.[8]

Bryant's apologists have made the case he tried to integrate as early as when he coached at Kentucky (1946-53), but if Bryant truly *was* intent on searching for a way to integrate his teams prior to Alabama's first integrated team in 1971, meeting Thornhill in Roanoke was a golden opportunity.

If Bryant had recruited Thornhill or another black athlete to enroll as a freshman in the fall of 1963, it would have been three months after Alabama's student body integrated, when Viviane Malone and James

Hood were admitted on June 11 at Foster Auditorium. That was the schoolhouse door where Governor George Wallace stepped aside.

The Alabama historical moment is depicted in a scene from the movie *Forrest Gump*, whose title character, portrayed by actor Tom Hanks, is an Alabama football player inquisitively standing nearby. In retrospect, art imitated life with Namath playing an Alabama football player watching along with fellow students. Namath said years later he had registered moments earlier and remained on the scene.

"The National Guard surrounded the campus," Namath said. "I remember gathering myself 30, 40 feet away and could hear every word...'This is a federal issue, step aside.'...Governor Wallace stepped aside. Vivian went in, man. And that was special. Those of us that understood, their goose bumps burst. It was a big change."[9]

Bear Bryant was one of those who failed to understand. On that same historic June day, Bryant says in his book he was eating at a restaurant in Chicago on his way to a clinic in Montana. Bryant was well aware national public opinion was turning against Alabama and segregation. At the restaurant, the coach said he left "a tip that was more than I could afford," but the waiter chased him down and gave it back to him saying he "didn't want his money."

"He was a white guy, too," Bryant wrote. "I put the money back in my pocket. If he wanted to cut off his nose to spite his face, that was all right with me."[10]

The historic day concluded with an evening address by President John F. Kennedy on TV and radio. He explained the National Guard was called in to peacefully carry out the enrollment of Malone and Hood as ordered by the U.S. District Court of the Northern District of Alabama, but there were no riots as there had been a year earlier at the University of Mississippi when James Meredith was admitted. Kennedy's speech credited the cooperative behavior of the Alabama students. The Alabama student newspaper had also supported the admission of Malone and Hood.

From the Kennedy address: "That they were admitted peacefully on the campus is due in good measure to the conduct of the students of the University of Alabama, who met their responsibilities in a constructive way.

"I hope every American, regardless of where he lives, will stop and examine his conscience about this and other related incidents. This nation was founded by men of many nations and backgrounds. It was founded on the principle that all men are created equal, and that rights of every man are diminished when rights of one man are threatened."

For Bryant, Kennedy's plea on national television to examine his conscience fell on deaf ears for another eight years before John Mitchell and Wilbur Jackson took the field in an Alabama uniform.

Folklore portraying Bryant as a legendary figure in the South fits together as smoothly as a center-quarterback exchange. But to give Bryant credit for scouting and finding Thornhill and informing Daugherty about him diminishes Daugherty's leadership in pushing the cause of integration in the 1960s. Daugherty found players in the South from putting on clinics for black coaches who were barred by Jim Crow laws from attending clinics at the southern colleges. He and his assistants had their boots on the recruiting turf.

There was a six-year lapse between the integration of Alabama's student body in 1963 and the lawsuit that was filed, but the 1969 case never went to trial. Alabama's 1969 team stumbled to a 6-4 record after a 49-26 loss to Auburn, its worst regular season mark since 1958. The Crimson Tide's final record was 6-5 following a 47-33 defeat to an integrated Colorado team in the Liberty Bowl at Memphis. A few weeks later Bryant signed his first African-American player, Wilbur Jackson of Ozark, Alabama. The lawsuit went away, even though Jackson was the only black player in Bryant's 1970 recruiting class.

What ultimately may have played a role in Bryant recruiting black players was the desegregation of the Alabama public-school system. Jackson attended an all-black high school until his senior year when he and his black classmates were moved to a previously all-white school. There was no reason for Bryant's teams to remain all white if the Alabama high schools were desegregated.

Jackson was ineligible for the 1970 varsity team by NCAA freshman eligibility rules, but he was joined on the varsity in 1971 by junior-college transfer John Mitchell of Mobile, Alabama. Bryant admitted in his 1974 book that he was unaware of Mitchell. He writes he was at a Houston hotel talking with his good friend John McKay, the USC head coach, when McKay slipped up by telling Bryant he had recruited Mitchell as a junior-college transfer out of East Arizona College. McKay laughed at Bryant once he realized Bryant did not know about Mitchell or that he was from Alabama.

At that point, Bryant instructed assistant coach Clem Gryska to track down the talented black athlete from Alabama's backyard. Mobile, it should be noted, was more than just another town to Bryant and Alabama football. The Crimson Tide played one of their home games in Mobile's Ladd Peebles Stadium during the 1961, 1963, 1964, 1965, 1966, 1967, and 1968 seasons. Mitchell was a senior at Mobile's Williamson High in the 1968 season.

Mitchell had committed to USC by the time Alabama had recruited him, but he signed with Alabama once Gryska began to recruit him so that his parents could attend his games.

Bear Bryant's failure to recruit a black athlete until the 1970s meant dozens upon dozens of young black athletes in the South in the 1950s and 1960s were forced to look North for an opportunity if they wanted to play major conference football, much as Jesse Jackson had when he attended the University of Illinois in 1959 as a quarterback from Greenville. "I grew up down the street from Furman University, but I could not apply," Jackson said. "I was 30 miles from Clemson University, but I could not apply. The University of South Carolina, I could not apply. So I ended up at the University of Illinois in 1959. Most of the best athletes from that era—the Bubba Smiths, the Jimmy Rayes—they had to go North. The Big Ten schools had all the talent then that the University of Alabama and LSU have now."

Notes

1. *Roanoke Times,* Jan. 15, 1963.

2. *Ibid.*

3. *The Last Coach,* Allen Barra. W.W. Norton and Company, p. 375.

4. HBO, *Breaking the Huddle,* 2008.

5. *Ibid.*

6. *Bear, The Hard Life and Good Times of Alabama's Coach Bryant,* Bear Bryant and John Underwood. Little, Brown, 1975, p. 183.

7. HBO, *Namath,* 2012.

8. HBO, *Breaking the Huddle*, 2008.

9. HBO, *Namath*, 2012.

10. *Bear*, p. 269.

11

THE PASSENGERS

"I told my mother I was never coming back to the South. I broke her heart. She cried. When I left to get on the train, she couldn't come with us. She told my dad, 'Take his suitcases and put him on the train. I can't watch him leave.'"—Clifton Roaf

The Underground Railroad's first player to book passage was Clifton Roaf, a lineman from segregated Pine Bluff, Arkansas. He arrived at Michigan State in the fall of 1959 eager to play Big Ten football and intent on showing his teachers at all-black Merrill High School that they had adequately prepared him to graduate from a major university, despite the limited resources of a segregated school system.

Roaf owed his scholarship to Raymond Hatch, a Michigan State School of Education professor, as well as Michigan State's reputation throughout the South of fielding integrated teams, a reputation established via the power of televised games. Hatch visited Merrill's campus in 1958 when the university was contracted by International Paper Company to evaluate the Pine Bluff school systems. The company wanted to ensure that graduates of both the white and black high schools were properly educated for jobs at the new mill.

Merrill principal M.D. Jordan and football coach Ervin Phillips welcomed the Michigan State professor to Pine Bluff's black school. Jordan and Phillips also told Hatch about Roaf, a star athlete and pupil they believed had the potential needed to attend the Big Ten school. They knew Michigan State fielded integrated teams from having seen the

Spartans in the Rose Bowl, and they asked Hatch to help them contact Daugherty about a scholarship opportunity.

"My high-school coach had a new Pontiac and drove me from Pine Bluff to East Lansing," Roaf said. "We stayed at the Kellogg Center and the next day we walked across the bridge over the Red Center River to Jenison Fieldhouse to meet Duffy Daugherty."

One misperception about Daugherty's success recruiting the South is that he brought to the North only a handful of All-America players. In reality, there were more Clifton Roaf-like stories than Bubba Smith-like stories. These were players who never found stardom yet remained grateful to Daugherty and Michigan State for their opportunity to earn a degree and start a successful career.

In all, 44 black high-school recruits from the South boarded Daugherty's Underground Railroad from 1959 through his final season in 1972. Thirty of the forty-four recruits graduated—68 percent, double the nationwide rate when the NCAA was forced to address the poor graduation record of African-American football players in the 1970s and 1980s.

The NCAA first tracked graduation rates with the incoming recruiting class in the fall of 1984. According to figures provided by the NCAA's Ellen Summers, the nationwide graduation rate for African-American football players was 34 percent. The graduation rate for Michigan State's African-American players in this class was 30 percent. The 1984 recruits comprised George Perles's second class.

On the field, only 10 of the 44 earned postseason honors, ranging from first-team All-America to All-Big Ten honorable mention. Some were never starters. Others, such as Roaf, never played in a game.

Despite failing to earn a varsity letter, Clifton Roaf's Michigan State degree led to a career of 40-plus years as a dentist in his hometown. On Roaf's recruiting trip, he met Daugherty, along with assistant coach Bill Yeoman and freshman coach Burt Smith.

Bill Yeoman went on to become the head coach at the University of Houston from 1962 to 1986, integrating the Cougars' football program in 1964 when he signed running back Warren McVea. Yeoman also recruited Andre Ware, the first black quarterback to win the Heisman Trophy, although the coach retired before the 1987 season and Ware never played for him. Burt Smith went on to succeed Biggie Munn as Michigan State's athletic director from 1971 to 1975.

"They knew I had a knee injury in high school, and while we talked Coach Yeoman rubbed my knee to see how it responded," Roaf said. "I guess they decided it was OK. They gave me a scholarship. It was an amazing experience for me as a kid coming from the South to visit Michigan State."

Jimmy Raye and Clifton Roaf. Photo by Ray Black.

Roaf was elated with the opportunity college afforded him, and happy to escape segregation. His hometown of Pine Bluff is only 44 miles from Little Rock, where the turmoil of the Little Rock Nine erupted in the 1957-58 school year. President Dwight Eisenhower sent federal troops to protect the Little Rock Nine and enforce the desegregation of Central High School. The memory of the Little Rock Nine was burned into Roaf's mind as he prepared to leave home.

"I told my mother I was never coming back to the South," Roaf said. "I broke her heart. She cried. When I left to get on the train, she couldn't come with us. She told my dad, 'Take his suitcases and put him on the train. I can't watch him leave.'"

He boarded a train that was segregated until it reached Cairo, Illinois, on his way to East Lansing by way of Chicago. His Michigan State athletic scholarship was essentially a passport to cross the Mason-Dixon Line into what seemed a different nation.

Roaf earned his Michigan State zoology degree and then a dental degree at Howard University in Washington, D.C. As life unfolded, he returned home to Pine Bluff, after all. He worked at his dental practice at age 72 until he retired after 40 years in 2013.

"What do we know when we're young?" he said with a laugh. "My parents were still alive, and I decided I wanted to give back to my community."

Roaf and his wife, Andree Layton Roaf, met at Michigan State and were both graduates of the school. While he earned his dental degree at Howard, his wife worked in Washington as a scientist for the U.S. Food and Drug Administration. They moved to Pine Bluff in 1969, where they raised four children. Clifton opened his dental practice. Andree switched careers and earned a law degree in 1975 from the University of Arkansas-Little Rock.

Andree taught law for a year at UALR before she went into private practice with a Little Rock firm, Walker, Roaf, Campbell, Ivory and Dunkin. In 1995, she became the first African-American woman named to the Arkansas Supreme Court. She passed away at age 68 in 2009.

"I'm indebted to the people of Michigan State," Roaf said. "I came from very humble beginnings. My father was a laborer for the railroad who could never have afforded to send me to college. I grew up on that campus. I met a beautiful woman that I married. I'll never forget my Michigan State experiences."

Roaf entered the 1961 spring drills thinking he was positioned to break into the playing rotation for his junior season in fall, but on a kickoff coverage drill a blocker struck the same knee he had first injured in high school. He was never the same. He finished that spring with a walking stick to help him across campus to classes and labs. The next two years, he showed up for practice and dressed for home games despite never taking the field.

"My dad told always taught me to finish what you start," Roaf said. "I felt if you could survive Michigan State's practices, you could survive anything."

He also felt a responsibility to his dedicated teachers at Merrill to graduate. His senior teammates noticed his work ethic on and off the practice field and voted him a team ring.

"I still have that ring," Roaf said. "I'm very proud of that, and I felt a part of the team. We beat Michigan all four years I was there."

When Michigan State ran off a four-year winning streak against Michigan from 2008-11, Roaf read stories that noted it was the first time since 1959-62. He felt he was reading about his team, even though you won't find his name listed among varsity lettermen in Michigan State's media guide.

"I wouldn't trade being on those teams for the world," he said. "Hank Bullough was an assistant coach when I was there, and one year when I came back for a reunion he gave me a Michigan State hat. When Michigan State plays, no matter where I am, I'm always wearing my Sparty stuff."

The football gods ultimately paid back Roaf for his lost playing career. His son Willie Roaf—named William for Andree's father William Layton, an Urban League official in Michigan—was inducted into the Pro Football Hall of Fame in 2012. A product of Louisiana Tech, Willie wore No. 77 during a standout career as an 11-time Pro Bowl offensive tackle with the New Orleans Saints and Kansas City Chiefs.

Willie Roaf was lightly recruited as a senior at Pine Bluff High in 1990, so naturally Clifton wondered if his alma mater would be take a look at his son. He placed a call to the Michigan State football office when head coach George Perles was the program's steward.

"They told me they didn't recruit Arkansas," Clifton said. "I didn't push the issue. I just let it go. Duffy Daugherty would have listened."

Roaf thought back to his Michigan State days on that August 2012 afternoon while he watched his son's induction into the Pro Football Hall of Fame in Canton, Ohio.

"I felt Will validated me as an athlete," Roaf said. "We'll never know how good I would have been if it wasn't for that block that hurt my knee, but there is no doubt in anyone's mind that No. 77 can *play*."

By the time Roaf enrolled, Daugherty had staged his first clinics in the South for black high-school coaches. The black coaches began to tip Daugherty with a trickle followed by the gusher of Bubba Smith, George Webster, Gene Washington, Charlie Thornhill, and Jimmy Raye as the Underground Railroad gained steam.

But there always was another Roaf-like story. Ernie Pasteur of Queen Street High in Beaufort, North Carolina, arrived at Michigan State highly recruited as fullback/linebacker in the 1963 class before an injury ended his career. Still, he loved his time at Michigan State and the education he received.

Pasteur owes Earl Tootle and Norm Clark for his Michigan State opportunity. Tootle was his older brother's high-school football team-mate and Clark, who Tootle knew, was a white high-school coach at nearby Morehead City. Pasteur thought he'd follow his brother Joe to play at North Carolina A&T until Tootle drove Pasteur to meet Clark.

"I had never met the guy," Pasteur said. "I told him I was planning to go to A&T or Grambling. He said, 'Ernie, you're better than that. I've been following your career—let me write some letters.'"

Michigan State was among the Big Ten schools that began to recruit Pasteur. He had suffered a pinched nerve in his shoulder in high school, but he kept the injury quiet for fear of jeopardizing a scholarship opportunity.

At Michigan State he practiced with the freshmen team in the fall of 1963 in the NCAA era when freshmen were ineligible for the varsity. As a sophomore in 1964, he was switched to offensive guard. The pounding of Big Ten-level play on his shoulder began to take a toll, but he played through the shooting pains down his side.

"I didn't want to lose my scholarship," Pasteur said. "There was an expectation when I left North Carolina that I would graduate. Every time I came home, the coaches and teachers had me talk to kids at my high school."

Pasteur saw limited playing time his sophomore year, spending the year on the "White Rocks"—the Spartans' term for the practice squad. But Michigan State assistant coach Vince Carillot said the coaches recognized Pasteur stood out in his otherwise anonymous role.

"Ernie was an integral part of the team," Carillot said. "He was on the White Rocks, but he helped the varsity. The first-stringers will tell you Ernie was tougher to face than some of the players on teams we faced."

Pasteur's playing time was still limited as a junior midway through the 1965 season when the pain shooting from his shoulder down his side turned unbearable. Jeff Richardson, an All-Big Ten tackle and Big Ten wrestling heavyweight champion, convinced Pasteur to have his shoulder checked. The team doctors told him he risked further serious injury. The diagnosis ended his career, but not his education.

"Duffy and Burt Smith told me not to worry about my scholarship," Pasteur said. "Burt asked me to come out and help him coach the freshman team. God bless Burt Smith. To this day I love that man."

Pasteur graduated, began his career as a teacher and added master's and educational specialist degrees in administration. He was a teacher, vice-principal, principal, and later a campus director at a juvenile facility. His career concluded as a consultant for Central Michigan University, establishing charter schools throughout the state of Michigan.

Similar to Roaf, Ernie Pasteur and his future wife met as Michigan State students, but here Pasteur's story took a complicated interracial twist—his girlfriend was white. Ernie was a sophomore and Micki a freshman when they met in 1964. The black players of the 1950s and 1960s widely felt there was an unwritten rule against dating white women on campus. The penalty was doled out in reduced playing time.

Ernie Pasteur and family. Photo courtesy Ernie Pasteur.

When Jimmy Raye made his recruiting trip to Michigan State, linebacker Charlie Thornhill was his host and picked him up at night in a car driven by a white girl. When they crossed by the Brody Complex and Kellogg Center by a well-lit area, Thornhill ducked down in the front passenger seat and instructed Raye to do the same in back seat. He explained it was not a good idea to be seen with a white girl.

"Duffy didn't come out and say it, but we knew about the unwritten rule from the older players," Pasteur said. "Sherman Lewis told us and players before Sherman told him. It was handed down. There was retribution—unless you were a star like Bubba or George. It affected my playing time—I know it did.... I know it did. The coaches knew Micki and I were dating, but I didn't care. We were in love. It was a campus of 40,000 students and back then there were only about 350 black students."

Ernie and Micki, a lawyer, had two daughters and a son. E.J. Pasteur served as a U.S. Army officer after graduating from West Point, where he was a member of the wrestling team. Nicole Dandridge teaches law at Michigan State. Tracy Pasteur is their oldest daughter, and Ernie likes to joke "she ran away from home" to the University of Michigan, where she earned bachelor's and master's degrees.

Younger generations may not appreciate the harsh prejudice against interracial dating that existed not so long ago. There were laws against interracial dating in states like Virginia that were struck down in 1967 by the U.S. Supreme Court. A kiss between a black actor and white actress on television could set off a firestorm of controversy for networks, alienating viewers and advertisers.

At the end of spring drills in 1966, when Clinton Jones and George Webster were elected by a player vote as Michigan State's first two black team captains without a white co-captain to share the leadership role, they were approached by black teammates who wanted them to ask Daugherty to end the unwritten rule.

"Maurice Haynes and some other guys said they didn't want there to be retribution anymore for interracial dating," Jones said. "We told Duffy, and Duffy said, 'O.K.'"

Whatever bitterness Pasteur felt was overridden by his opportunity to graduate. He pays back his school by serving on the board of the Michigan State Football Players Association, taking care of behind-the-scene details for reunions that allow the old stars to come home and shine again. Micki has served on the MSU Mid-Michigan Alumni Board.

"Michigan State has given me a lot and I've given back to Michigan State," Pasteur said. "It's been a warm place and a place of comfort."

Jim Garrett, who arrived at Michigan State in 1962 as a highly touted quarterback from Columbia, South Carolina, left the school bitter about being switched to halfback. He only earned only one varsity letter as a little-used backup in 1965, but he put together one of Michigan State's finest track and field careers as a five-time Big Ten champion and eight-time Big Ten medalist in indoor and outdoor track and a two-time NCAA indoor meet medalist.

Garrett's individual points were crucial to three Big Ten team titles for the Spartans—two outdoor (1965 and 1966) and one indoor (1966). A case could be made that he belongs in the Michigan State Hall of Fame based on his track career alone.

Jim Garrett also graduated with a degree in education. He and his college girlfriend Linda married and became teachers. He later was a human resources director for 3M in Minnesota, passing away in 1997. With time, his degree and track success outweighed his football disappointment. His family established the James T. Garrett Memorial Scholarship Fund through the MSU Black Alumni Association. Each year an African-American student at Michigan State receives a $1,000 to $1,500 scholarship.

"Jim was stubborn and independent, which didn't help his football career," Linda Garrett said. "But he loved his track career. He was the first person in his family to go to college and graduate. With his degree and track success, that was important to him. The scholarship was a way to honor his life."

Jim and Linda's son Chris was a four-year letterman as a wide receiver at Arizona State. Among other ASU games, they traveled to two Michigan State-Arizona State games in 1985 in East Lansing and in 1986 in Tempe.

The list of 44 Underground Railroad players, starting with Roaf as the lone passenger in 1959, ends symbolically with quarterback Charlie Baggett. Baggett arrived in 1972 as a transfer from the University of North Carolina, joining four black freshmen from the South in Daugherty's final 1972 recruiting class. NCAA rules required Baggett to sit out 1972 as a transfer, but he was a three-year starter from 1973 to 1975.

A gross misunderstanding of Daugherty's Underground Railroad is that it ended with the 1966 team's success, prompting Southern schools to finally integrate and keep talent home. The numbers don't add up that way. Among Daugherty's 44 Underground Railroad passengers, 26 were on the varsity roster in Daugherty's final six seasons—1967 to 1972.

Those 26 players represent 59 percent of the total number of southern black players Daugherty recruited from 1959 onward.

In addition, Michigan State's number of Underground Railroad players on the varsity team remained consistent from 1964 through 1972: There were 8 in 1964, 11 in 1965, 12 in 1966; 11 in 1967; 11 in 1968; 10 in 1969; 10 in 1970; 7 in 1971; and 13 in 1972.

The 1966 season was a starting point for integration, in part because television shone a light on Michigan State's successful integrated roster. Still, many southern schools and coaches continued to drag their feet. It's true that by the early 1970s southern schoolhouse doors had finally opened to black athletes as well as black students, but there was no clean sweep of the talent pool by Alabama's Bear Bryant and his colleagues. In the early days, they signed only one or two black recruits a year, so other prospects from the South were still forced to look North for an opportunity. The pipeline from the South was not turned off like a faucet.

Only five of the ten SEC schools had integrated before the 1971 season, when Alabama was joined by Vanderbilt. The last three SEC schools to integrate were Georgia, LSU, and Ole Miss in 1972: Georgia with three black players and LSU and Ole Miss with one black player each.

Tight end Billy Joe DuPree was recruited in 1968 by the Spartans out of segregated Richardson High in West Monroe, Louisiana. He says every time he's invited to play in a celebrity golf tournament he can count on one question.

"I hear all the time, 'Why didn't you go to LSU?'" DuPree said. "I say, 'Let's take a little trip back in time, guys. There was something called segregation. My other options were historically black schools in the South.'"

The 1972 college football season was the first year the NCAA permitted freshmen eligibility on the varsity. Michigan State's 1972 roster had eight southern black players among the sophomore, junior, and senior classes and 13 total when four freshmen and a redshirt freshman transfer (Baggett) are included. The eight sophomores, juniors, and seniors in 1972 are equal to the eight Underground Railroad players on the 1964 varsity team that included future College Football Hall of Famers Bubba Smith, George Webster, and Gene Washington.

Michigan State's decline from a national powerhouse to a .500 program from the 1967 to 1972 seasons was about Daugherty and his changing cast of assistants—not desegregation in the South. The new staffs failed to identify and develop recruits as successfully as Daugh-erty's staffs that built the 1965 and 1966 rosters. The 1966 team alone had six Underground Railroad players earn all-star honors. In that sin-gle season, there were three consensus All-Americas (Smith, Webster and Washington), two more first-team All-Big Ten picks (Charlie Thornhill and Jess Phillips), and one more second-team All-Big Ten choice (Jimmy Raye).

By contrast, the total number of southern black recruits garnering postseason honors from 1967 to 1972 was only six in six seasons. Of those six, none was consensus All-America and three were limited to honorable mention All-Big Ten. A winning record has other factors, such as a lack of injuries and team chemistry, and the 1967 team was devastated by injuries. Raye missed games with a rib injury and played hurt. All-America fullback Bob Apisa missed most of the season due to knee injuries.

Daugherty may have failed to win games at the end of his career, but his larger contribution was the opportunities he provided 44 Under-ground Railroad passengers in an era of segregation. He was progressive when his southern brethren at best tacitly approved of segregation.

"My love for Michigan State began in high school when I saw Sher-man Lewis and Dewey Lincoln on TV," Ernie Pasteur said. "It stood out as an integrated school. Before then, my path was set for North Carolina A&T or Grambling. Duffy, Cal Stoll, and Burt Smith did so much for me."

12

MR. MSU

"We were more than a sports story at Michigan State. A lot of athletes and youths today don't know the history of the 1960s. There were people being murdered and put in jail over voting. Things were boiling over in the country with civil unrest, but at Michigan State we were an oasis."—Clinton Jones

Clinton Jones basked in the glow of the Michigan State Athletics Hall of Fame as he was enshrined on Sept. 20, 2012, at the Wharton Center. The two-time All-American halfback expressed no disappointment that his alma mater waited 46 years to induct him alongside teammates and fellow two-time All-Americas Bubba Smith, George Webster, and Gene Washington.

Similar emotions coursed through him when he learned he had been named to College Football Hall of Fame's Class of 2015, joining Webster (1987), Smith (1988) and Washington (2011). Michigan State is only the fourth school with four players from the same class named to the College Football Hall of Fame and the first since 1940. More significantly, they are the first foursome of black athletes, another illustration of the Underground Railroad's influence.

Jones was from Cleveland, Ohio, and thus didn't ride the Underground Railroad, but he suffered the institutional racism of the North as a youth in the 1950s and 1960s in the Lake Erie factory city. He viewed Michigan State as his escape route to opportunity, much like his teammates from the segregated South.

The 6-foot, 215-pound halfback's success propelled him to the

National Football League as the second overall pick of the 1967 draft by the Minnesota Vikings. His professional career did not match his college days as his first marriage, to a Michigan State girlfriend, ended in divorce, but he is a man at peace with himself. He has practiced Soka Gakkai, a Japanese Buddhism, since the end of his pro playing days and throughout his second career as a chiropractor for 30-plus years in Southern California.

"I never even thought about the Hall of Fame until someone asked me about it a year ago," Jones said the night of the ceremony. "I didn't feel unfulfilled, but now that I'm in, I feel more responsibility to represent Michigan State. It's a great school."

Jones's speech was thoughtful but likely one of the shortest heard in the historic venue. "I had a coach, Bud Grant," Jones began, "who said when you get up to give a speech, stand tall so people can see you, speak loud so people can hear you, and sit down so people will like you." He followed that directive to the letter, speaking for just three minutes.

Short and sweet, however, was insufficient for the interview session that preceded the Hall of Fame ceremony. Jones and the other Hall of Fame inductees in the six-member Class of 2012 sat at individual tables in a Wharton Center conference room. None of them had waited longer for the moment than Jones—not even 91-year-old gymnastics coach George Syzpula, who guided the Spartans to a national title in 1958. Syzpula had been retired only 24 years.

A crowd of media members with tape recorders and video cameras huddled around Jones. He spoke of his pride having played on the first fully integrated team in college football—one that changed the face of the college game.

"We had people from all over the world at Michigan State," Jones explained. "It's a testament to Michigan State's history. We came together. We never had racial overtones on our team. We had black guys from the South with no association with white players and white players with no association with black players. When we squabbled, it was like a family—like brothers. It wasn't racial."

One reporter expressed skepticism. "Clint, there was so much racism back in that time, and I know Michigan State was in the forefront of trying to end that, but how were the students? Did you encounter much racism back then?"

"I didn't encounter any," Clinton Jones promptly replied. "None. My sophomore year I lived in Wonders Hall, and I don't know how this happened, but I was voted Mr. MSU."

Then Jones paused. "I take that back—there was some racism. Miss MSU wouldn't dance with me. I was a sophomore and the first black Mr. MSU. The tradition was Mr. MSU and Miss MSU would lead off the ball, but she wouldn't dance with me."

Miss MSU in the spring of 1965 was Anne Lawrenz, a comely white sophomore from Franklin, Michigan. Jones's first indication she was unhappy sharing the honor with a black man was when they met for a photo arranged by the *State News*, the student newspaper.

On the front page of the March 4, 1965 edition, Jones and Lawrenz were posed together before Beaumont Tower, a campus landmark. Lawrenz had a forced smile, and Jones a stoic look. Two or three feet separated them in a three-quarter turn toward the camera. They tucked their hands in their coat pockets. There was no story, only a photo with a headline and caption: Surveying Their Realm; "Anne Lawrenz, Franklin sophomore, and Clint Jones, Cleveland sophomore, survey the realm in which they reign as Miss MSU and Mr. MSU."

Jones tells the Miss MSU story with regret in his voice. He sounds as if he wishes he could wipe away what he considers the only racial scar on his Michigan State days.

"We were more than a sports story at Michigan State," he said. "A lot of athletes and youth today don't know the history of the times. There were people being murdered and put in jail over voting. Things were boiling over in the country with civil unrest in the 1960s, but at Michigan State we were an oasis.

"What we accomplished was a paradigm shift into a positive energy and synergy instead of polarization. We became a family. We were more important to each other than anything else. We bridged gaps of racism and negativity. We just jelled that way. We'd do anything for our brothers, and when I say brothers I don't mean black brothers. I mean the whole team."

Jones said he never heard his white teammates using the N-word or other racial slurs. Then after a pause he added a footnote with a laugh, "The only person at Michigan State who ever called me a nigger was George Webster, but we could do that with each other."

Webster and Jones were voted by the players as team captains for the 1966 season. They weren't the Spartans' first black team captains, but they were the first two black captains who didn't share the team leadership role with a white teammate.

"To have two black captains and Jimmy Raye as a black quarterback in that period of time was incredible," Jones said. "Kids today don't understand how incredible that was."

Team captains Clinton Jones (#26) and George Webster (#90), as voted on by teammates. It was the first time two black team captains shared honors without a white co-captain. Courtesy Michigan State University.

Clinton Jones' first experience as an integration leader came during his high-school years at Cathedral Latin (the Catholic school has since closed its downtown site and merged with a Catholic girls school to form Notre Dame-Cathedral Latin in suburban Chadron). He rode public buses 45 minutes each way between the school and his home in the blue-collar section of town known as Mt. Pleasant. He was the only black varsity football player on the team at a school with about 20 black students in an enrollment of 1,100. Unlike his Michigan State days, Jones did hear the N-word at Cathedral Latin.

"I was sitting at a table once with a guy named Tim McNeal who was talking about 'those niggers,'" Jones said. "The other guys looked at him because I was sitting there at the time. He looked at me and said, 'Oh, but you're different, Clinton.' I was only different because I was on the team and they knew me.

"Cleveland was as racist as any place in the South. The neighborhood I grew up in was Italian, Sicilian, Eastern European, and Orthodox Jews. We lived together, but we didn't socialize. My children never knew any of that. We had people at our house of all cultural groups."

Clinton Jones's children grew up in Southern California, where he and his second wife, Rosielee, are practicing chiropractors. They own Jones Chiropractic Wellness and Sports Center in Lake Balboa in the San Fernando Valley. Rosielee had one daughter, Dywana, whom Jones considers his daughter, and together they had four more girls, Stephanie, Tiffany, Shani, and Cara Ren. Their daughters grew up a world away from his gritty Cleveland childhood.

Jones was born to a 15-year-old mother, Emma Lee Jones, and a 19-year-old father, also named Clinton, who turned alcoholic and physically abusive. When Jones was six years old, his father beat him so badly his grandmother wanted him arrested. Clinton's grandmother, Eula Riggins, remained upset with his mother for months for not calling the police. His parents ultimately divorced when he was nine.

Jones opened up about this period of his childhood in 2012 when he fulfilled a request from Soka Gokkai International to compile a brief biography.

"I developed learning disabilities and I had low self-esteem as a child," he wrote. "I would strike out at anything that made me unhappy. I felt powerless and seemed always to be searching for something. Cleveland was a very violent environment for blacks in the 1950s. There

was always racism and rampant slander by everybody in my environment. I saw the injustice in the community and many unhappy families.
I wanted a better life and I wanted to get out of Cleveland. These strug-
gles as a child would become the foundation for the rest of my life."

Following his parents' divorce, he was raised by his mother, who
worked two to three jobs, and his grandmother, who was born in the
South and knew segregation's brand of racism. His first escape was to
Cathedral Latin outside of Cleveland's east-side borders.

"I chose a high school out of my neighborhood so I could get out of
the environment I was raised in," Jones said. "I really started to blossom
there because I had mentors who cared about me and my mother."

Clinton Jones was lightly recruited in football due to a broken wrist
his senior year. He had planned to attend the University of Detroit until
one of his high-school coaches, Dick Marabito, informed him Detroit
was about to drop its football program and had a track club but no varsity track team. Marabito made a call to John McVay, then a Michigan
State assistant coach. McVay and Marabito were old friends, and McVay
trusted Marabito's recruiting eye. He invited Jones on a recruiting trip
to Michigan State.

"I went to the spring game and fell in love with the campus," said
Jones of his commitment to the Spartans.

Ohio State coach Woody Hayes learned about Jones by watching the
Cleveland product sweep state titles in the high hurdles and low hurdles at the Ohio state meet, contested on the track at Ohio Stadium in
Columbus. Hayes congratulated Jones and said he would call him about
a recruiting trip, expecting the Ohio kid to jump at the possible scholarship offer.

"Clint was too polite to say he had already committed to Michigan
State," Marabito said. "When Woody called and Clint told him he was
going to Michigan State, Woody cussed him out. Can you imagine that?
He was cussing out an 18-year-old kid on the phone. That was Woody."

Jones arrived at Michigan State on the freshman team in the fall
of 1963 amongst a bumper recruiting crop that included Bubba Smith,
George Webster, Gene Washington, Charlie Thornhill, and Jimmy Summers. They played under freshman coach Burt Smith, who went on to
become Biggie Munn's successor as athletic director from 1971-1975.
Smith was Jones's first Michigan State mentor in his development into
All-America stature.

"Burt Smith molded us as a team," Clinton Jones says with conviction. "He made sure we left our high-school accolades at home. Burt doesn't get enough credit for the job he did with us. When he took us up the 'hill' to scrimmage the varsity, we started kicking ass. I got in a fight with a varsity linebacker and kicked his ass. Duffy could see then he had something special with the freshmen."

Jones, falling back on his experience at Cathedral Latin as a black kid with white teammates and classmates, took it upon himself to see that college football's first fully integrated roster had the same unity at team meals as on the football field. "The white guys were sitting with white guys and black guys with black guys. I felt I was the bridge. I had socialized with white guys in high school. I could sit with the black guys and the white guys and get us to sit together."

Duffy Daugherty also noticed the separate groups and instructed the players to sit without regard to race. He told them the only colors at Michigan State were green and white.

Jones also arrived with size and agility at the right time for his first varsity season as a sophomore. New substitution rules in 1964 permitted two-platoon football, a dividing line in the size of college football players past and present. Michigan State had previously thrived on small, quick running backs in the 1950s and early 1960s. Limited substitution rules favored one-platoon football and smaller players that could stay on the field for 60 minutes.

Daugherty changed his philosophy in spring drills to go with bigger backs as Jones arrived for his first varsity season. The Spartans suffered through a disappointing 4-5 record, but Jones gained experience to set up his breakout year. As a junior in 1965, Jones's first career 100-yard game was against Ohio State and Hayes.

Hayes, a run-the-ball-first coach most closely associated with the phrase "three-yards-and-a-cloud-of-dust," watched as Michigan State's defense held his team to minus-21 yards rushing while the kid from Cleveland shredded the Buckeyes' defense with 132 yards. Jones scored touchdowns on an 80-yard run and a 12-yard reception as the Spartans beat Ohio State 32-7 before 75,288 at Spartan Stadium.

"He went 80 against Ohio State on a short-side toss," Raye said. "He got jammed, made a stiff arm, broke the run, and turned the game."

The dominant victory improved Michigan State to 5-0 in a season that had started with the Spartans unranked in the Associated Press preseason poll. Michigan State was ranked No. 2 after the Ohio State game and climbed to No. 1 the following week with a win over Purdue.

Jones finished the 1965 season leading the team with 787 yards rushing and 4.8 yards a carry. He also won the Big Ten scoring title with 68 points—11 touchdowns (10 rushing, one receiving) and one 2-point conversion. As a senior in 1966, he led the Spartans again with 784 yards rushing and 4.9 yards a carry.

"I wouldn't trade Jones for any halfback in the country," Daugherty said during the 1966 season. "He's the greatest back at eluding and breaking tackles I have ever seen. He has remarkable balance, speed, and power. Jones is also big, so he can run either around tacklers or over them, and that's the same thing that made Jim Brown so great."

No statistic better illustrates Daugherty's desire for a balanced offense than Michigan State's 1966 individual touchdown totals. Daugherty considered Jones the best running back in college football, yet his six rushing touchdowns ranked third on the team.

All-American fullback Bob Apisa led the Spartans with nine rushing scores. Regis Cavender, who took over at fullback when Apisa was hurt, scored seven. Jones's six-touchdown total was followed by quarterback Jimmy Raye (five TDs), and halfback Dwight Lee, who lined up opposite Jones (three touchdowns).

"There was only one ball," said Raye. "In the backfield, we had Clinton Jones, Bob Apisa, Dwight Lee, Regis Cavender, and Jimmy Raye. We had Gene Washington and Allen Brenner as receivers. Duffy's philosophy was to spread the ball around. It was a true team concept. You had to be humble to exist on our team. Without that personality on our team, it would have been different—it would have been chaotic."

That team play with the Spartans never diminished.

"We were an unselfish team, and I think that's why the friendships and relationships have endured," Raye said. "Everybody was in it for the ultimate goal—to win a ring. In our team meetings, we used to say, 'Don't blow the diamonds.'"

Clinton Jones finished as Michigan State's second-leading rusher, amassing 1,921 yards in his career, second only to All-American Lynn Chandois's 2,013 career rushing yards. He totaled 2,549 career all-purpose yards and 23 touchdowns and finished sixth in the 1966 Heisman Trophy voting won by Florida quarterback Steve Spurrier. It was a year when Purdue All-American quarterback Bob Griese was the runner-up and Notre Dame fullback Nick Eddy placed third to account for most of the Midwest votes.

"I've said this all along," Apisa said. "Clinton Jones is the best running back I ever saw or played with."

Jones followed his first 100-yard game against Ohio State with four more in his career, including a 200-yarder in 1966 against Iowa.

His other two 100-yard games in 1965 were 20 carries for 117 in a 12-3 win at Notre Dame and 20 for 113 in the Rose Bowl 14-12 loss to UCLA.

As a senior, Jones carried 19 times for 129 yards against North Carolina State in the 1966 opener and had 21 rushes for 268 yards against Iowa to improve to 8-0. In the Iowa game, he scored on runs of 79, 70, and 2 yards.

"We never felt we were on a long field with him," Raye said. "He could go 70, 60, 40, or 20 yards. We never felt trapped on a short field."

In track, Jones was a five-time Big Ten medalist as a hurdler and a 1965 All-American on the 440-yard relay team. In the hurdles, he pushed Gene Washington, an NCAA indoor champion and three-time track All-American. Their competition was mostly indoors once Jones's role in the backfield increased. During the track outdoor season, Daugherty expected Jones to be with the football team during spring drills. Washington, as an All-American offensive end in a run-oriented offense, was permitted more time to compete in outdoor track.

Jones's sophomore track season was his best. At the indoor Big Ten championships, he finished third in the high hurdles and fourth in the low hurdles. In the outdoor season, Jones was third in the high hurdles in the Big Ten meet. In the NCAA meet at UC-Berkeley, the 440-yard relay team came in third to earn All-American honors.

Jones led off the relay followed by two football teammates, Jimmy Summers and Gene Washington, on the second and third legs. Daswell Campbell was the anchor. The Spartans clocked a time of 41.1 seconds, losing to a San Jose State team that was anchored by 1968 Olympic 200-meter gold medalist Tommie Smith in 40.5, and a Nebraska foursome anchored by 1968 Olympic 100-meter bronze medalist Charlie Greene in 40.9.

In Jones's junior year at the Big Ten indoor championships, he came in second in both the high hurdles and low hurdles. He also teamed with

Washington to set a shuttle hurdles national record of 57.4 seconds at the Drake Relays.

The NFL agreed with Duffy Daugherty's evaluation of Jones as a running back; the only player drafted ahead of him was his Michigan State teammate, defensive end Bubba Smith, taken by the Baltimore Colts. Jones was joined in Minnesota by Gene Washington, selected with the No. 8 pick.

"Gene and I mirrored each other throughout our careers," Jones said. "We ran the hurdles, we were in Big Brothers of America together, we were roommates, we pushed each other in the hurdles, we both went to Minnesota, we got married the same day, and I have all daughters and he has all daughters."

Clinton Jones played seven NFL seasons—six with the Vikings and one with the San Diego Chargers. His six years at Minnesota included a 1969 NFL title, though the Vikings went on to lose in the Super Bowl to the AFL champion Kansas City Chiefs.

In Jones's three best years, he was second on the team to Bill Brown in rushing with 536 yards in 1968, led the team in touchdowns with nine in 1970, and led the team in rushing with 675 yards in 1971. Those numbers might sound modest by today's 16-game standards, but the numbers in a 14-game season were consistent with leading rushers from other teams in an era of two-back offenses. The Vikings' conservative offense failed to produce a 1,000-yard rushing season during Jones's six seasons in Minnesota, while the NFL overall produced just one 1,000-yard rusher in 1967 (Leroy Kelly), 1968 (Leroy Kelly), and 1969 (Gale Sayers).

Jones's finest season, 1971, was followed by a contract dispute with the organization that turned so bitter he did not speak to general manager Jim Finks for a year. In 1972, he suffered a broken arm in practice and finished the season with only 52 attempts for 164 yards and two touchdowns.

At this point Jones realized he lacked the direction in life he gained from mentors at Michigan State and Cathedral Latin. He battled depression over both his career and failing marriage to his first wife, but he kept it from everyone—including his close friend, Gene Washington.

"I had plenty of money, plenty of friends, plenty of partying, and doing whatever I pleased," Jones said. "It destroyed my marriage, my dreams and my self-esteem, but no one except my wife really knew what I was going through."

Clinton Jones was traded to the San Diego Chargers in 1973, but he needed more than a new team to change his life. He played the 1973 season but missed the following year with a knee injury. When Jones realized his knee was not fit for the 1975 campaign, he retired from football and enrolled in chiropractic school.

He had already explored Buddhism in the early 1970s, but says he found what he was looking for through his second wife, Rosielee. They met in chiropractic school and became friends as Jones's marriage ended. Rosielee practiced Japanese Buddhism and took Jones with her to a meeting in the fall of 1977. He says he would not have been alive to receive his Michigan State Hall of Fame honor without the revelation he experienced.

"I started to chant and I started crying," Jones said. "Rosielee asked me what's wrong. I told her, 'I found what I've been looking for all these years.'" He felt he found his true self.

He and his former wife were still separated at the time, but they have since established a new friendship. Clinton also reconciled with his father, whom he persuaded to chant with him before his father's death in 2006.

"My life and practice are devoted to helping people with their health, happiness, and prosperity," said Jones. "I try to be a husband, father, chiropractor, neighbor, and a friend."

Jones hoped to help Bubba Smith before he died on August 3, 2011. The Michigan State legend also was living in the Los Angeles area, thanks to his Hollywood career. Jones called Smith on what turned out to be the morning of his death from his Lake Balboa San Fernando office.

"I had finally convinced Bubba to come to my health clinics so I could treat him," Jones said. "Bubba was having a lot of problems. He had to have a rod put down his back, he had a knee operation, and he had prostate surgery. He was in good spirits, though, and finally said he was going to come."

Smith also was battling his weight, and the Los Angeles County Coroner report attributed his death to an overdose of the diet drug phentermine.

"I called him at 10:15 in the morning, and his friend said he was in the shower and to call back in 30 minutes," Jones said. "I called back later and no one answered. I found out at 3:30 that day he had passed away."

Jones also stayed in close contact with George Webster in his final days. Webster had battled throat cancer and had both legs amputated due to circulation problems before he died from heart failure in 2007.

"I was calling him and telling him jokes every day," Jones said. "I wanted to keep him laughing. I pray for Bubba and George twice a day. It's part of my religion."

Clinton Jones may not have needed the validation associated with the Hall of Fame, but he was nevertheless emotional when the phone call came to inform him he had been voted in. Asked by a reporter three months later, before the Hall of Fame ceremony, about his reaction, Jones choked up. "A lot of appreciation and tears—just like now," he said in a halting voice.

The great running back only has one football regret, the results of the final 1966 AP and UPI polls ranking Notre Dame above Michigan State despite the 10-10 tie in the Game of the Century and identical 9-0-1 records. "We should be No. 1 alone," he says, as if still holding out for a re-vote. "Truly in my mind we were the undefeated national champions. They didn't play anyone but Mount St. Mary's Angels. You look at their schedule and our schedule and there is no comparison. In the game itself, we kicked their butts."

The standing that he values the most is Michigan State's role in the integration of college football—a station in history that is secure, if sometimes overlooked with the passage of time.

"I have a debt of gratitude to pay to all those guys I played with," says Jones. "You can't plan something like what happened with us. Our team was monumental because of the times. We were breaking ground. We were doing things that had never happened."

Clinton Jones's Hall of Fame speech included advice to the 82 Michigan State athletes and team managers receiving their varsity jacket and letter that night.

"I want to give to you what I learned—to have been mentored means everything in life," he said. "It keeps you from being arrogant. It allows you to see the highbrows you otherwise cannot see. I was mentored and accomplished great things because of the people surrounding me and the people supporting me. Follow your mentors with determination. You will achieve great things, not only in sports, but in life. Michigan State has given me so much in life—as you can see by the testament of my teammates. I congratulate all of you and wish you good health, happiness, and prosperity."

13

First All-American Samoan

"Bob Apisa was Junior Seau before Junior Seau."—Carter Kamana

Michigan State's Bob Apisa wrote history in 1965 as college football's first Samoan All-America player. He was a 6-foot-1, 225-pound sophomore with fullback power and halfback agility who helped the Spartans to a Big Ten title and the national championship by collecting 715 yards (5.7 yards a carry) and ten touchdowns in just eight games.

He might have made more history in the National Football League—the kind Junior Seau carved out for Samoans as a linebacker in the 1990s—if his knees hadn't been shredded by his senior year. Otherwise, Apisa fit the prototype of the 1960s NFL fullback. Pro Football Hall of Fame fullbacks Jim Brown and Jim Taylor were 1,000-yard rushers—Brown seven times and Taylor five. They were unlike the one-dimensional blocking backs that fullbacks have been reduced to in football's modern era. Additionally, Apisa had the rare ability to run inside with power or carry the ball outside with agility NFL teams sought.

"If Bob doesn't get hurt, he has a stellar NFL career," Raye said. "If he had stayed healthy in college, he would have been one of the greatest Spartan runners of all time. He had the foot quickness to go outside and the power to go inside. His knee injuries robbed him of his ability."

NFL teams knew Apisa was damaged goods, but his reputation as a prodigious talent was enough for a certain Green Bay Packers general manager to take a chance on him with the hope his knee would recover. The iconic Vince Lombardi had just stepped down as the Packers' head coach after winning the second of his two straight Super Bowls titles that would later bear his name. He chose to use a ninth-round pick on Apisa.

"I was honored that Vince Lombardi drafted me, but I was injured throughout my senior year," Apisa said. "The Dallas Cowboys timed me in 4.5 seconds for 40 yards before the draft, but my knee just wouldn't hold up for training camp with the Packers."

An injury-free Apisa might have entered the 1968 NFL draft as the nation's top fullback prospect, but that distinction belonged to Syracuse University's Larry Csonka. As an example of the value the NFL placed on a fullback in the 1960s, all four backs taken in the first round of the 1968 draft were fullbacks.

Csonka was selected as the eighth pick by the Miami Dolphins, Utah State fullback MacArthur Lane went thirteenth to the St. Louis Cardinals, USC fullback Mike Hull sixteenth by the Chicago Bears, and Weber State fullback Lee White one pick later at seventeenth by the New York Jets. Among the four, Csonka carved out a Pro Football Hall of Fame career. He won two Super Bowls with the Dolphins and was inducted in Canton, Ohio, in 1987.

"Bob would have been an ideal NFL fullback for that era with his size and speed," Raye said. "Czonk was a bruiser and collision runner. Bob could bruise you and he could make you miss. He could run inside and outside. Czonk was strictly an inside runner."

The injuries robbed Apisa of a pro career and nearly all of his senior year at Michigan State, but he only needed his first two seasons to put Hawaii football on the map as a key player on Michigan State's back-to-back unbeaten Big Ten championship teams with national titles.

Few colleges recruited the islands when Apisa graduated from Honolulu Farrington in 1964. Hawaii football was so sleepy that the University of Hawaii did not elevate its program to Division I status until 1974. Apisa was the original South Pacific tsunami in Samoan and Polynesian football circles.

"Bob Apisa was Junior Seau before Junior Seau," says Carter Kamana, Michigan State's last recruit in the Hawaiian Pipeline and a defensive back from 1981 to 1984.

Naval Academy football coach Ken Niumatalolo, the first Samoan college head coach at any level, is also from Hawaii and respects Apisa's place in Samoan football history despite his own significant history. He was named the Midshipmen's head coach in 2008 after having served as offensive coordinator.

"I see Bob Apisa as not only a trailblazer for Samoan and Polynesians players but for coaches as well," Niumatalolo observed. "You have to be a player before you're a coach. There are a lot of Samoans and Polynesians coaching now. Bob was a pioneer who opened doors for us."

Niumatalolo was born in Hawaii in 1965 and went on to play quarterback at Honolulu Radford and then the University of Hawaii in the late 1980s. He and the players of his generation were well aware of Apisa's legend without ever having seen him play.

"Everybody I grew up with knew about Bob Apisa," Niumatalolo said. "He went to the mainland and was the first one to make a name for himself. I don't know if the younger kids these days still know about Bob Apisa, but they should."

Apisa was among the 10 players from the islands Daugherty recruited between 1955 and 1972 to form his Hawaiian Pipeline to Michigan State. Kamana, from Honolulu Kamehameha, became the eleventh and final Hawaiian Spartans recruit, playing a decade later under Muddy Waters.

Apisa came to the United States the same way as many of the first Samoan high-school stars in Hawaii and on the West Coast—his father was in the military. More specifically, Tailepeua Apisa was a chief petty officer in the Navy who fought in World War II and in Korea.

In 1872, the U.S. Navy first established a base in Pago Pago, American Samoa, serving as a coaling station. Twenty-eight years later, the United States annexed American Samoa. The outbreak of World War II led to expansion of the U.S. military's presence in Pago Pago after the Japanese bombed Pearl Harbor in Hawaii on Dec. 7, 1941. The history of Samoans serving in the U.S. military includes fighting the Japanese alongside U.S. Marines in World War II. The Samoan migration to Hawaii and Southern California—and later across the mainland—began after the U.S. Navy closed its base in America Samoa in 1950. Soon, sons of Samoan fathers stationed at Navy and Marine bases in Hawaii and California showed up on football rosters at high schools near military bases. In California, there were Navy bases in San Diego and Long Beach and the sprawling Camp Pendleton Marine base in Oceanside.

The Honolulu Advertiser 10¢

SATURDAY, JANUARY 6, 1968

Hula Bowl Classic

NORTH vs. SOUTH

BOB APISA
(Michigan State fullback)

LARRY CSONKA
(Syracuse fullback)

GARY BEBAN
(UCLA quarterback)

WARREN McVEA
(Houston halfback)

JIMMY RAYE
(Michigan State quarterback)

EDGAR CHANDLER
(Georgia guard)

Football coaches realized Samoans were naturals for their sport as large men with nimble feet and an affinity for physical contact.

Charles "Kale" Ane was part of the first wave of Samoan stars to follow Apisa into major college football. He played at Michigan State from 1972 to 1974 out of Honolulu Punahou and went on to play seven seasons as a center in the NFL with the Kansas City Chiefs and Green

Bay Packers. Ane followed Apisa's Michigan State career, including the Spartans' 1966 Game of the Century against Notre Dame, the first live broadcast in the islands.

"All of us knew about Bob's exploits," Ane said. "Bob was such a great story and a great representative for Hawaii football. He was very humble and competed hard. The rest of us followed in his footsteps. He allowed us to believe we could play Division I football. We're very grateful for that."

Over the past 30 years, Samoan and Polynesian stars like Mosi Tatupu, Manu Tuiasosopo, and Junior Seau made an increasing impact upon mainland American football at the high school, college, and NFL levels.

Bob Apisa understood his place in Samoan football history and the value of his name recognition as an All-America player. He used it to stage the first football clinic in America Samoa in 1973. "Those are things I'm very proud of," Apisa said. "When I went to Michigan State, I wanted to represent my family, Hawaii, and Samoans."

The early trickle of Samoan and Polynesian football players in the 1960s and early 1970s turned into a steady flow by the late 1970s, 1980s, and 1990s and into the 21st century.

By 2005, Samoans dotted the mainland to such an extent that Neli A'asa, a 6-foot-2, 290-pound Samoan defensive tackle, accepted a scholarship from the University of Utah out of the small northern Michigan town of Big Rapids, picking Utah over Michigan State, Michigan, and Colorado. During A'asa's recruiting process, a story was published on the Internet subscription recruiting service *Scout.com* with the headline, "What's a Big Samoan guy doing in Big Rapids?" The answer: Neli A'asa's father had attended Ferris State University as a graduate student.

The start of the Samoan football revolution includes similar biographies for Bob Apisa and Junior Seau—not to mention others.

Apisa and Seau were both born in American Samoa and came to the United States at the age of seven speaking limited English. They adapted quickly to American sports and personified the archetypal All-American boy as multisport stars in high school. Apisa played football, basketball, baseball, and track at Honolulu Farrington; Seau played football, basketball, and track at Oceanside High near San Diego. Both were best known for football, but they were good enough all-around athletes in track season to flirt with the shotput's 60-foot barrier. They likely would have broken the boundary, too, if they had spent more time honing fundamental techniques. Apisa was a shot putter as a freshman and sophomore, but he only threw the shot one time his senior year to help the track team win a meet contested between games of a Farrington baseball doubleheader. Similarly, Seau spent the spring of his senior year locked in the weight room until someone knocked on the door and told him it was time to emerge and throw the shot in the track meet.

Apisa credited track with improving his speed while competing in the sprint events, but he dropped track after his sophomore year to focus on baseball. As a junior first baseman and outfielder on Farrington's baseball team, he led the league in home runs as the Governors won the state title.

In the spring of Apisa's senior year, Farrington had an important track meet with Punahou when track coach George Nomura asked Farrington baseball coach Dick Kitamura if he could borrow Apisa for the meet.

"The baseball team had a doubleheader with about an hour-and-a-half break between games," Apisa said. "The baseball coach said it was OK as long as the track coach got me back in time for the second game. It was just a short drive to the track meet from the baseball field—a couple of miles. I took off my baseball jersey and threw the shot in a tank top and my baseball pants."

On his first throw, Apisa heaved the 12-pound shot a Hawaii state record of 56 feet, 3¾ inches.

"I just whirled as fast as I could and got a big arc on it," Apisa said. "People were aghast, but I acted like I knew what I was doing—which I didn't. My next two throws probably didn't add up to my state-record throw. Samoans have innate strength, and I just got off a perfect throw on that first one. Duffy was really happy when he saw the story in the newspaper."

Daugherty first learned about Apisa through longtime friend and Hawaiian Eye on the recruiting trail, Tommy Kaulukukui, Sr. It was Kaulukukui who kept the Hawaiian Pipeline flowing to Michigan State.

Kaulukukui was a Hawaii football legend as a 1935 honorable mention All-America halfback at the University of Hawaii. He later served as his alma mater's head coach from 1946 to 1950. When the Spartans played home-and-home games with Hawaii in 1947 and 1948, Duffy Daugherty was a Michigan State assistant under Biggie Munn.

Daugherty took over as head coach in 1954 and told Kaulukukui he had one scholarship a year to give to a Hawaii prospect. One of those scholarships went to William Kaae, a Hawaiian who played at Farrington and was a halfback on the Spartans 1955 team that won the Big Ten title and the 1956 Rose Bowl. Still, Hawaii was considered virgin recruiting turf in the 1960s. That began to change with Apisa's All-America success at Michigan State.

Daugherty likely would not have landed Apisa without Kaulukukui. Apisa was the Back of the Year on Hawaii's all-state team and earned honorable mention on an All-America team. He took recruiting trips to USC, the University of Washington, BYU and, as the lone non-western school, Michigan State, thanks to Tommy Kaulukukui, Sr.

Kaulukukui's son, Tom Kaulukukui, Jr., was a year ahead of Apisa when he enrolled at Michigan State in 1963. Tom Jr. didn't play football for the Spartans, but he served as the recruiting host for Apisa and other prospects from Hawaii when they visited Michigan State. Apisa and Kaulukukui Jr. have been lifelong friends since then.

"Bob once told me that my Dad said, 'Bob, I've got one scholarship to Michigan State and I want it to be you,'" recalled Tom Jr. "Bob said for a kid that came to Hawaii from American Samoa unable to speak much English, it changed his life."

On the day Bob Apisa signed his Michigan State scholarship commitment in the Farrington principal's office, he was having a tough time deciding between Michigan State and USC. Tommy Kaulukukui, Sr., was on hand to answer all of Apisa's final questions and seal the deal for Daugherty.

Apisa also expected to speak with an assistant from USC, but the coach failed to show up.

"I thought USC had gone in another direction, but I found out later the coach missed his flight," said Apisa. "It made my choice a lot easier. I thought it was best for me, my family, and the state of Hawaii. That's how I looked at it. I ended up at Michigan State by fate."

Another person influential in making Apisa feel comfortable was Eki Espinda, one of Farrington's assistant football coaches. The Hawaiian Espinda had played football in the Big Ten at Purdue University.

Recalled Apisa, "Eki said, 'Bob, I know you've got a lot of schools recruiting you, but the Big Ten is where you want to be. If you're going to get your butt kicked, get it kicked by the best.'" Espinda was referring to such Big Ten legends as Dick Butkus. Apisa's senior high-school season was the fall of 1963, and Butkus had just led the University of Illinois to the Big Ten title. Apisa understood what Epinda meant. In those days, the Big Ten was as dominant a force on the college football landscape as the Southeastern Conference is now.

Apisa's impact at Michigan State was immediate as a sophomore in 1965. The Spartans opened their national championship season—the first of back-to-back unbeaten Big Ten titles and national championship crowns—with a 13-3 win over UCLA at Spartan Stadium. On Apisa's first carry, he showed both his inside power and outside running ability. He took the handoff, bounced off two tacklers, and broke away for a 21-yard touchdown run.

"I was sitting in the stadium with other friends from Hawaii who were attending Michigan State," remembered Tom Kaulukukui, Jr. "When Bob broke those tackles and scored a touchdown, we were jumping around and yelling."

Apisa soon supplanted senior Eddie Cotton as the starter. He had rushed for 666 yards through seven games (in an offense that spread the ball around in a four-man backfield) before a knee injury sidelined him for the 1965 season's final three regular-season games.

Apisa's All-American stature drew more headlines than Daugherty's previous Hawaiian recruits, but he was still considered a novelty as his legend grew. He had to teach geographically challenged sportswriters that American Samoa was a United States territory in the South Pacific—5,000 miles from California and 7,000 miles from Michigan State's campus.

"I remember sitting in my locker-room cubicle at Spartan Stadium and newspaper writers asked me where I was from," Apisa said. "I had to explain I was born in American Samoa but raised in Hawaii. They thought everyone from the South Pacific was from Hawaii. I was surprised they didn't know there was an island named American Samoa."

After missing the last three 1965 regular-season games, he returned to the field for the Rose Bowl against UCLA. His mother came to Los Angeles to see him play on the mainland for the first time. Apisa contributed a 38-yard touchdown run and finished with four carries for 49 yards, but was tackled on a potential game-tying 2-point conversion with 31 seconds remaining. The seemingly invincible Spartans suffered a shocking 14-12 upset loss.

The highlight of Apisa's junior season in 1966 occurred when he led the Spartans to a second straight win over Michigan. He carried 18 times for 140 yards and one touchdown in a 20-7 victory before an overflow crowd of 78,833 at Spartan Stadium. Apisa scored on a seven-yard run and had a long gain of 49 yards. His power inside and finesse and speed outside overwhelmed an archrival in a game that was a slugfest. There were so many hard hits that Daugherty told the media afterward, "It wasn't a day for the timid."[1]

The Michigan game was Apisa's last 100-yard performance of his career. He finished his junior year leading the team in touchdowns with nine and repeated as an All-Big Ten pick, but his knee injuries had taken a toll: he missed the Game of the Century against Notre Dame. In his absence, backup sophomore fullback Regis Cavender scored Michigan State's only touchdown in the 10-10 tie.

Apisa then missed most of his senior year—only 50 carries for 183 yards—but he still managed to finish as Michigan State's career-rushing leader among fullbacks, with 1,343 yards. He was limited to 86 carries for 445 yards during his junior year, but he was called upon near the goal line to score eight touchdowns. His career total was accumulated in essentially little more than a season-and-a-half.

Despite the injuries, Apisa has been named among the Spartan's Top 10 all-time running backs in fan votes. Raye believes an injury-free Apisa would be among the top two or three alongside Clinton Jones and Lorenzo White, a pair of All-Americas who finished in the top ten of Heisman Trophy voting and were NFL first-round draft picks.

His legendary status from his sophomore and junior seasons stood the test of time, as Carter Kamana learned when he arrived at Michigan State in the early 1980s out of Honolulu Kemehameha.

"When I would go to my classes," Kamana said, "I'd have professors say, 'Oh, you're the Hawaiian kid on the football team. How is Bob Apisa doing?' "

Another reason for the special affection that developed between Hawaii football fans and Michigan State was the Spartans' 1966 comeback 11-8 win at Ohio State. Michigan State needed the victory to remain unbeaten at 5-0 in their march to a showdown with also unbeaten Notre Dame in the season finale. In heavy rain blowing sideways in 35-mph winds at Ohio Stadium, the Spartans' three Hawaiian Punch players accounted for all 11 points.

Senior kicker Dick Kenney, of Honolulu Iolani, connected on a 27-yard field goal for a 3-2 lead in the third quarter. Late in the fourth quarter, with Michigan State trailing 8-3, Apisa scored a touchdown on a fourth-and-1 dive for a 9-8 lead. On the ensuing extra-point attempt, backup quarterback Charlie Wedemeyer—a Honolulu Punahou alum and Herman Wedemeyer's younger brother—knelt down for the hold, but the ball was snapped instead to Kenney. Wedemeyer got up and drifted into the right corner of the end zone. Kenney, a pitcher on the Spartans' baseball team, hit him with the 2-point conversion pass. The three-point lead meant Ohio State would need a touchdown to beat the Spartans.

"I got a phone call from a friend waking me up saying, 'Bob, you've got to see this headline,'" Apisa said.

The headline in the *Honolulu Star-Bulletin* newspaper read: "Hawaiians 11, Ohio State 8." With no Division I football in the islands until 1974, Hawaii football fans felt validated by the three Hawaii players preserving No. 1-ranked Michigan State's unbeaten record.

Kenney was a senior, Apisa a junior, and Wedemeyer a sophomore in 1966, but they knew each other well dating back to competing against each other in Hawaii. All three were multisport athletes at rival high schools. Kenney also was a multisport athlete at Michigan State, participating in football as a kicker and punter and serving as a pitcher on the Spartans' baseball team. He was a fan favorite at Spartan Stadium, the Hawaiian barefoot kicker.

"He'd take that shoe off, snow, rain, zero-degree weather," Apisa said. "The fans loved him."[2]

The last time Apisa saw Kenney was when Michigan State played its regular-season finale at Hawaii on December 4, 2004. Kenney died at age 59 less than three months later.

"He and I gave speeches at the tailgate for the alumni," Apisa said. "He seemed fine, but you could tell he was looking forward to his retirement."

To Apisa and his two Michigan State teammates from Hawaii, a college-football opportunity was his chance to follow in the footsteps of Hawaii legends Tommy Kaulukukui, Sr. and Herman Wedemeyer. They had earned All-America honors and were his Polynesian football inspirations. Tommy Kaulukukui, Sr., was of Hawaiian ancestry and Wedemeyer was German/Hawaiian.

Wedemeyer followed Kaulukukui Sr. as the state of Hawaii's second All-American in 1945 while playing for St. Mary's University, then a college football power in Moraga, California, near the Bay Area.

Wedemeyer was inducted into the College Football Hall of Fame in 1979, having finished fourth in the 1945 Heisman Trophy voting to Army fullback Doc Blanchard and sixth in the 1946 voting to Army halfback Glenn Davis. But with no TV games showcasing Wedemeyer, Heisman voters in most of the country likely thought they were voting for a St. Mary's kid of German ancestry. Football fans in general may not have realized his Hawaiian heritage until decades later, when the same Herman Wedemeyer was a regular cast member as a Hawaiian detective on the TV series *Hawaii Five-O* in the 1960s and 1970s.

Apisa also followed his playing days with a career in entertainment similar to Wedemeyer. He spent 30-plus years as character actor and stunt coordinator in movies and TV. Apisa appeared frequently in *Hawaii Five-O* and in another Hawaii-based TV series in the 1980s, *Magnum P.I.*

For Bob Apisa, his family history has come full circle with his two daughters' medical careers supporting the military. Kelly Anne Apisa Beck, his older daughter, graduated from University of Redlands in California and is a family resource specialist for the U.S. Coast Guard in Virginia Beach, Virginia. She works with a special needs program for veterans who have been diagnosed with medical, psychological, physical, or educational special needs, providing support as well as resources to military dependents. Dr. Amy Apisa Hitzeman graduated from Michigan State in 1993. She is an optometrist, specializing in low vision, at Tripler Army-Naval Hospital in Honolulu, treating military vets and dependents. "I'm very proud of my daughters and the work they do to help our veterans," said Apisa.

His story began with a Navy father bringing his seven-year-old kid from American Samoa, speaking limited English, to Hawaii. And now the first Samoan All-America football player has daughters with their own military-influenced careers.

Notes

1. *Detroit Free Press,* Oct. 9, 1966.

2. *Honolulu Star-Bulletin,* Feb. 24, 2005.

14

THE HAWAIIAN PIPELINE

"There are a lot of us here who would like to see Michigan State recruit Hawaii. They would be welcomed back. All of us who played at Michigan State have great memories, and we'd like to see other kids have that opportunity."—Charles *"Kale"* Ane

The remarkable number of Samoans playing college and pro football caught the attention of CBS's *60 Minutes,* with a report by Scott Pelley that first aired on September 19, 2010. Pelley cited these eye-raising statistics: "From an island of just 65,000 people, there are more than 30 players of Samoan descent in the NFL and over 200 in Division I college ball. That's like 30 current NFL players out of Sparks, Nevada, or Gastonia, North Carolina.

"It's estimated a boy born to Samoan parents is 56 times more likely to get to the NFL than any other in America."

Pelley added, "What coach doesn't wish he had thought of this first?"

That coach was Michigan State's Duffy Daugherty—in the 1950s.

William Kaae, a halfback from Farrington High in Honolulu, was the first of ten Samoan and Polynesian players Daugherty recruited from paradise through his final season as the Spartans' head coach in 1972. But most prominent among Daugherty's Hawaiian recruits was Apisa.

"Hawaii was his baby," Apisa said. "Duffy would always go to Hawaii. He had a lot of friends there and people respected him. He was an honorary member at the Waialae Country Club in Honolulu, where they play the Hawaiian Open."

Larry Cundiff, the oldest living Hawaiian Pipeline Spartan, was an honorable mention All-Big Ten lineman in 1959 from Honolulu Iolani. He and his wife had dinner with Daugherty and his wife when they visited paradise during his coaching years and into his retirement.

"Duffy coached 19 years, but he could sit there and tell me what everyone one of my teammates was doing," Cundiff said. "He kept track of his guys. That's how Duffy was. He was a terrific guy. I loved that guy."

Daugherty liked to joke that when he divided up the recruiting map of the United States with his assistant coaches he took California, Hawaii—and his golf clubs. It was a funny line to tell on the banquet circuit, and it was not far from the truth. Daugherty landed more recruits from Hawaii than the more populous state of California, thanks to the Hawaiian Pipeline he built with the helping hand of his Hawaiian Eye, Hawaii football legend Tommy Kaulukukui, Sr. Daugherty could touch down in the islands and hit the links, confident Kaulukukui had Hawaii's recruiting turf blanketed.

"Duffy trusted my Dad's recruiting eye," said Tom Kaulukukui, Jr. "He told my Dad he had one scholarship a year to give out to a player if he thought he could play at Michigan State."

Cundiff, a three-year letterman in 1957-59, was Daugherty's second Hawaiian recruit. He had narrowed his choice to UCLA and Washington until Daugherty and Kaulukukui knocked on his family's door at 10 o'clock one morning.

"Duffy was talking with my parents and telling stories," Cundiff said. "They all had lunch and then they had dinner. When he left at 10:30 that night, my Dad turned to me and said, 'You're going to Michigan State.'"

For entirely different reasons and historical significance, Daugherty's career opened up two distinct untapped talent pools. The Underground Railroad to the South began to correct a social injustice of black coaches unable to attend clinics and black athletes denied a chance to attend their home-state school. Hawaii was much simpler—for the undervalued Polynesian players and the golf. Eventually, Daugherty's trailblazing in the South was overwhelmed by the Civil Rights movement, while other schools followed his path to Hawaii thanks to the jet age and television satellites shrinking the distance between Hawaii and the mainland.

Daugherty first discovered he could tap into a Hawaiian pipeline as an assistant under head coach Biggie Munn. Munn and Daugherty met

Kaulukukui, the University of Hawaii's head coach from 1946 to 1950, at a clinic on the mainland. Munn and Kaulukukui scheduled a home-and-home series in 1947 and 1948. The 1947 trip to Honolulu served as a quasi-bowl game for the Spartans, who were not yet members of the Big Ten and searched for games as an independent. Hawaii traveled to East Lansing in 1948.

Thomas K. Kaulukukui, Sr., wife Felice Kaulukukui, Francie Daugherty, Duffy Daugherty. Courtesy Tom Kaulukukui, Jr.

The Spartans routed the undermanned Rainbow Warriors both times, winning 58-19 at Honolulu Stadium and 68-21 at Spartan Stadium. In the 1948 game at Spartan Stadium, Tommy Sr.'s brother Sol was Hawaii's quarterback.

Tom Jr. said his father and family were so close to Daugherty and Munn that he has been "bleeding green and white" since the day he landed at Lansing's Capital City Airport in the fall of 1963. He arrived with his cousin, Dick Kenney, who was a freshman about to launch his career as Michigan State's bare-footed kicker and a baseball pitcher.

"Dick and I had never been anywhere and we were so green when we landed we thought we were on campus," Kaulukukui Jr. said. "We asked some guy if this was the campus and he said, 'No, you idiots. You have to take a cab.' We had no money, but my Dad had given me three phone numbers—John Hannah, Biggie Munn, and Duffy Daugherty. I picked the name in the middle and called Biggie. His wife Vera answered the phone. She said Biggie was out of town, but 'I'll come and get you boys.'

"She came out in a big Oldsmobile, took us to their home and put us up in the den. The next day Biggie came home and he took us to our dorms. Dick was staying at Wonders Hall and I was staying at Shaw Hall. Biggie was helping us carry our suitcases in and people would say, 'Oh, Mr. Munn, can I help you?' He'd say, 'No, I've got it.'"

The only sight that might have been more startling would have been to see President Hannah or the 5-foot-8 Daugherty carrying luggage into the dorms.

More important to Michigan State's future success as a football program than the victories over Hawaii was the friendship Munn and Daugherty struck up with Tommy Kaulukukui, Sr. The elder Kaulukukui was an all-around athlete in football, basketball, baseball, and track, an early Hawaiian sports legend along with Duke Kahanamoku, a five-time Olympic swimming medalist known as the ambassador of surfing.

Kaulukukui, who was 94 years old when he passed away in 2007, was Hawaii's first All-America football player as honorable mention in 1935. His 1935 season as a halfback included a 103-yard kickoff return for a touchdown against UCLA at the Los Angeles Coliseum. Immortal sportswriter Grantland Rice nicknamed him "Grass Shack," which helped him earn his All-American attention.

After serving as Hawaii's head coach for five seasons, Kaulukukui spent 1951 pursuing a graduate degree at Michigan State. He also served as a volunteer coach on the staff with Munn and Daugherty. In the fall, he soaked up football knowledge. In the winter, he trudged through the snow delivering the U.S. Mail with a job Daugherty found for him.

Once his father returned to the islands, Tom Jr. remembers as a kid seeing Daugherty at their family home as a frequent visitor on recruiting/golfing trips. Charles "Kale" Ane, Arnold Morgado, and Douglas Won were Daugherty's last three Hawaiian recruits as freshmen in 1971, the trio earning varsity letters as sophomores in 1972, Daugherty's final season. Ane was a center who went on to play seven NFL seasons, Morgado a fullback who played four NFL seasons, and Won a safety.

However, Denny Stolz succeeded Daugherty, and Morgado returned home to finish his career at Hawaii. Ane was entrenched at center and earned three letters, but Won suffered knee injuries that ended his career following the 1972 season. Stolz told Morgado he would be switched to linebacker. Worse, he also told Morgado he had no plans to continue Daugherty's tradition of recruiting Hawaii. That meant there was no risk of recruiting fallout on the islands if he didn't play Morgado.

"That's why I left Michigan State," said Morgado. "When you come from a Duffy Daugherty recruiting experience and then run into a Denny Stolz at such a young age, it makes a tremendous impact. I refused to switch, but he wasn't going to play me anyway. I wouldn't waste a second breath on Denny, but I will talk to anybody about how great Duffy was."

Ane was drawn to Michigan State as an eighth-grader when he watched the 1966 Game of the Century. The Notre Dame-Michigan State broadcast was the first live telecast of a football game in Hawaii, thanks to the new space technology of satellites. The game was also in demand on the islands to see Michigan State's three Hawaiian players—senior Dick Kenney, junior Bob Apisa and sophomore Charlie Wedemeyer.

"We used to have to wait a week to see the games—it was terrible," Ane said. "We all gathered around the TV set at my mom and dad's house to watch the game. When it was over, I said to myself, 'I want to go to one of those two schools.'"

Michigan State recruited Ane out of Honolulu Punahou, where he had played for his father, Charlie Ane. Charlie, like his son, had a seven-year career in the NFL, playing with the Detroit Lions (1953-59). He played at a California junior college, Compton College, and transferred to USC.

"Duffy was a great guy and he knew the right people in Hawaii," said Kale Ane, who took over as the head coach at Punahou in 1999. "His passion and love of the game of football matched everybody here. In reality, nobody was recruiting Hawaii before Duffy."

Stolz severed the pipeline and it was left unpatched by his successor, Darryl Rogers. But when Rogers departed, Muddy Waters took over with an understanding of the pipeline's tradition. He had played under Munn and Daugherty, including the Hawaii-Michigan State games in 1947 and 1948. He re-tapped the pipeline when he landed Carter Kamana of Honolulu Kamehameha in 1981. Waters was fired after the 1982 season and Kamana finished the last two years of his career in 1983 and 1984 under George Perles. The pipeline subsequently dried up on Perles' watch, even though Perles was a Daugherty disciple as a player and assistant coach. Kamana remains Michigan State's last link to Daugherty's Hawaiian Pipeline.

The list of Michigan State's 11 Hawaii recruits with their high school, their Michigan State varsity letters, their ethnicity and any honors:

- William Kaae, HB, Farrington, 1955, Hawaiian
- Larry Cundiff, T/C, Iolani, 1957-59, Welsh/Portuguese/ Hawaiian, 1959 All-Big Ten honorable mention
- Roger Lopes, FB, Iolani, 1961-63, Portuguese/Hawaiian, 1963 All-Big Ten second-team
- Dick Kenney, K/P, Iolani, 1964-66, Irish/Hawaiian, 1966 All-Big Ten first-team
- Bob Apisa, FB, Farrington, 1965-67, Samoan, 1965 All-American, 1965 All-Big Ten second-team, 1966 All-Big Ten first-team
- Charlie Wedemeyer, QB/flanker/holder, Punahou, 1966-68, German/Hawaiian
- Jim Nicholson, OT, St. Louis, 1970-72, Irish/Samoan, 1972 All-Big Ten second-team
- Arnold Morgado, FB, Punahou, 1972, Chinese/Japanese/ Italian/Hawaiian
- Douglas Won, S, St. Louis, 1972, Chinese/Hawaiian
- Charles "Kale" Ane, C, Punahou, 1972-74, Hawaiian
- Carter Kamana, CB, Kamehameha, 1981-84, Hawaiian

Five of Daugherty's ten Hawaiian recruits earned All-Big Ten recognition, a 50 percent batting average any recruiter would envy. Three of the five went on to play in the NFL, another impressive batting average.

Nicholson played for the Kansas City Chiefs, 1974-79; Morgado with Kansas City, 1977-79; and Ane with Kansas City (1975-80) and the Green Bay Packers (1981).

The former Spartans also have remained influential in Hawaii high-school football. Cundiff was an assistant coach at Iolani and St. Louis. Kenney was an assistant football and baseball coach at Pearl City High. Ane has been the head coach since 1999 at Punahou, a traditional Hawaii state power and the alma mater of President Barack Obama. Morgado helps him coach at Punahou, his alma mater, too.

Kenney, who died in 2009 at age 59, was a two-sport athlete in football and baseball as a pitcher. He was third on the Spartans' all-time strikeouts list at end of his career. In the spring, he would trot over from baseball practice to spring football practice to kick field goals in his baseball uniform. He quickly became a fan favorite for his barefoot kicking in an era before the soccer-style revolution in the 1970s, when kickers were relatively anonymous. Kenney kicked straight-on with his toes balled up.

"When we were born in 1945 and '46, Hawaii was still a relatively small, sleepy, tropical paradise," Tom Jr. said. "Island kids rarely wore shoes, not even flip-flops. We all grew up running around and playing sports barefoot. Dick and I did not wear shoes to school until the seventh grade. The soles of our feet were so hard that in college, I used to amaze my classmates by grinding out lighted cigarettes with my bare feet."

Kenney was an outreach counselor at a Pearl City High bordering Honolulu. He coached baseball in addition to football. When he died in 2005 at age 59, he was the pitching coach at Honolulu Damien on the staff of a longtime friend, John Matias.

Wedemeyer arrived at Michigan State as a three-sport athlete in football, basketball and baseball at Punahou. He is considered one of Hawaii's greatest multisport high school athletes and was known as the younger brother of Herman Wedemeyer. "Squirmin' Herman" was the state of Hawaii's second All-American pick (after Kaulukukui Sr.) as a halfback at St. Mary's College, a college power in Moraga, California, near San Francisco.

The Wedemeyer brothers, both now deceased, also carved out additional identities. Charlie was a high-school coach in Los Gatos, California, who continued working after he was afflicted with amyotrophic lateral sclerosis (ALS), better known as Lou Gehrig's Disease. Wedemeyer and his wife Lucy wrote a book, *Charlie's Victory*. His story was turned into an Emmy Award-winning PBS documentary, *One More Season*, and a 1988 television movie, *Quiet Victory: The Charlie Wedemeyer Story*.

Herman played Sgt. Duke Lukela in *Hawaii Five-O*, in the late 1960s and 1970s. He also was an elected politician serving on the Honolulu City Council and the Hawaii House of State Representatives. (Morgado also served on the Honolulu City Council.)

Apisa's name, though, is the one that came along at the dawn of the television age and gained lasting recognition. His All-America honors embedded the Spartans' strong identity in Hawaii. A Michigan State alum or fan wearing Spartans attire in Hawaii is often asked by old-timers about Bob Apisa and Duffy Daugherty. The ties between the state and Michigan State University were a storyline that followed the Spartans to Hawaii for the 1989 Aloha Bowl. This was two years after Michigan State had won the 1988 Rose Bowl (concluding the 1987 season).

Then-Michigan State head coach George Perles led the Spartans to a 33-13 win over Hawaii at Aloha Stadium. Perles, who liked to highlight his ties to Daugherty, mentioned the Michigan State-Hawaii tradition during the bowl trip, but the 1989 season was his sixth at Michigan State and he had yet to land a Hawaii recruit. He was fired after the 1994 season without re-tapping the Daugherty pipeline to Hawaii.

In addition to failing to maintain the Hawaiian pipeline, Perles was oblivious to the Munn-Daugherty example of creative scheduling. Before Michigan State was a Big Ten member, Munn and Daugherty wanted an exotic season-ending road trip as a substitute for a bowl game. Michigan State traveled for regular season finales to Hawaii in 1947, the Bay Area to play Santa Clara in 1948, and Arizona in 1949.

Perles needed to apply this tradition in 1993 to save face when the season went sour late in the year. Michigan State had agreed to play Wisconsin in the 1993 regular season finale in Tokyo, but by gametime the Spartans had little to play for while Wisconsin needed a victory to clinch its first Big Ten title and its first Rose Bowl berth in 31 years.

The pregame functions included a banquet for school dignitaries and Japanese sponsors and hosts. Daugherty the quipster might have made himself the butt of a joke over his team playing in the shadows for something less aromatic than roses. Instead, Perles took the microphone and directed it toward Wisconsin coach Barry Alvarez, saying "I just want you to know, I don't give a shit about this game."[1]

The shocked Japanese, accustomed to a culture of courtesy and hiding personal feelings, repeated and translated Perles's words as a murmur spread across the room. The Spartans' play reflected Perles's attitude, as they were routed 41-20 at the Tokyo Dome.

Perles coached one more season in 1994 before he was fired. Subsequent Michigan State coaches Nick Saban and Bobby Williams also failed to land a recruit from Hawaii.

John L. Smith, who succeeded the fired Williams, told the Hawaiian media that he wanted to re-tap the pipeline when Michigan State played its 2004 regular season finale on December 4 against Hawaii at Aloha Stadium. Smith, in his second year as Michigan State's head coach, noted the talent pool in Hawaii and the proliferation of Samoan and Polynesian football players in college football in the previous two decades. That plan was thwarted when bad blood developed between Smith, known for his sideline outbursts, and Hawaii coach June Jones. Michigan State suffered a 41-38 loss to end a disappointing season with a 5-7 record. The game turned ugly with shoving matches, including the ejection of MSU defensive end Clifton Ryan, the Spartans' star player, later bound for the NFL with the St. Louis Rams.

Smith got into a running feud with Jones, and by extension Hawaii's fans, that was still smouldering by 2005 when Hawaii played the second half of the contract at Spartan Stadium. Both coaches accused the other of failing to send videotape from the previous game as is customary, but Jones offered more specific evidence than Smith, accusing the Michigan State coach of telling the Kent State coaches not to send Hawaii tape of the Michigan State-Kent State game.

"The Michigan State coaches asked the Kent State coaches not to send it to us because we wouldn't send them ours," said Jones. "I have no idea why they would lie to them. It's kind of a bad deal. But you do what you do to win, I guess."[2]

Smith, declining further comment, only said, "We're not sending tapes. They're not sending tapes. It's that simple."

The bad blood spilled over to basketball season when the Spartans opened their 2005-06 season ranked No. 4 and played Hawaii at Sheriff Center on campus en route to the Maui Invitational. Michigan State's players suffered leg cramps, delaying the game, and Hawaii's fans booed unmercifully as the Warriors pulled away to an 84-62 victory.

Left to right: Tom Kaulukukui, Jr., Carter Kamana, Doug Won, Jim Nicholson, Kale Ane, Larry Cundiff. Photo by Lia Kamana.

The Hawaiian Spartans lament the rupture of the pipeline and remain hopeful the Spartans will rebuild Daugherty's tradition.

"There are a lot of us out here who would like to see Michigan State recruit Hawaii," Ane said. "They would be welcomed back. All of us who played at Michigan State have great memories, and we'd like to see other kids have that opportunity."

Carter Kamana said Muddy Waters re-tapped the Hawaiian Pipeline with the help of Ron Marcial, one of Hawaii's legendary high-school coaches who had earned his master's degree at Michigan State. Marcial led Waters to John Kamana—Carter's older brother—and Leroy Lutu in the 1980 recruiting class.

John Kamana came out of Punahou, where he played on the basketball team with a gangly kid named Barry Obama—now President

Barack Obama. John Kamana picked USC and went on to play in the NFL; Lutu was from University High in Honolulu and committed to the University of Washington. Waters, despite missing out on the two targets, returned to Hawaii for the 1981 recruiting class. This time he landed Carter Kamana out of Honolulu Kemehameha.

"Guys like my brother and Leroy were going to the Pac-10," said Carter. "I was thinking about Arizona State in the Pac-10, but then I talked to guys like Nicholson, Morgado, and Kale. They said there was a great following of Hawaiian players at Michigan State and they felt at home. They sold me on the tradition."

Morgado only told Kamana how much he enjoyed his time at Michigan State without allowing his conflict with Stolz to color his comments.

Kamana also committed to Michigan State for the school's highly rated hotel and restaurant business school. He knew he could use his degree to return to Hawaii and work in the tourism industry, which he does now for Avendra. Kamana's daughter Lia Kamana chose to attend Michigan State in 2011, where she majors in journalism.

"She was accepted at Michigan State, Iowa, Miami, and Texas," Carter said. "I told her if she had a problem, 'Dad has friends within 30 minutes of campus. At the other schools, it's a plane trip.'"

When Kamana's son, Tim, played at Punahou, he twice attended Michigan State summer football camps. Tim had a preferred walk-on invitation from the Spartans in the 2012 recruiting class, but he accepted an appointment from West Point to play for Army. He stayed one year before deciding the military commitment wasn't for him, and he transferred to Wyoming, which also had offered him a scholarship coming out of high school. Wyoming will play at Michigan State for the Spartans' 2014 homecoming.

Carter Kamana says he and his fellow Michigan State alums in Hawaii are eager to assist the Spartans coaching staff as a latter-day Tommy Kaulukukui, Sr. Kamana says he has communicated with head coach Mark Dantonio and offensive line coach Mark Staten.

"I send Mark Staten emails about players that might be a possibility," Kamana said. "It's sad Michigan State no longer has a pipeline to this market. Kale has a lot of great players coming out of Punahou. I keep telling Mark Dantonio he's only got to hit it one time. Bob Apisa tells me, 'Let's keep pushing it.'"

As a Michigan State alumnus and a proud Hawaiian, Tom Kaulukukui Jr. is bothered that the Spartans stopped recruiting Hawaii. Tom Jr. graduated from Michigan State and served as a paratrooper in the Army, and then he returned to Michigan State to earn his Master's degree in education. He was a teacher and coach in Okemos, near East Lansing, and in Hawaii before earning a law degree. He then practiced law before serving as a judge. Now he's a retired judge and managing trustee of Queen Lili'uokalani Trust.

"The pipeline has dried up, and I think it's a mistake," Tom Kaulukukui, Jr. said. "There is a lot of talent in Hawaii. Michigan State was the first school to recruit Hawaii. The best athletes in Hawaii back then wanted to go to Michigan State. They wanted to play football for a school with tradition, and Michigan State has a lot of tradition."

That lost history was particularly painful on September 15, 2012, as Kaulukukui watched two Punahou alums play a key role in Notre Dame beating Michigan State 20-3. All-American linebacker Manti Te'o recorded 12 tackles and starting wide receiver Robby Toma caught five balls for 58 yards on a night Michigan State's receivers repeatedly dropped balls. At Punahou, Te'o and Toma played for Ane and were named Under Armour High School All-Americas.

"Manti Te'o made all those tackles for Notre Dame," said Tom Kaulukukui, Jr., "and Manti's high-school coach played at Michigan State."

Kaulukukui Jr. recognizes that college recruiting has grown more sophisticated and a figure such as his father no longer carries enough influence to steer prospects. Still, it's disappointing to him that the Big Ten school that put Hawaii football on the map has let its history with the islands wash away with the tide.

"I took two of my grandsons to a Michigan State game against Purdue that was the last home game of the year," said Kaulukukui Jr., referring to the 2010 season. "Bob got us seats in the press box, but I wanted them to sit outside for the first half to see the band, the big crowd, and everything. They were astonished. Then at the end of the game in the press box, they had their faces pressed against the glass window and they said, 'Papa, why are those players doing pushups in the middle of the field?' I said, 'No, boys. They're not doing pushups. They're kissing the S. It's their last home game.' One of my grandsons told me he wanted to play for Michigan State."

Notes

1. Lynn Henning, *Spartan Seasons II*, Sports Seasons Publishing, 2006, p. 79.

2. AP story, Sept. 6, 2005.

15

SPARTAN POET LAUREATE

"If I had to pick the five toughest guys I ever coached, Pat Gallinagh would be in my top five."—Hank Bullough

Michigan State defensive tackle Pat Gallinagh earned Academic All-America honors in 1966 as a gritty second-team All-Big Ten pick, but the kid from Detroit's blue-collar east side holds no such exalted title as poet laureate from his alma mater. He gained such a de facto role among his teammates when he pumped out tributes with the passing of legends from the Spartans' 1965 and 1966 Big Ten and national championship teams. Teammates of Gallinagh, a retired high-school history teacher and football coach, enjoyed sharing his reflections on their giant of a coach, Duffy Daugherty, and two giant teammates on the playing field and in the history of college football, Bubba Smith and George Webster.

Clinton Jones, the Spartans' two-time All-American halfback, choked up when reading aloud a portion of Gallinagh's poem, "What is a Spartan?"

A Spartan is an artist, a creative soul and muse

An architect of beauty, song and verse for common use

A Spartan is an activist who speak out when they see wrong

Who combats ignorance and hatred with truths buried for so long

The last time Gallinagh, Jones, Smith, Webster, Jimmy Raye, and the other 1965 and 1966 Spartans saw Smith and Webster together was when they returned to campus for the 2006 Notre Dame-Michigan

State game, played on the fortieth anniversary of the Game of the Century. Michigan State also chose that night to retire Smith's No. 95 jersey alongside Webster's No. 90. Names from those Underground Railroad teams are enshrined on the Ring of Fame along with Gene Washington, head coach Duffy Daugherty, and athletic director Biggie Munn at Spartan Stadium.

The old 1966 teammates gathered before the 2006 on-field festivities in the lounge at Spartan Stadium. They didn't know it at the time, but the men were at that age when they start to unknowingly experience final farewells more frequently than they're ready to accept. All-Big Ten linebacker Charlie Thornhill passed away three months after the 40th reunion. Webster died a year later in 2007. Smith passed in 2011.

"We never know when it's going to be the last time to see an old friend," said Jones when he was back on campus in 2012 to be inducted into Michigan State's Hall of Fame.

Gallinagh crafted "A Tribute to Hugh 'Duffy' Daugherty," "A Tribute to George 'Mickey' Webster," and "Remembering Charles A. 'Bubba' Smith," sensitive poems that belied his onfield persona. (Check them out for yourself: they're presented in an appendix.) Michigan State defensive coordinator Hank Bullough, who coached on Daugherty's staff from 1959 to 1969 and another two decades in the NFL, called Gallinagh "a bulldog—like Rocky Marciano. If I had to pick the five toughest guys I ever coached, Pat Gallinagh would be in my top five."

Including NFL players?

"Anybody," said Bullough.

It's a hackneyed phrase for coaches to compliment an intense athlete by saying he practices likes he plays, but it's more than a tired cliché for Gallinagh.

"It would take him two hours to get ready for practice," Bullough said. "He treated every practice like a game."

Gallinagh's pregame energy was legendary. He once slammed his head—with his helmet on—against a locker, drawing blood.

Another time, he nearly sidelined Michigan State quarterback Jimmy Raye.

After Raye and the quarterbacks met with Daugherty in a routine pregame meeting, Raye composed himself in the Spartan Stadium locker room before he took the field. Michigan State was about to play Purdue and All-American quarterback Bob Griese that afternoon.

Raye, a first-year starter, was recovering from a shoulder strain suffered two weeks earlier against Michigan, though he had played through the injury the following week while directing an 11-8 comeback victory at Ohio State. The shoulder was still tender before the Purdue game.

"Gallinagh was going into his growl, getting fired up, throwing up and butting his head against the locker-room door," he recalled. "It was his normal routine. I thought he was crazy and tried to stay out of his way. I guess I didn't look fired up enough for him. He comes by me and with double fists slams down on my shoulder pads. He said, 'Get fired up, Jimmy Raye!' Well, quarterbacks wear smaller shoulder pads, so it hurt when he hit me. But I still had one of my better games." In fact, Raye was awarded a game ball for the second time that season following the Spartans' 41-20 victory before 78,014 fans. Michigan State led 35-7 in the fourth quarter before Daugherty inserted the backups. Raye was 11 of 21 for 168 yards with one touchdown passing, one interception, and one rushing TD. Griese was 18 of 30 for 186 yards with one touchdown and one interception. He also rushed for two TDs—the second one late in the fourth quarter.

Pat Gallinagh was an overachiever who broke into the 1966 starting lineup as one of the strongest players on the team, thanks to dedicated weight-lifting. He earned his first varsity letter as a junior in 1965, having climbed up from so far down the depth chart, he says, that the coaches tried to run him off the team as a sophomore—a common practice around the nation for that era.

"They had drills that would probably get you sued now," Gallinagh said. "If they wanted to run you off, they'd have you be the ball carrier against some of the best defensive players. I decided if they were going to run me off, I was going to take one of them with me. I'm going to be like a bowling ball. I went six inches above the knee."

Defensive ends Bubba Smith and Robert Viney were among the defenders in the four-on-one drill facing Gallinagh. Bullough quickly sized up potential disaster.

"Hank had them stop the drill before he lost half his defense," Gallinagh said.

In 1966, Gallinagh's senior year, the Spartans played a 6-2-3 scheme that was an early version of the modern 4-3. There were four defensive tackles and two defensive ends, but the ends played like outside linebackers without the pass coverage responsibilities of the modern game. Five of the six defensive linemen earned All-Big Ten honors.

Gallinagh (second team) and Nicholas Jordan (first team) were two of four tackles and Smith (first team and All-America) and Phil Hoag (second team) the starting ends. George Chatlos (honorable mention) was a third defensive end that entered the game in certain situations. He would play Smith's end position while Smith shifted inside to a nose tackle.

Behind the linemen were George Webster, All-American roverback; Charlie Thornhill, first-team All-Big Ten linebacker; Jess Phillips, first-team All-Big Ten safety; and Drake Garrett, Big Ten honorable mention cornerback.

Gallinagh earned a niche among this all-star cast, but his high-strung nature also was the reason he found himself in a locker-room altercation with the gentle giant, Smith.

"I was the only one dumb enough to get in a fight with Bubba, but there was nothing racial about it," Gallinagh said. "Families have fights and it was like a fight between brothers. Actually, Bubba and I got closer after that. The bond that our team formed in those four years is unbreakable. I don't remember a racial incident the entire time I was there."

The fight started in the locker room after a Friday walk-through practice before the Spartans played on November 12 at Indiana. Michigan State's record was 8-0, and the Spartans needed only a victory to do its part to set up The Game of the Century with Notre Dame one week later at Spartan Stadium.

Tension was building with Michigan State in the vulnerable position of bring ranked No. 2 behind No. 1 Notre Dame. The Spartans believed Notre Dame was running up scores to protect its No. 1 ranking. They felt they not only had to beat Indiana but win convincingly. After all, voters had compared scores four weeks earlier when Michigan State won 11-8 at Ohio State in monsoon-like conditions on the same day that Notre Dame won at home 32-0 over North Carolina. The result: Michigan State lost its No. 1 ranking to No. 2 Notre Dame in a flip-flop of positions.

Adding to the stress in the locker room the Friday before the Indiana game—and leading to the Gallinagh-Smith tussle—was a *Chicago Daily*

News column written by Tom Fitzpatrick two weeks earlier calling Smith overrated following Michigan State's 22-0 win at Northwestern.

Gallinagh says Smith brushed off the article on the outside, but in reality was sensitive and easily bothered by such criticism.

"He was truly hurt," Gallingah said. "He said, 'What did I do to deserve that?'"

The Chicago story also brought back a moment from Smith's sophomore year that he never lived down. The Spartans lost 27-20 at Indiana, their record falling to 1-3 overall in what would turn out to be a disappointing 4-5 season. Smith was criticized throughout his career for taking plays off; after the Indiana loss, an angry Daugherty said in the privacy of the locker room, "Bubba, I thought you were a stretcher case out there."

Two years later, Gallinagh felt the Spartans needed to relieve some pressure as they left the walkthrough for the visitor's locker room. Smith, a prankster, might have been trying to break the building tension with some levity when he directed a sexual remark at Gallinagh, but he threw a towel at Gallinagh as he made the comment. Gallinagh threw the towel back at Bubba and dredged up Duffy's two-year-old "stretcher" comment. The towel knocked off Smith's green beret that the defensive players proudly wore that season (the offensive players wore gray berets).

"Bubba said, 'You're crazier than I thought,' and everything escalated from there," Gallinagh recalled. "Bubba hit me and I went down because the floor was slippery and I had on some new shoes. I got back up and went after him. The thing that got me is they all grabbed me to break up the fight and nobody grabbed Bubba. He sucker-punched me and was whaling on me and I was trying to grab him like a wrestling match."

Daugherty was furious when he learned about the tussle. He called Smith and Gallinagh into a locker-room office.

"He really reamed us both out," Gallinagh said. "He said, 'Bubba, you've got no business complaining about that Indiana game.' And to me he said, 'You've got no business talking to Bubba about it.'"

When the players gathered for their team dinner, Daugherty made both players apologize.

"Bubba got up and said he was sorry," Gallinagh said. "I was a little more long-winded. I said I was sorry and lucky I wasn't killed. I didn't hear it, but I learned later guys were saying to shut up and sit down so they could eat. That was probably Jerry West saying that."

Clinton Jones said the players waved off the incident as another Bubba-ism.

"That was Bubba's nature," Jones said. "He was an instigator. He used to piss everybody off at one time or another—especially Duffy. He was so mischievous. We had arguments, but we always got over it."

When the Smith-Gallinagh tussle broke out, an Indiana trainer was in the visitors' locker room. He reported the fight to the Indiana coaching staff with the suggestion the Spartans would not be ready to play Saturday afternoon's game.

The Spartans won 37-19. Jimmy Raye completed 7 of 9 passes for 173 yards and three touchdowns.

In that same time frame at other schools, racial incidents occurred in games and on the practice field. Jerry Levias was the Southwestern Conference's first black scholarship player as a sophomore on the varsity at Southern Methodist University in 1966.

"The first day of practice was when I realized this was going to be tough," Levias said. "When your own teammate spits on you and you're on the ground about to get up, and then he kicks you in the back and breaks your ribs."[1]

Michigan State's black and white players repeated a common theme when recounting their time at Michigan State: they had no such problems. Daugherty told them the only colors on the team were green and white.

"We were a football family," Gallinagh said. "In the four years I was there, I can't give you one a single racial incident."

Another memorable moment in Gallinagh's career occurred in the Illinois game during the third week of the 1966 season. Chatlos jarred the ball loose from an Illinois ball carrier into the hands of Hoag, who pitched the ball to Gallinagh. He rumbled his way to the goal line, 40 yards away.

"I was so tired when I finally got to the end zone I almost passed out," Gallinagh said.

Michigan State Sports Information Director Fred Stabley, who set the standard for the modern-day SID, grabbed Raye and Gallinagh at practice the next week to pose for a photo. Gallinagh received a mock handoff from Raye in Spartan Stadium. Stabley never missed a photo op.

Gallinagh learned as early as his March 1963 recruiting trip to Michigan State that the campus was a historic place in the integration of college athletics. His trip was the same weekend as the NCAA Mideast Regional basketball tournament at Jenison Fieldhouse. The field featured the famed Mississippi State-Loyola Chicago game that came to be known as "The Game of the Change" after the documentary of the same name. Mississippi State's all-white team defied a state court order prohibiting it from facing Loyola's integrated team with four black starters. The Mississippi State players and coaches surreptitiously left town to cross the state border and catch a flight to Michigan.

Coincidentally, George Webster was on his recruiting trip to Michigan State the same weekend with Gallinagh. Webster's future was football, but he was also a basketball and track and field star in Anderson, South Carolina.

"I met George for the first time at the Kellogg Center," Gallinagh said. "We shook hands and (assistant coach) Vince Carillot said it was probably the first time he'd shaken hands with a white player. I didn't care about basketball, but I did attend one game. George was a basketball fan and he went to all the games."

Loyola defeated Mississippi State en route to the regional title and the national championship. Michigan State commemorated the 50th anniversary with a plaque placed outside Jenison. Michigan State also played a nonconference contest against historically black Tuskegee University on Dec. 15, 2012. The game was the Spartans' first contest played at Jenison since the Breslin Center opened in 1990.

After Pat Gallinagh graduated, Michigan State assistant coach Danny Boisture landed the head job at Eastern Michigan University. He brought Gallinagh with him as a graduate assistant. Gallinagh hoped to be promoted to a full-time position, but he felt he was passed over when a job came open. Rather than remain a graduate assistant for another year, he began a 29-year-career as a high-school coach and teacher in Michigan's Upper Peninsula. He spent 24 years at Bessemer High and five at Ironwood High. One of his quarterbacks at Bessemer was Kevin Borseth, who went on to become the women's basketball coach at the University of Michigan. Bobby Jurasin, one of his defensive linemen, won a Canadian Football League Gray Cup title in 1989 and is in the CFL Hall of Fame.

Gallinagh was inducted into the Michigan High School Football

Coaches Association Hall of Fame as well as the Upper Peninsula Hall of Fame. (The Upper Peninsula Hall of Fame also includes Michigan State basketball coach Tom Izzo, a teammate at Iron Mountain with another Upper Peninsula Hall of Famer, college and NFL coach Steve Mariucci.)

With the move to the Upper Peninsula, Gallinagh met his wife, Deloris. The kid from Detroit's blue-collar neighborhoods was now closer geographically to the Green Bay Packers in Wisconsin than the Detroit Lions. He adopted a rural lifestyle that was 180 degrees removed from Detroit's urban streets.

Gallinagh is proud of Michigan State's role at integrating college football—as indicated in his poem "What is a Spartan?" But he knows it went easier on Michigan State's football roster than anywhere else.

"Affirmative action upset a lot of people, but there had to be a way to break the dam," Gallinagh said. "That's what we did at Michigan State—we broke the dam. Alabama didn't have one black player in 1966. Now look at them today—you'd never know that."

Notes

1. HBO, *Breaking the Huddle*, 2008.

16

ROSE THORNS AND WOODY'S TANTRUM

"Duffy said, 'Whatever you do, pitch the ball to Bob.' He said, 'You got it? I said yes. I started onto the field and he grabs me again and says, 'Pitch the ball to Bob.' I said, 'OK, I got it.' It made sense to pitch the ball to Bob. He weighed 245 pounds."—Jimmy Raye

The 1965 college football season drew a line in the sand on how coaches, teams, fans, and the media viewed the purpose of bowl games then and now. Bowl games, created as tourist destinations, were limited in number and not part of the national championship equation. Bowl game statistics also were excluded from an athlete's final season statistics.

National championships were voted upon by the Associated Press poll, debuting in 1934, and by the United Press International poll that began in 1950 after the regular season. They did not wait for bowl games. Notre Dame and Army won multiple national titles without playing in bowl games.

The last Notre Dame national title claimed without a bowl game was in 1966, after the Irish and Michigan State played to a 10-10 tie in the Game of the Century. In 1965, in response to media clamor, AP held voting after bowl games before reverting to traditional pre-bowl voting in 1966. The AP switched permanently to post-bowl voting in 1968. The UPI poll, voted upon by coaches, followed in 1969.

In the 1965 experimental season, Michigan State's 10-0 and No.

1-ranked team suffered the consequence of the first post-bowl vote. The UPI stuck to tradition and named Michigan State its national champion following the regular season. So too did the Football Writers Association (FWAA) and the National Football Foundation (NFF), the latter awarding the Spartans its prestigious MacArthur Bowl Trophy.

Michigan State coach Duffy Daugherty was ahead of the times in many ways, but some Spartans felt their progressive coach was stuck in the past with his view of bowl games. He treated the Rose Bowl as a reward—particularly for his seniors.

At the conclusion of the 1965 season, the Spartans lost to UCLA 14-12 in the 1966 Rose Bowl, a stunning result that remains one of the all-time upsets in college football. Michigan State's final 10-1 record was superior to Alabama's final mark of 9-1-1, but the Crimson Tide beat Nebraska in the Orange Bowl and was voted the AP national champion. Times had changed. In the minds of the AP voters, Michigan State's lone loss in a bowl game to a Top 5 opponent (No. 5 UCLA, 8-2-1) outweighed Alabama's regular-season defeat to an unranked team (Georgia, 6-4) and regular season tie to a Top 10 team (No. 7 Tennessee, 8-1-2).

Michigan State dropped to No. 2, the prior No. 2 Arkansas (10-1) fell to No. 3 following a Cotton Bowl loss to LSU, and the prior No. 3 Nebraska (10-1) slipped to No. 5 after its Orange Bowl defeat. Alabama jumped from No. 4 to No. 1, UCLA rose to No. 4, and Tennessee remained No. 7.

The Michigan State Spartans had beaten UCLA 13-3 in the 1965 season opener at Spartan Stadium in a game that was not as close as the score indicates. When UCLA earned the Rose Bowl bid with a 20-16 upset of USC in the regular season finale, *Los Angeles Times* columnist Jim Murray wrote about impending doom for the hometown team. "A terrible thing happened to the UCLA Bruins in the Coliseum Saturday afternoon. They won the right to go to the Rose Bowl—an invitation to bleed....Playing Michigan State is a job that calls for volunteers, not victors."[1]

Another Murray punchline stated that the Spartans' line was "so big that when they ran a picture of it on the front page of the Detroit Free Press, they had to make it 'Continued on Page 11.' And even then, they only got to the left guard."

Statistically, the Spartans set a Big Ten record that still stands, allowing only 34.6 yards rushing per game in conference contests. Overall, the defense limited its opposition to 47.3 yards rushing and 6.2 points per contest.

In MSU's three rivalry games in 1965, the Spartans held Michigan to minus 51 yards rushing, Ohio State to minus 21 yards rushing and Notre Dame to minus 12 yards rushing. Notre Dame's 24 passing yards gave the Irish a net total of just 12 yards for the contest. "I don't recall anything like this before," Notre Dame coach Ara Parseghian said afterward. "As far as we're concerned, MSU is No. 1. They are a great team deserving of their ranking."[2]

But the Spartans felt the seeds to their upset loss were sown three years earlier when Wisconsin played on the same Rose Bowl turf. In 1960s America, the Rose Bowl (known as "The Granddaddy of Them All") presented a unique opportunity to play before a large national audience. Wisconsin senior quarterback Ron Vander Kelen made a national splash in the 1963 Rose Bowl (1962 season) against USC, completing 33 of 48 passes for 401 yards—all Rose Bowl records and staggering numbers for the era—in a dramatic comeback that ended in a 42-37 loss for the Badgers.

Michigan State defensive end Bubba Smith, a junior in 1965, said what other players had long thought about their baffling loss to the Bruins in his 1983 book, *Kill, Bubba, Kill!* He felt Daugherty wanted a Vander Kelen-like moment for his two senior captains, All-American quarterback Steve Juday and All-Big Ten cornerback Don Japinga, while UCLA coach Tommy Prothro "... had his team geared for victory...And we're geared for the Steve Juday showcase.

"Daugherty also changed the punt return man, from Drake Garrett to a little dude named Don Japinga. Both captains were being massaged."[3]

Duffy Daugherty had been seduced by fawning Southern California media coverage into thinking he could tinker with the lineup. Meanwhile, the overconfident players stayed out late upon arriving in Southern California early in the week until an alarmed Daugherty moved the team to a monastery in the mountains above Los Angeles.

On game day, Don Japinga was placed in a difficult position. Daugherty called on him to return punts in place of the Spartans' two regulars, Drake Garrett and Jess Phillips. In the regular season, Garrett had returned 22 punts, Phillips ten and Japinga one.

Japinga quickly dug a 7-0 hole by fumbling a punt on the Spartans' 6-yard line. UCLA quarterback Gary Beban, who would win the Heisman Trophy in 1967, needed only two plays to score—a five-yard rush and a one-yard touchdown.

Gifted with a early 7-0 lead, UCLA stayed aggressive and attempted an onside kick. Michigan State was caught sleeping, even though the Bruins had used an onside kick to upset USC to earn the Rose Bowl bid. UCLA recovered the kick and scored with a seven-play, 42-yard drive capped by another Beban one-yard touchdown run.

UCLA led 14-0 with 11:50 left in the second quarter despite Michigan State's defense already having forced three punts. By halftime UCLA had punted seven times and Michigan State All-American roverback George Webster had recovered a fumble, yet the Spartans still trailed by two touchdowns.

For the game, UCLA's longest drive was a 44-yarder that ended in a punt. The Bruins finished with 212 total yards—65 rushing and 147 passing. Michigan State gave up more yards than expected, but it was a sputtering offense with Steve Juday's four turnovers—three interceptions and one fumble—that cost the Spartans the game. Juday, a two-year starter and an AP All-American, played his worst game in his final start. Bubba Smith felt Daugherty stayed with Juday too long and should have substituted sophomore backup quarterback Jimmy Raye earlier.

The Spartans' three first-quarter possessions included a pair of three-and-outs and a Juday interception. In the second quarter, Michigan State started with a three-and-out, Juday fumble, three-and-out and Juday's second interception. On the Spartans' final possession of the first half, Dick Kenney missed a 23-yard field goal that was set up by 47 yards in UCLA penalties. The kick drifted slightly over the right upright. Daugherty said it "couldn't have been closer to being good."[4]

At halftime, Juday was 2 of 8 passing for 15 yards with two interceptions, a lost fumble and two sacks for 7 yards. Daugherty told the team in the locker room that Raye would start the second half.

"It was consistent with during the season when he had put me in games," Raye said. "He told the team I was going in, but when we were in the tunnel going back on the field, he pulled me back. He said he was going to start Steve one more series to see if he could get it going. He told me when I was a senior, I would understand."

The Spartans fielded the second-half kickoff and again went three-

and-out. Juday remained behind center on the second possession. Clinton Jones broke off a 26-yard run to reach midfield, but the Spartans gave the ball back when a fourth-and-1 play was stopped at the UCLA 45. Juday returned to the field for the third possession of the third quarter and threw his third interception. After three quarters, he was 2-for-11 passing for 15 yards with three interceptions.

In the second half, Daugherty told Raye to warm up three times before he finally inserted him in the lineup in the game's final seven minutes. Bubba Smith's father Willie Ray Smith had a sidelines pass.

"He asked me why Duffy kept telling me to warm up but didn't put me in," Raye said.

Juday started Michigan State's first fourth-quarter possession and completed a 9-yard pass to Gene Washington, but the Spartans were stopped on fourth-and-1 at their 29-yard line. UCLA could have put the game away but failed to capitalize with a missed 34-yard field goal.

Juday was under center again for the fourth quarter's second possession and completed a first-down pass of 42 yards to Gene Washington to the UCLA 38. Daugherty then sent Raye into the game for his first snap.

Raye ran the sprint option right and pitched to fullback Bob Apisa, who ran 38 yards down the sideline for a touchdown, with 6:13 left in the game. Daugherty, as he had done in previous games in a comeback situation, opted for the 2-point conversion after an early score rather than with the game on the line if the Spartans managed to score again. "That's the time to go for two," he said. "If there's going to be an element of surprise, that's when you'll have it."[5]

Daugherty sent Steve Juday back onto the field for the 2-point conversion, but his pass on a fake kick was deflected.

With the clock ticking down, Michigan State forced a three-and-out. Bubba Smith partially blocked the punt, giving the Spartans the ball at the Michigan State 49-yard line.

Juday started the third and final possession of the quarter and was sacked for the third time for a 7-yard loss by 195-pound defensive tackle Terry Donahue, the future UCLA head coach from 1976 to 1995. The next two plays, Raye and Juday both threw an incomplete pass before Raye returned to the huddle for fourth-and-17.

The Rose Bowl came down to a quarterback from Fayetteville, North Carolina, and an end from LaPorte, Texas, unwelcome at their home-state schools, to keep the drive alive. They connected—Gene Washington ran his pattern precisely 18 yards, Raye delivered the ball on time and Washington secured the catch and ran three more yards for a 21-yard gain. Michigan State had a first down at the UCLA 37.

Juday returned and completed a nine-yard toss to Washington. Raye followed with back-to-back snaps, rushing for four yards and a first down and then passing nine yards to halfback Dwight Lee to the UCLA 15. After incomplete passes by both Juday and Raye, Apisa gained 5 yards on third-and-1 for a first down. The ball was placed a half-yard outside of the 10-yard line.

With the ball spotted officially on the 11-yard line, Michigan State had room to gain a first down without scoring. Juday began the series with an incomplete pass. Fullback Eddie Cotton bulled for three yards on second down. Juday completed a third-down pass to Lee for six yards. Raye came in on fourth-and-1 and gained enough to set up a first-and-goal. Juday returned and scored on a first-down plunge to trim the deficit to 14-12 with 31 seconds remaining.

Daugherty called timeout and huddled with Raye on the sideline. He instructed Raye to tell the official to move the ball from the middle of the field to the left hash mark—leaving the right side as the wide side. Daugherty wanted the ball in Apisa's hands, and Apisa ran better to the right following his knee injury. Daugherty called for sprint option right—the same play Apisa scored a touchdown on earlier.

"Duffy said, 'Whatever you do, pitch the ball to Bob,'" Raye recalled. "He said, 'You got it?' I said yes. I started onto the field and he grabs me again and says, 'Pitch the ball to Bob.' I said, 'OK, I got it.' It made sense to pitch the ball to Bob. He weighed 245 pounds."

UCLA's undersized defensive line featured two players who would go on to longtime coaching careers. Donahue was a head coach at UCLA and Jim Colletto a longtime college and the NFL assistant. They did not need coach to tell them what Michigan State had in mind. Once the official granted Daugherty's request relayed by Raye, the UCLA defense knew the play was designed to go right.

"I got the ball and started to go down the line on the sprint option," Raye said. "Everybody flew out to Bob. I could have run from California to Fayetteville before anyone touched me, but I flipped the ball to Bob."

Apisa was hit first by Colletto and second by linebacker Dallas Grider. Despite the two hits, Apisa still plowed forward with momentum toward the goal line before 175-pound defensive back Bob Stiles—who already had two interceptions—launched his body missile-like into Apisa. The effort stopped Apisa short of the score.

Sports Illustrated reported, "It was the hardest blow of the game, and one of the most damaging ever inflicted on the Big Ten. Apisa crashed two feet shy of the end zone, and Bob Stiles had to be revived and helped off the field to accept the most valuable player trophy."[6]

With handcuffs Raye's high-school coach never placed on him, he was forced to pitch rather than make his own read and cut inside to score. A 14-14 tie might have protected Michigan State's No. 1 ranking in the AP poll. He would have earned a place in Rose Bowl and Michigan State lore. He also probably would not have faced a challenge for the starting job in both 1966's spring drills and fall camp.

Raye finished with modest totals of 2-of-4 rushing for 5 yards and 2-of-4 passing for 30 yards, but he was on the field for the crucial plays. He took the snap for Apisa's touchdown. On the second TD drive, he was under center for all four first downs. Three of those first downs were gutsy fourth-down plays.

Raye and Apisa lived in private anguish with the failed 2-point conversion attempt and the devastating upset loss, Raye because Daugherty had tied his hands, Apisa because he felt he was to blame for costing the Spartans the AP national title.

Michigan State's Rose Bowl loss meant the Spartans were no longer considered invincible. In 1966, when No. 1 Michigan State beat Ohio State 11-8 in conditions considered "monsoon-like" on the same afternoon that No. 2 Notre Dame routed lowly North Carolina 32-0, AP voters did not give the Spartans the benefit of the doubt. 5-0 Notre Dame was voted No. 1 and 5-0 Michigan State dropped to No. 2. The two unbeaten teams remained ranked in that order the rest of the season. If the Spartans had won the Rose Bowl, would they have received a mulligan at Ohio State for the win in bad weather over a rival looking for revenge on the road?

Raye was Michigan State's starting quarterback as a junior when Spartans traveled to their fateful October 15 game at Ohio Stadium in Columbus. Those conditions were referred to as "monsoon-like" because the temperature was 72 degrees despite 35-mph winds that blew heavy rain sideways.

The Spartans came from behind to beat the Buckeyes with a fourth-quarter drive for the ages. The victory should be better remembered in Michigan State lore as one of the Spartans' finest hours in the two-year run of back-to-back unbeaten Big Ten titles; instead, MSU fell from No. 1 and the victory faded from memory. Perhaps if the game had been televised, it would be accorded its proper place in history, but fans had to listen to the radio as the Spartans pulled out the dramatic finish.

The Spartans' 1966 comeback task at Ohio State included beating a vengeful Woody Hayes. He had circled the game on his calendar to avenge the Buckeyes' 32-7 loss a year earlier. The night before the game, Hayes was believed to have ordered the field watered to slow down the bigger and quicker Spartans. The field was soaked even before heavy rain fell for the afternoon kickoff.

After the season, Michigan State defensive lineman Pat Gallinagh met Ohio State halfback Bo Rein at the North-South Shrine All-Star game. (Rein was named LSU's head coach following the 1979 season, but he died in a plane crash in January 1980 without ever coaching a game.)

"He told me Woody was so mad they practiced for us for a whole year for that game," Gallinagh said. "He said their spring game was the Green and Red game."

Once the 1966 mud bowl was underway, Michigan State committed the first mistake in the sloppy conditions midway through the first quarter. The Spartans faced fourth-and-8 at their 31-yard line when Ron Ranieri—playing his first game of the year after a fall camp injury—snapped the ball more than 42 yards out of the end zone to give Ohio State a 2-0 lead.

The *Detroit Free Press* story by Hal McCoy said of the snap, "In Tiger Stadium, Ranieri's pitch would have been in the upper deck."

Daugherty took the blame for putting Ranieri, the backup long-snapper, in a difficult situation. Ranieri was a talented player who was the starter in 1966 and earned honorable mention All-Big Ten at the position in 1967. Daugherty explained he left regular long-snapper Keith Redd at home due to starting guard Dave Techlin's injury. He brought Ranieri to handle the long-snapping and for depth if Techlin could not finish the game.

Midway through the third quarter, Michigan State rallied for a 3-2 lead when barefooted Hawaiian kicker Kenney trotted onto the muddy field to boot a 27-yard field goal. The score was set up by a 20-yard Ohio State punt that provided field position.

A 3-2 lead appeared sufficient, thanks to the conditions and a Michigan State defense that forced seven Ohio State punts and four turnovers. But on the first play of the fourth quarter, the Buckeyes caught the Spartans overplaying the run. Billy Anders got behind the secondary and caught a 47-yard catch-and-run touchdown pass from quarterback Bill Long. The extra-point failed, but Ohio State still led 8-3 with 14:53 to play.

With Michigan State's unbeaten season stuck in the mud, Raye mounted a 16-play, 84-yard drive. Bob Apisa scored the game-winning touchdown on a fourth-and-goal dive from the 1-yard line.

"It was a terrible day, the rain pouring down, the field a quagmire and a strong wind blowing," said Michigan State assistant coach Al Dorow. "...It was a dark moment for us."[7]

The drive started at the MSU 16-yard line. Jimmy Raye hooked up with Washington for 28 yards and then connected on two passes with Allen Brenner—a 14-yard on second and 10, and a 17-yarder on third-and-10—to advance the ball to the Buckeyes' 25.

"Jimmy found himself in the Ohio State game," Dorow said. "That was the day he grew up and became the master, the day his teammates gained solid confidence in him....Jimmy drove the team with the expertness of a craftsman, and we got the winning touchdown."

The next four snaps were running plays with Raye, Clinton Jones, and Michigander Dick Berlinski, representing the Upper Peninsula from the small town of Quinnesec. The running plays set up a third-and-10 at the Ohio State 12-yard line. Raye and Washington proved a clutch combination again, with Washington catching a 10-yard pass from Raye for a first-and-goal at the 2-yard line.

Raye was 4-of-7 passing for 69 yards on the drive, and Robert Markus of the *Chicago Tribune* wrote in his game story that the three incompletions were all dropped balls. The Ohio State game was only Raye's fifth start. Pundits and fans were still evaluating whether he could prove himself to be a team leader and effective passer under pressure for the No. 1-ranked team.

Wrote Markus: "With desperation born of despair, Raye had put the soggy, slippery football in the air seven times on this advance and he connected four times. The other three passes were on target, too, but his receivers simply could not hold on to the treacherous ball."[8]

Clinton Jones said years later, "We don't win the Ohio State game without Jimmy. He was magnificent."

On first-and-goal from the 2, the Spartans called Raye's number for three straight dives, but he only managed to nudge the ball to the 1-yard line. The season had come down to a fourth-and-goal from the 1. The play sent in from the sideline called for Apisa to carry the ball.

"Ohio State put up a good defense, but the problem was the footing," Apisa said. "If it was dry, Jimmy would have marched in there. We knew fourth down was our last hurrah. If we lose, we won't be No. 1. Dick Berlinski came in as a substitute halfback. He was short and squatty, but a good blocker. When the play was called, I looked at him and I said, 'Dick, just give me a crease. All I need is a crease.'

"That's what happened. When the ball was snapped, I saw a smidgen of light. Everybody was converging on me, and I went up in the air. I got hit, but I instinctively extended my arms to put the ball out to break the plane. The ball got slapped out of my hands on the way down and I ended up on my back, but I knew I had broken the plane."

Bob Apisa looked up from the ground to the official, who raised his arms to signal a touchdown. Apisa felt a monkey hop off his back. He had been unfairly blaming himself for 288 days following the failed 2-point conversion play at the Rose Bowl.

"To this day, the Rose Bowl is the toughest loss for me to take," Apisa said. "That was one of the things that came to mind at the Ohio State game when the play came in and for me. I didn't want to re-live that horror story. I said, 'You know what, Bob, you were one yard short of the AP national title. You can't afford to do this to your teammates again and lose the undefeated season and national title.'

"I knew I had to deliver the mail, and thank God I did. It was good fortune, good blocking and Jimmy was the captain with the way he handled the play and the ball."

When Apisa says "good fortune," he understood how easily it would have been for the official to rule the play was stopped short of a touchdown. The play also could have been ruled a fumble with the ball slapped from Apisa's hands.

"The official knew I had broken the plane, but I had been hit and when I came down I wasn't in the end zone," Apisa said. "The crowd went nuts thinking I had been stopped. The referee was very courageous. He knew 84,000 Ohio State fans were ready to string him up. It was bedlam when he signaled touchdown. The fans booed and rained all kinds of debris down on us."

Apisa remembers well Hayes's ensuing sideline tantrum protesting the touchdown call.

"Woody Hayes was just going nuts, and he incited the crowd. He was a madman after that touchdown. I have never seen a coach display that kind of sideline behavior. I look at the way Duffy behaved as a coach and the way Woody behaved, and it was night and day."

When order was restored, Michigan State added a 2-point conversion on a pass from kicker Dick Kenney to holder Charlie Wedemeyer.

Ohio State found itself confronted with an 11-8 margin with 7:09 left in the game. The Buckeyes got the ball back three times—twice inside Michigan State territory.

On third-and-10 play from Michigan State's 35-yard line, Long's pass was intercepted by Jimmy Summers at the Spartans' 9-yard line with 3:37 to play.

A short Michigan State punt and 15-yard penalty on the Spartans gave the ball back to Ohio State with a first-and-10 at MSU's 24-yard line. This time Drake Garrett intercepted a pass with 1:23 to play.

Ohio State had time for one final desperation pass in the final seconds. It was picked off again by Garrett.

Ironically, when the game ended, the sun came out. The only remaining rain was debris from Ohio State's fans.

"We got bombarded as we ran to our locker room," said Apisa. "We needed a police escort when we left the stadium."

Hayes had calmed down by the post-game interview session. He called Michigan State "the best team in the country." About his sideline tantrum, he said, "I never saw the official signal their touchdown. He must have just made it over by a whisker. I'm not implying that Michigan State didn't score—but I just didn't see it."[9]

Two days after the game, Michigan State's joy at preserving its unbeaten season turned to disbelief when the AP and UPI polls came out. Without Michigan State having suffered a loss, the No. 1 Spartans and No. 2 Notre Dame switched positions. Notre Dame's easy victory over North Carolina had swayed enough voters.

On October 10, the Monday before the Ohio State/North Carolina results, Michigan State was 4-0 and No. 1 with 18 first-place votes and

369 points. Notre Dame was 3-0 and No. 2 with 15 first-place votes and 353 points.

On October 17, the Monday after the Ohio State/North Carolina results, Notre Dame was 4-0 and No. 1 with 31 first-place votes and 443 points. Michigan State was No. 2 and 5-0 with 10 first-place votes and 416 points.

The polls remained No. 1 Notre Dame and No. 2 Michigan State through the rest of the season and the final votes.

"I always thought the object of the game was to win," Daugherty said when the Spartans dropped to No. 2. "Apparently, they expect more of us."[10]

Notes

1. *Los Angeles Times*, Nov. 21, 1965.

2. *Flint Journal*, Nov. 21, 1965.

3. *Kill, Bubba, Kill!*, p. 92.

4. Post-game notes.

5. *Los Angeles Times*, Jan. 3, 1966.

6. *Sports Illustrated*, Jan. 10, 1966.

7. *Fayetteville Observer*, Dec. 20, 1966.

8. *Chicago Tribune*, Oct. 16; *Biggest Game*, p. 154.

9. Official Ohio State gamebook.

10. *Biggest Game*, p. 164.

17

TRUE NATIONAL CHAMPIONS

"The reasons are rather obvious why we divided the award. It seemed like the only fair thing to do with a couple excellent teams like Notre Dame and Michigan State."—Vincent DePaul Draddy, National Football Foundation

George McGovern carried only one state against Richard Nixon in the 1972 Presidential election, but history proved the Massachusetts electorate prescient once the Watergate scandal forced Nixon to resign in 1974. Much later, McGovern demonstrated wit and wisdom when he said Massachusetts was the only state in the union to demonstrate good sense in 1972.

Michigan State coach Duffy Daugherty, always a quipster, could have used such a line to paraphrase in 1966. The Associated Press and United Press International polls voted Notre Dame No. 1 over Michigan State, but the National Football Foundation presented the MacArthur Bowl Trophy to the Spartans and Notre Dame as national co-champions.

"The MacArthur Bowl was the only national title award with good sense," Daugherty could have said.

Separating Michigan State and Notre Dame was not easy then—or now. In addition to the 10-10 tie and identical 9-0-1 records, Michigan State was ranked No. 1 the first five weeks and Notre Dame the final five.

"The reasons are rather obvious why we divided the award," said Vincent DePaul Draddy, the chairman of the MacArthur Bowl. "It seemed like the only fair thing to do with a couple of excellent teams like Notre Dame and Michigan State."[1]

The MacArthur Bowl, named for General Douglas MacArthur, went one step further. The NFF also split its national coach-of-the-year award between Daugherty and Notre Dame coach Ara Parseghian. In fact, the coaches held a three-year stranglehold on the award—Parseghian in 1964 and Daugherty in 1965.

"We were the No. 1-ranked team in the nation and we didn't lose a game," Michigan State quarterback Jimmy Raye said. "Duffy said we were national champions. He never used the word co-champions. I think the '66 team felt then and now it was a national championship season."

The MacArthur Bowl Trophy was first presented in 1959, but since 1998 it has been claimed by the winner of the Bowl Championship Series game. But in the 1960s newspapers dutifully reported the National Football Foundation's selection as the MacArthur Bowl recipient. General MacArthur, who attended the NFF dinners before he passed away in 1964, was a passionate football fan throughout his life. During World War II, while directing the U.S. forces in the Pacific Theater, MacArthur sent a telegram to Army's undefeated football team following a 1944 season-ending win over Navy: *"The greatest of Army teams. We have stopped the war to celebrate your success."*[2]

The MacArthur Bowl Trophy was not equal to the AP or UPI titles in prestige, but it gave the Spartans a slice of the national title they felt had been denied them by the whims of poll voting favoring Notre Dame's history and tradition. Neither team lacked a case as the best in the nation. Ultimately, the two varsity rosters of sophomores, juniors, and seniors included 10 first-round draft picks, 42 overall draft picks, 33 pro players, and 25 All-America picks.

In those days underclassmen were ineligible for the draft, so seniors dominated the NFL drafts. The two senior classes in the Game of the Century combined to produce seven first-round draft picks and 17 choices overall—nearly a full starting lineup of NFL prospects just among the seniors representing two schools.

Michigan State had four first-round choices: defensive end Bubba Smith (1st overall), halfback Clinton Jones (2nd), roverback George Webster (5th) and offensive end Gene Washington (8th). The other four Michigan State seniors drafted were defensive end Jeff Richardson (6th round), cornerback Jimmy Summers (9th), linebacker Charlie Thornhill (9th), and kicker Dick Kenney (14th).

Notre Dame had three first-rounders: left tackle Paul Seiler (12th), defensive tackle Alan Page (15th) and left guard Tom Regner (23rd). The other six Notre Dame seniors drafted were linebacker Jim Lynch (2nd), halfback Nick Eddy (2nd), halfback Larry Conjar (2nd), center George Goeddeke (3rd), defensive end Tom Rhoads (3rd), and linebacker Allen Sack (16th).

Coach Duffy Daugherty of Michigan State, left, and coach Ara Parseghian of Notre Dame beam over the MacArthur Bowl, which was presented jointly to their teams at the National Football Association's awards dinner in New York, Dec. 6, 1966. [AP]

"To this day, I still think it's the two best teams ever to play each other," said Notre Dame quarterback Terry Hanratty, a sophomore then who was drafted in 1968 by the Pittsburgh Steelers in the second round. "You look on both sides, both teams, the All-Americans, the Hall of Famers, the all-pros, whatever. I mean, those are two great, great football teams."[3]

Another person with an NFL future who considered the Game of the Century unprecedented was Jerry Markbreit, the back judge on the referee crew. He would go on to work as an NFL referee for 23 years, including four Super Bowls.

"The atmosphere was like that of a Super Bowl game today," Markbreit said in 1988. "It was late November, but people were driving around like it was summertime, hanging out their windows and honking their horns; the press was 20 deep....It was the most highly charged pregame atmosphere I had ever experienced."[4]

Game day arrived with a 33-degree temperature, 5-to-12 mile easterly swirling winds, lead-gray skies, and a record crowd of 80,011 crammed into 76,000-seat Spartan Stadium. Notre Dame's Mike Burgener, now a USA Weightlifting coach who upon graduation served in Vietnam as a U.S. Marine Corps reconnaissance officer for Special Forces, said the chill never tempered the crowd's rabid enthusiasm.

"I remember you couldn't hear the guy standing next to you," Burgener said. "I still get chills thinking about it."

Burgener, from the small town of Marion, Illinois, was a backup safety and special-teams regular who was one of only two defensive substitutes to see playing time in the Game of the Century. His kickoff coverage role was to launch his 5-foot-10, 182-pound body at three wedge-buster blockers on kickoff coverage. The strategy is now outlawed.

Notre Dame won the coin toss, but the Irish already had lost a starter. Fullback Nick Eddy aggravated a shoulder injury on Friday when he slipped as he deboarded the team train at the Lansing Grand Funk station. Two other starters, Hanratty and center George Goeddeke, were knocked out of the game in the first quarter.

Notre Dame's offense was otherwise thought to have an advantage with its passing attack. Hanratty was a 6-foot-1, 210-pound dropback passer and glamour boy, featured on the cover of *Time* magazine on Oct. 28, 1966, with offensive end Jim Seymour.

The smaller Raye was considered more of a running quarterback, but he entered the game with a better touchdown-to-interception ratio. Raye had compiled 10 touchdowns compared to six interceptions; Hanratty had eight TDs and 10 picks. Raye's 10 touchdown passes in 1966 were the most by a Spartans quarterback since All-American Tom Yewicic threw 10 in 1952.

Notre Dame's defense arrived in East Lansing having allowed only 28 points with five shutouts in eight games. Irish defensive coordinator John Ray was most concerned with Jimmy Raye as the Irish practiced during the week.

"Ray was emphatic about containing Jimmy Raye," Burgener said. "He was constantly telling our defensive ends and linebackers, 'You've got to contain! You've got to wrap up! You can't let him run amok!' He was worried about Jimmy Raye's athleticism and ability to get outside."

The Game of the Century turned out to be a defensive struggle, as was often the case for the era in big games. Both teams were forced to punt eight times, and neither one gained field position from the returns. The coverage teams also were playing at a national championship level. Michigan State sophomore Allen Brenner returned only three for minus-8 yards. Notre Dame junior Tom Schoen returned only two for 5 yards.

Notre Dame punted first after it received the opening kickoff. An injury had forced Notre Dame defensive lineman Kevin Hardy into also handling the punting duties, but the big guy had a leg. His first punt was a 40-yarder; after aggressive coverage by junior Bob Gladieux resulting in a 2-yard loss, Michigan State revved up its first drive from its 11-yard line.

The Spartans started in reverse. Raye lost two yards on first down. On second down he dropped back to pass, but was engulfed by the pass rush of Tom Rhoads and Alan Page. In tucking the ball, Raye fumbled, but fullback Regis Cavender, playing for injured All-American Bob Apisa, recovered at the 4-yard line. A delay of game penalty pushed the ball back two more yards.

On fourth-and-13 from the 8, Dick Kenney lined up five yards deep in his end zone. His 54-yard Hawaiian punch, benefitting from a generous bounce, rolled dead across midfield at the Notre Dame 38-yard line.

Notre Dame's second series was Hanratty's last. The quarterback completed his only pass of the game (in four attempts) on a third-and-10 play, connecting with Gladieux for 26 yards to the Michigan State 36 despite junior safety Jess Phillips draped all over the Irish player in coverage. Two plays later, Hanratty rolled right. Charlie Thornhill wrapped up Hanratty just as Bubba Smith caught up to the play. The 285-pound Smith was described as a freight train hitting Hanratty, driving his left shoulder into the turf.

Hanratty was sent to the locker room for an examination. He watched the rest of the game with a separated shoulder and his arm in a sling. On fourth-and-7 from the Michigan State 33, Parseghian opted to punt.

Kenney's 54-yard punt had made a vital difference in field position. If Kenney's punt had been only, say, a very respectable 44 yards, Notre Dame would have faced a fourth-and-7 from the Michigan State 23 instead of the 33. From the 23, Parseghian could have called for a 40-yard field-goal attempt rather than punt. But from the 33, a 50-yard field-goal attempt was rare in the college game in the days preceding soccer-style kickers.

Michigan State responded with the first scoring drive, a 10-play, 73-yarder. Raye completed a 42-yard pass to Gene Washington to the Notre Dame 31. Clinton Jones gained 5 and 4 yards on the next two plays, including breaking a tackle by Lynch at the line of scrimmage.

Raye was stopped on third-and-1, but here Daugherty made his first critical coaching decision.

Daugherty went for it on fourth-and-1. The move paid off, as Raye gained two yards on a sneak behind center Larry Smith for a first down at the Notre Dame 20-yard line. On first-and-10 from the 20, Cavender gained 11 yards for first-and-goal at the 9. Two plays later on a third-and-goal from the 4-yard line, Cavender ran over right tackle for a touchdown. Right tackle Jerry West blocked his man left and offensive end Gene Washington forced his man right to open the hole. Clinton Jones led Cavender through the hole and cleared out a linebacker. Michigan State led 7-0 with 13:40 left in the second quarter.

Bedlam overtook Spartan Stadium. The momentum had shifted.

Michigan State kicked off and sophomore Coley O'Brien took the field as Hanratty's replacement. Notre Dame managed a first down before it was forced to punt from its 40-yard line.

The Spartans took over at their 19. On second-and-10, Raye ran to the right behind a block by Jones and gained 30 yards before he was knocked out of bounds by junior Jim Smithberger. It was the sort of play that had Notre Dame's John Ray fretting all week in practice.

"As we saw in the game, Jimmy had the speed to get outside and also throw," said O'Brien, who lives near Washington, D.C., and is a fan of Redskins quarterback Robert Griffin III. "He could roll out and throw or he could run. He presented to the defense a lot of the threat that RG3 does for Redskins' opponents."

Regis Cavender scoring a touchdown against Notre Dame. Photo courtesy Jimmy Raye.

The block Clinton Jones threw to help Raye break containment wasn't his only big hit on the possession. Two plays later, Jim Lynch intercepted a pass. On his return, Jones upended the All-American, causing a fumble as Lynch's head came down first on the turf. The Spartan standout pounced on the loose ball.

The intensity of the hit has been the source of a running debate between the two All-Americans. Lynch says it wasn't so hard. When they crossed paths years later, Lynch had undergone a knee replacement. That decided the issue in Clinton Jones's mind.

"Yeah, I knew I got him," Jones said with a chuckle.

With Jones's fumble recovery putting the Spartans back in business,

Gene Washington, who would catch five balls for 123 yards, brought a 17-yard pass to Notre Dame's 26. From there, the drive stalled.

Kenney was known for a big leg and he trotted onto the chilly field with his bare foot. His subsequent 47-yard field goal extended the Michigan State lead to 10-0 with 5:47 left in the first half.

To that point the Spartans had outgained Notre Dame, 153 yards to 68. The Irish faced the task of mounting a comeback without three starters, Eddy, Hanratty, and Goeddeke, directed by a sophomore QB who had missed the Navy game three weeks earlier when he was diagnosed and treated for diabetes.

The situation was precarious, but the son of U.S. Navy captain Jim O'Brien, commander of the USS Midway in the South Pacific in 1965, took the helm. He showed remarkable poise for a sophomore thrust into the Game of the Century, but he was aided by playing time the two previous weeks in routs of Pittsburgh (40-0) and Duke (64-0).

"All of the sudden, Terry goes down—I didn't see him get hurt—and they're calling my name, 'Coley, get ready!'" O'Brien recalled. "I didn't have time to get nervous. I had practiced all week and you prepare for the moment. Now if they had told me on Friday that Terry slipped on the train like Nick Eddy, then I would have had time to get nervous and might have had a rougher time."

After the game, Bubba Smith lamented how the Spartans prepared for a Hanratty in the pocket and instead faced a more mobile O'Brien.

"I always wanted to meet Bubba and thank him for his kind comments, but I never had the chance," Coley O'Brien said. "He said, 'They brought in this quick guy O'Brien and we hadn't practiced for him. He gave us a hard time.'"

The young quarterback put together a four-play, 54-yard touchdown drive with three straight pass completions. He connected for 11 yards to Gladieux and 9 to junior halfback Rocky Bleier to the Michigan State 34. On a play-action pass, Gladieux got behind the secondary and O'Brien hit him at goal line for a 34-yard touchdown pass with 4:30 left in the half. Notre Dame trailed 10-7 at halftime.

The second half opened with another exchange of turnovers. First, Raye fumbled at the Spartans' 31-yard line. Notre Dame went for a quick strike as O'Brien threw long, but Phillips intercepted a ball intended for Bleier at the 2-yard line.

That prompted another exchange of punts before O'Brien put

together a 10-play, 70-yard drive that finished with Joe Azzaro kicking a 28-yard field goal with 14:57 left in the game. Michigan State senior defensive back Sterling Armstrong recovered a fumble earlier in the possession, but Smith was flagged offside to negate the play.

Michigan State's best scoring opportunity in the second half came early in the fourth quarter when Jimmy Raye broke off a 20-yard run for a first down at Notre Dame's 46. Raye ran right, away from Alan Page, and cut back left before Lynch tackled him.

"I look back on that play as a missed opportunity," said Raye. "If I would have cut harder to the right than to the left, I might have taken it to the house. I thought I would get another chance, but I didn't."

Raye's big gainer was followed by a one-yard run by Jones, a two-yard loss by Raye, and an incomplete pass that forced the Spartans to punt.

An exchange of punts in the fourth quarter favored Notre Dame, since the game was being played in Michigan State territory. As a result, the Fighting Irish's best scoring opportunity was a first down at Michigan State's 18-yard line after Schoen intercepted a Raye pass. But the Spartans' defense pushed Notre Dame back when Bubba Smith and Philip Hoag sacked O'Brien for an 8-yard loss to the Michigan State 24. On third-and-16, O'Brien's pass was incomplete.

The sack forced Azzaro to attempt a 41-yard field goal rather than from the mid-30s. His attempt was long enough but drifted right. Markbreit signaled it wide as Spartan Stadium erupted in relief.

There was 4:39 left in the game when Michigan State took over at its 20-yard line. On first down, Jones was tackled for a six-yard loss. On second down, Raye threw an incomplete pass. Then Cavender ran up the middle on third-and-16 for a 15-yard gain that called for a measurement. The chains were stretched, and the referees determined Cavender was six inches short. Michigan State faced fourth-and-1 from its 29.

A punt was the safe play since Notre Dame would be in position for a long field goal with a stop, but Daugherty went for it. History might have labeled Daugherty a gambler who cost his team a national championship if the play had failed, but Raye sneaked between center Larry Smith and left guard Tony Conti to move the chains.

It was the Spartans' final first down.

Jones lost two yards, Brenner caught a pass for eight yards, and Raye's pass on third-and-4 at the Michigan State 36 was incomplete with two minutes to play. Daugherty decided fourth-and-4 was too risky and punted, hoping to get the ball back on a turnover or use time-outs to force a punt.

The coach almost got his wish. Tom Schoen fumbled the punt, but he was able to pounce on his own loose ball.

Notre Dame had a first down at its 30-yard line with 1:24 to play and all of its timeouts at its disposal.

There was enough time for the Irish to reach Michigan State territory to try a field goal. At least, that was how most football fans saw it. Parseghian opted instead to safely run out the clock.

As Dan Jenkins wrote in *Sports Illustrated* in a line that forever haunted Parseghian, "Tie, tie for old Notre Dame."

Jim Murray of the *Los Angeles Times* wrote, 'The Four Horsemen indeed!...Outlined against a blue-gray October sky, the Four Mice went into hiding again today'...May George Gipp never hear of it.'"

Notre Dame's final sequence of plays:

- 1st-and-10 at Notre Dame 30-yard line: O'Brien 4-yard run
- 2nd-and-6 34: Bleier 3-yard run
- 3rd-and-3 37: Conjar 2-yard run (Michigan State called timeout)
- 4th-and-1 39: O'Brien 2-yard run, first down (Michigan State called timeout)
- 1st-and-10 at Notre Dame 41-yard line: O'Brien sacked minus-7 yards by Smith (Michigan State called timeout)
- 2nd-and-17 34: O'Brien 5-run (time expired)

Parseghian's successful decision to go for it on fourth-and-1 from the Irish 39 was overshadowed by the fact he failed to use his timeouts. Notre Dame had a first down at its 41 with 30 seconds remaining, but it was Michigan State—not the Irish, as football pundits have noted ever since—who called a timeout.

Michigan State's players turned to the sidelines, screaming at Parseghian, and then turned back to Notre Dame's players, challenging them. Parseghian finally called for a pass. The Spartans had five defensive backs deployed, but O'Brien never had a chance to look for an open receiver. Bubba Smith jumped past backup center Tim Monty to sack O'Brien for a seven-yard loss.

"Bubba just leaped over him and squashed me," O'Brien said.

Smith had frequently shifted to nose tackle in the 1966 season so defensive coordinator Hank Bullough could get George Chatlos on the field at Smith's end position.

Jimmy Raye (#16) and Duffy Daugherty. Photo courtesy Jimmy Raye.

Parseghian sent in the final play, but instead of another pass as O'Brien expected, Parseghian instructed him to run the ball. He gained five yards as time expired.

"Walking off the field, I wondered why we ran the ball," O'Brien said. "I remember thinking we had lost the national championship. I was depressed in the locker room and so were other guys. But then Ara explained, 'Look, they didn't beat us and we didn't beat them. It was a tie, and we had a lot of injuries. We've still got a game to play. Michigan State is done—they don't have another game. We've got to go out Los Angeles. If we play well against Southern California, we can still win it.' I didn't think about it that way. He was right. We had a great week of practice and whipped Southern Cal."

In the November 21st AP poll after the 10-10 tie, Notre Dame ranked No. 1 with 37 first-place votes and 556 points. Michigan State received 27 first-place votes but nearly topped the Irish with 553 points.

Interestingly, Michigan State was actually the UPI national champion for one week after the 10-10 tie. In the November 21st voting of 35 coaches, Michigan State rated No. 1 with 318 points and Notre Dame No. 2 with 315. The Irish received 14 first-place votes to Michigan State's 12, with two coaches voting for a co-championship. The other first-place votes went to Nebraska (3), Alabama (2), Georgia Tech (1) and UCLA (1).

The coaches may have been influenced by Michigan State playing to win, but that would change after Notre Dame routed USC 51-0 on November 26. Parseghian took no chances with poll voters, keeping Eddy in the game until he scored a touchdown for a 43-0 lead. Michigan State could only sit by helplessly.

The UPI joined the AP voting with Notre Dame No. 1 and Michigan State No. 2. In the AP poll, Notre Dame had 40 first-place votes and 505 points to Michigan State's 10 first-place votes and 471 points. Without Michigan State playing a game, the Spartans lost 17 first-place votes and 82 overall points in the AP voting.

One final poll remained to be voted, waiting until No. 3-ranked Alabama's game on December 3 against Auburn. The Crimson Tide rolled 31-0 over an Auburn team that finished 4-6, but they remained a distant third.

The final AP and UPI votes were released on December 5, 1966:

1. Notre Dame, 41 first-place votes, 506 points

2. Michigan State, 8 first-place votes, 471 points
3. Alabama, 7 first-place votes, 427 points

Without playing a game during the final two poll votes, Michigan State lost 19 first-place votes and 82 overall points. The MacArthur Bowl Trophy would not be so capricious in naming its national co-champions.

Parseghian's strategy may have paid off, but the taunts of "Tie one for the Gipper" have followed him and his players since then. The ribbing riles Mike Burgener more than the reactions of any Vietnam War protestors when he was a Marine. Burgener said he ignored the Department of Defense advice that military personnel not to wear their uniform in airports.

"When I walked through airports, I always had my uniform on," Burgener said. "I didn't shy away from it like other branches of the service. I never got spit on or yelled at, but we were told if anything like that happened to us to not retaliate; just keep walking."

But ask Burgener about Parseghian playing for a tie, and he's quickly riled up. "I still get calls and we hash it all out again. I know it's all in fun, but I always say, 'No, no, Ara did the right thing. Do you want to see my national championship ring?'"

The debate has never abated and the scenario will never be duplicated for two reasons. First, the Bowl Championship Series (to be replaced by the four-team College Football Playoff in 2014) has decided the national champion since 1998. Second, tiebreaker rules have been in place since 1996.

In a side story to the Game of the Century, Alabama players and fans have long complained they were victims of prejudicial voting because of an all-white roster—an absurd reverse-discrimination argument—and played an insulated all-white schedule. A hole to punch in that argument: Texas' all-white roster was voted No. 1 in 1969. The Longhorns were the last all-white national championship team. Another hole: Steve Spurrier at segregated Florida was voted the 1966 Heisman Trophy winner. As for their insulated schedule: In 1966, the Crimson Tide played eight games in the state of Alabama at one of their three home stadiums (Tuscaloosa, Birmingham, and Mobile) and traveled only twice, visiting neighboring states Tennessee and Mississippi. In a six-game SEC schedule, Alabama did not face No. 4-ranked Georgia. None of the Crimson Tide's 10 opponents finished the season with a national ranking.

At least one writer in the South had no sympathy for Alabama's case. Dick Herbert of the *Raleigh News and Observer* wrote Alabama was fortunate to win the AP national title in 1965 with a 9-1-1 record that was inferior to UPI national champion Michigan State's 10-1 mark. He also wrote Alabama was only a victim of having a strong team in a year there were two stronger teams at Michigan State and Notre Dame.[5]

"Michigan State and Notre Dame were the two best teams in the country—no question," Coley O'Brien said. "We didn't consider Alabama. We lost our last game of the year in 1965 at home to Michigan State, 12-3, and we knew since that game they would be our competition for the national title. And it came down to the last game with that great buildup all year."

Time healed some of Michigan State's wounds by 1995 when the Spartans held a 30th reunion for the 1965 and 1966 teams. Duffy Daugherty had passed away in 1987, but Ara Parseghian wrote a touching letter to the players delivered through Michigan State left guard Tony Conti.[6]

Parseghian's respect for the Spartans was evident from his words and length of the two-page letter he took the time to compose. This was more than a courtesy letter.

"In view of the importance of your event I broke out the 1966 game-day program. I was tempted to go back to the film room to check out to see how you really performed in that game, but time didn't allow me to do so. Thus, it's my memory you must trust.

"In all honesty, the game brought together two of the finest college teams in history. Documentation of that is to review the number of players from both teams that distinguished themselves in pro ball. There was great talent on both sides and in spite of the fact the game ended in a tie, it is still recognized as a classic.

"You had a great coach in Duffy and an outstanding staff and I always felt that we had a terrific staff too. Much criticism was heaped on me because of the tie. I have said many times the game ended in a tie and if Duffy or I could have done anything about it we would have. Certainly, I won't debate with you the logic that was used in our last possession. Much has been written, including a book, addressing the entire season, as well as, the game itself. After 30 years I have no intention of attempting to influence anyone particularly the opposition. The best I can say is I made your team immortal. The game will live on forever and for that you can thank me.

"I hope the past years have treated you well. I am sure at this stage of your life you have come to appreciate the value of being involved with a team. Even now as you meet, many friendships will be renewed and stories told. I am sure those runs, passes and tackles are all so much longer and devastating than they actually were, but that's what reunions are all about.

"I hope you have a wonderful time and the 1966 Spartans team will always have the greatest respect from the author of this letter. You were one hell of a team—I can't resist—almost as good as Notre Dame."

Penn State coach Joe Paterno, who died in 2012, also sent the players a letter for the 1995 reunion. Penn State was not a Big Ten member in 1966, but Penn State and Michigan State played a home-and-home non-conference series. Michigan State won 23-0 in 1965 at Penn State and 42-10 in 1966 at Spartan Stadium. Paterno's 1995 letter—written when he was in his 30th year as Penn State's head coach and had already collected two national titles in 1982 and 1986—also suggests the MacArthur Bowl had it correct with a national co-championship. He wrote: *"In one sentence, you were great. In the 47 years I have been in College Football, you guys were as good as anybody we played against or that I saw play."*

Notes

1. *The New York Times*, Nov. 29, 1966.

2. William Manchester, *America Caesar: Douglas MacArthur 1880-1964*.

3. Terry Hanratty, *UND.com*, September 10, 2012.

4. *The Biggest Game of Them All*, p. 247.

5. *News and Observer*, Dec. 6, 1966.

6. Conti was named first-team All-Big Ten in 1966.

18

LAST VESTIGES OF THE UNDERGROUND RAILROAD

"I was trying to do something for black kids coming behind me when I signed with North Carolina. For my own best interests, I should have gone to Michigan State to start with. They didn't have a quarterback in 1972. If I would have been on that team, maybe we would have had an opportunity to go to the Rose Bowl."—Charlie Baggett

The Underground Railroad's last vestige remains arguably the most electric ending to a game in Spartan Stadium history. On November 9, 1974, quarterback Charlie Baggett—Duffy Daugherty's final Underground Railroad passenger both chronologically and symbolically—led the Spartans to a stirring 16-13 upset of No. 1-ranked goliath Ohio State before 78,533 delirious fans jammed into a stadium with a capacity of 76,000.

The only other two times Michigan State has upset a No. 1-ranked team was at Michigan in 1990 and at Ohio State in 1998. The Rose Bowl victories of 1954 and 1956 were played on the West Coast. The 1966 Game of the Century rocked the foundation of Spartan Stadium, of course, but that game ended in an anti-climactic and controversial 10-10 tie.

In 1974, Baggett was a junior second-year starter after he had boarded the Underground Railroad in 1972, Daugherty's final season as the Spartans' head coach. He was a transfer from the University of

North Carolina by way of Fayetteville, North Carolina, joining the 1972 recruiting class with four black freshmen from the South: Brandon Barber from Georgetown, South Carolina; James Cordery from Louisville, Kentucky; Otto Smith from Columbia, South Carolina; and Tyrone Willingham from Jacksonville, North Carolina.

Baggett was the last of these players to join Michigan State's 1972 roster well after the team had assembled for fall camp and shortly before the season opener. Baggett went through all but one week of North Carolina's 1972 preseason camp before he left for East Lansing.

Symbolically, Baggett was the last Underground Railroad passenger due to the circumstances of his transfer. He says he left North Carolina when Tar Heels head coach Bill Dooley broke a promise he would not switch his position from quarterback. Nearly a decade earlier Jimmy Raye looked North from Fayetteville seeking a chance as a pioneer black quarterback. Now Baggett was following his footsteps.

Charlie Baggett was recruited by Michigan State out of high school, but he viewed North Carolina as an opportunity to blaze a trail as the Tar Heels' first starting black quarterback. Turning down Michigan State was difficult for him. The Baggett family home in Fayetteville was next door to the Raye residence. Young Charlie, seven years younger than Jimmy Raye, grew up idolizing his neighbor.

Baggett had followed in Raye's footsteps since his days at Seabrook Park. Like Raye, he was E.E. Smith's starting quarterback for legendary coach D.T. Carter. Baggett was in junior high when he he first met Daugherty in Fayetteville. "Jimmy introduced me to Duffy and said, 'This is the next Jimmy Raye.' Duffy told me, 'Well, I'll be back down here to recruit you.'"

When recruiting time arrived, Sherman Lewis was assigned as Charlie Baggett's primary recruiter. Raye was new to Daugherty's staff in 1971, but he also felt he would be putting Baggett in an unfair position to serve as the recruiter.

"Jimmy did not want to influence my decision and stayed out of it," Baggett said. "Sherm Lewis came down to Fayetteville, and I talked to Duffy on the phone."

Baggett arrived in Chapel Hill as a freshman in 1972 when NCAA rules still prevented freshmen eligibility on the varsity. He split time with a white quarterback in the same recruiting class, Chris Kupec. Baggett also went through North Carolina's 1972 spring drills and 1972 fall camp, but he felt his playing opportunities fading away. Nick Vidnovic, the eventual 1972 starter as a junior, and Kupec, the 1972 backup to Vidnovic, received more repetitions in practice—the telltale sign to a coach's early depth chart.

At the end of fall camp in 1972, Dooley called Charlie Baggett into his office. Baggett recounted the conversation—seared in his memory—when Dooley informed him he was being switched to wide receiver.

"Bill Dooley said, 'Charles, for the betterment of the team, I think you should switch positions. We want to move you to receiver.'

"I said, 'Well, Coach, you promised me in front of my parents if I signed with Carolina, you would never switch my position.' He said, 'Well, Charles, I think for the betterment of the team, I've got to move you.'

"I said, 'OK, sir, I appreciate everything.' I walked out of the office and immediately called Jimmy."

Baggett arrived at Michigan State in time to enroll for classes and qualify as a 1972 redshirt transfer per NCAA rules. His opportunity came in 1973, the first of his three seasons as the Spartans' starting quarterback under Stolz, who retained Raye and Lewis from Daugherty's staff.

"I never looked back," Baggett said. "I never thought negatively about the University of North Carolina. I never burned bridges or hollered racism. I just left and let everyone else do the talking. Everyone knows why I left and they talked about it, but I never verified it. This is the first time I've talked about it."

Baggett, who twice earned All-Big Ten honorable mention in 1974 and 1975, forever earned a place in Spartans lore with the Ohio State upset. Before his arrival, Michigan State had missed on its recruiting evaluation of quarterbacks.

"By 1974, we had chipped away with our recruiting and felt we had the right number of athletes," Raye said. "We had a quarterback we felt we could win with. Charlie was a run and pass threat. Ohio State had been dominating, but we felt we could compete with them. We were very good on defense and we thought we were equal or better with Charlie at quarterback."

The 1974 Buckeyes had come off a 42-17 Rose Bowl victory over USC in the 1973 season. Their star-studded backfield returned intact:

quarterback Cornelius Greene, halfbacks Archie Griffin and Brian Baschnagel, and fullbacks Champ Henson and Pete Johnson. Griffin won the Heisman Trophy in 1974 and 1975, but Greene was the Big Ten MVP over Griffin in 1975. Griffin, Henson, Johnson, and Baschnagel all went on to play in the NFL and Greene in the Canadian Football League.

Adding to the magnitude of the 1974 shocker was that top-ranked teams rarely suffered upsets to unranked opponents in that era. Upsets have become more common since implementation of parity-designed scholarship limitations reducing roster totals from 105 to 95 in 1978 and then from 95 to 85 in 1992.

The intimidating Buckeyes arrived in East Lansing with an average winning margin of 35.6 points through their 8-0 start. In the previous four Big Ten games, they had averaged 50.8 points and outscored opponents a combined 203-30—Wisconsin 52-7, Indiana 49-9, Northwestern 55-7, and Illinois 49-7.

"The way they were playing, no one thought we could beat them," Raye said. "I remember Denny Stolz came in to our Sunday meeting before the game and said we were throwing caution to the wind. We felt we had a good defense, and we were going to be aggressive."

Michigan State slowed the Buckeyes' offensive juggernaut in a hard-hitting game. One of the biggest blows was delivered by freshman safety Tommy Graves on Baschnagel. Graves, a 6-foot-4, 220-pounder, was recruited by Raye out of Norfolk, Virginia. He had All-American written all over him until he suffered knee injuries. He was a perfect fit for the Michigan State roverback/safety tradition, which included College Football Hall of Famers George Webster and Brad Van Pelt.

"Had it not been for injuries, he surely would have gone down as a two-time All-American and one of the greatest in Spartans history," said Raye. "He had the athleticism, range, size and he was a fierce competitor."

In the fourth quarter, Ohio State led only 13-3, needing to convert a fumble for their two-score lead. Henson scored on a touchdown plunge with 9:03 left in the game.

It turned out to be just enough time for the Spartans' offense to come alive for two electrifying touchdowns.

On the first score, Baggett threw across the field from the left hash mark to the right sideline to hit Mike Jones for a 44-yard touchdown pass with 5:30 to play, beating All-American safety Tim Fox, who went on to play 11 NFL seasons. The 2-point conversion failed, however, and the deficit remained 13-9.

Jimmy Raye (coaching with Kansas City Chiefs) and Charlie Baggett (coaching with Houston Oilers).

The Buckeyes were forced to punt on the ensuing possession, but a

55-yard boomer forced Baggett and the Spartans offense to take the field at their own 12-yard line with only 3:30 to play.

On first down, Baggett executed a sleight of hand that fooled the Ohio State linebackers and secondary, handing off to fullback Levi Jackson off right tackle before carrying out a fake wide to the right. As the cornerback and outside linebacker went with Baggett, Jackson burst through the hole. He was a fullback, true, but he had sprinter's speed, cutting to the right sideline for an 88-yard touchdown romp. Ohio State defensive back Bruce Ruhl and linebacker Jim Cope were pictured futilely chasing Jackson in one of Michigan State football's most iconic photographs.

The crowd erupted, with students in the southeast corner of Spartan Stadium celebrating so wildly that groups unknowingly relocated in a seismic shift. Members of Wonders Hall's Fourth Floor Northwest noted they were somehow standing on seats two or three rows and four or five seats in distance from their original seat location.

Ohio State regrouped after the touchdown and drove the length of the field, spearheaded by a 31-yard run from Archie Griffin. The Buckeyes kept pounding away until they advanced to the Spartans' 6.

Champ Henson gained five yards to the 1-yard line with 14 seconds remaining. Greene handed off to Henson again on the next play. The fullback had previously scored the Buckeyes' touchdown earlier in the quarter on a plunge, but this time his dive was stopped by a pile of bodies. With no timeouts for Ohio State, the clock expired before the players could untangle and line up. Greene took the snap anyway and ran into the end zone to create confusion, but the officials ruled time had expired and they left the field.

Michigan State fans swarmed out of the stands. Cantankerous Ohio State coach Woody Hayes lingered on the field during the wait, saying the game wasn't over. In a photo captured by the student newspaper *The State News*, Hayes took a swing at a Michigan State student who tried to swipe his distinctive cap with an "O" from his head.

Big Ten commissioner Wayne Duke left the press box saying he wanted to speak with the referees before the game was official. Duke waited 45 minutes to declare until he spoke with the referees to confirm Ohio State failed to score. (There was no doubt in the officials' minds; they had left the stadium grounds before Duke found them.)

Two weeks later, Ohio State beat Michigan 12-10 to earn the Rose

Bowl bid despite a co-championship with the Wolverines. Ohio State's win over Michigan would have created a Big Ten tri-championship with Michigan State, Ohio State, and Michigan were it not for the Spartans' early-season 21-21 tie against Illinois. The Spartans finished 7-3-1 overall and 6-1-1 in the Big Ten, while Ohio State and Michigan recorded 7-1-0 marks in Big Ten play. It would have been Michigan State's first Big Ten title since 1966 and the Spartans' first Rose Bowl since the 1965 title. The conference tiebreaker rule at the time would have sent Michigan State to Pasadena as the school with the longest lapse between Rose Bowl trips.

Ohio State was upset by USC 18-17 in the Rose Bowl, while Michigan and Michigan State stayed home in the archaic days when the Big Ten sent only its champion to a bowl game. In the final polls, the Spartans were ranked No. 18 by the AP and No. 12 by the UPI—Michigan State's first season-ending rankings since 1966.

Duffy Daugherty, serving in his role as a college football analyst, watched Michigan State's 1974 upset of Ohio State from the ABC-TV broadcast booth.

But Michigan State's revival under Stolz was short-lived. The NCAA launched a recruiting investigation—long speculated to have been fueled by Hayes' anger over losing recruits to Michigan State—and Stolz was dismissed following the 1975 season.

The Spartans' 1974 success still stands as the resurgence Daugherty hoped for with his underachieving 1972 team, which stumbled to a 5-5-1 record. The 1972 roster's preseason promise was evident by its postseason honors and NFL draft picks. There were two first-round picks, offense guard Joe DeLamielleure and tight end Billy Joe DuPree, and 10 draft choices overall. The honors included two College Football Hall of Famers (DeLamielleure, who is also in the Pro Football Hall of Fame, and safety Brad Van Pelt), three All-Americans (DeLamielleure, DuPree, and Van Pelt) and 11 with All-Big Ten recognition (first-team All-Big Ten players were DeLamiellielleure, Van Pelt, DuPree, safety Bill Simpson, and linebacker Gail Clark; second-teamers included offensive tackle Jim Nicholson, defensive tackle Gary Van Elst, and defensive end Brian McConnell; honorable mentions were offensive tackle Marvin Roberts, defensive tackle John Shinsky, and quarterback/safety Mark Niesen). Of the 11 All-Big Ten honorees, DuPree was the only skill-position player.

"That was a team that should have gone to the Rose Bowl, but we couldn't make enough big plays," DuPree said. "We should have won at least eight games. We were missing something. We never came together until the end."

Three of the Spartans' five losses were to ranked nonconference opponents: 1972 AP national champion USC (51-6), No. 14 Notre Dame (16-0), and No. 20 Georgia Tech (21-16). The conference losses were to No. 6 Michigan (10-0) and unranked Minnesota (14-10).

There was talent to build around, but a lack of game-breakers. Most significantly, the team did not have a capable quarterback. George Mihaiu led the team in passing with 367 yards, *zero* touchdowns, and four interceptions in six games. He completed 25 of 55 passes for 45.4 percent. Mark Niesen, a converted safety, was 15 of 59 (25.4 percent) for 280 yards with three touchdowns and eight interceptions.

DuPree was the team's leading receiver for the second straight year, but with no quarterback to hit him with passes, the All-American player finished with zero TD receptions. He had caught three in 1971.

Quarterback play had been a Spartans weakness since Raye graduated following his second year as a starter in 1967. Bill Triplett started in 1968 and 1969 before he was switched to receiver. Mike Rasmussen played quarterback in 1970 and 1971.

Despite 1971's underachieving 6-5 record, Daugherty felt optimistic about the upcoming 1972 season with the talent on paper. The Spartans opened the 1972 season with a 24-0 Big Ten victory over Illinois. They jumped from unranked to No. 18, but then reality hit. Daugherty once quipped earlier in his career at a Chicago Football Writers luncheon, "The trouble with Michigan State fans is that they get carried away with my enthusiasm."

Michigan State lost its second game to Georgia Tech to start a four-game losing streak. Daugherty says in his 1974 book he began to think it was time to retire before the 1972 season began, but he felt rejuvenated in preseason practice and by the 24-0 season-opening win over Illinois, which he considered perhaps Michigan State's best opener in his 19 seasons. However, he was dismayed by the loss to a Georgia Tech team he felt was inferior. Daugherty believed a good team made its most significant improvement between the first and second games. Instead, the Spartans had gone backward as they prepared for their third game at USC.

Daugherty would not make public his decision to leave for another five games, but DuPree says Daugherty had told him and team co-captain Van Pelt a month earlier in Los Angeles that 1972 would be his final season. "We had a night game at USC. We had a team meeting at the hotel right before lunch. Duffy pulled Brad and me aside to a little room and said he wanted to talk to us. We were in a quiet place and he said, 'I want you guys to know this will be my last season.' "

That night the Spartans were dominated by the eventual national champions, although DuPree finished with career-highs in catches (eight) and yards (134).

"I never tried to get in a person's head," DuPree said. "I didn't try figure out why he said that to me and Brad, but I know from all the time I was around Duffy, if he said something there was a 99 percent chance it would be true."

Daugherty did not give DuPree and Van Pelt a reason, but he says in his 1974 book he knew it was time to step down when coaching was no longer fun. The funding cutbacks following President John Hannah's departure in 1969 had frustrated Daugherty for some time.

Of the four-game losing streak, Daugherty says in his 1974 book a couple of bad calls cost the Spartans an upset in the 10-0 Michigan loss. The 1972 Spartans were 2-4-1 but coming off a win over Wisconsin and tie with Iowa when Daugherty stunned Michigan State fans the night before the Purdue game with the announcement he would retire at the end of the season.

Despite the disappointing season, the Daugherty mystique had one final run. Michigan State beat Purdue 22-12 and won three out of its final four games for a 5-5-1 final record. The Spartans followed Purdue with a 19-12 upset of No. 5-ranked Ohio State at Spartan Stadium. Daugherty had switched safety Mark Niesen to quarterback to run the wishbone offense. Michigan State improved to 4-4-1, but it was too late. The Daugherty era was coming to a close.

"When Duffy made his announcement, guys decided, 'Let's just go play,'" DuPree said. "Sometimes when you relax and quit trying to figure out what's wrong, you play better. Duffy was such a good person; we wanted to win for him and were no longer concerned about anything else."

So dramatic was the difference in Michigan State's offense with a safety at quarterback running a wishbone offense, Niesen was voted honorable mention on the All-Big Ten team as a quarterback. In 1973, he was a second-team All-Big Ten safety.

Baggett watched the 1972 Spartans struggle from the sidelines as an ineligible transfer. He says "things happen for a reason," but the 1972 season haunts him. What if he had gone directly to Michigan State from high school in 1971? What if he had been the Spartans' starting quarterback as a true sophomore in 1972 rather than as a third-year sophomore in 1973 following his transfer season?

"I was trying to do something for black kids coming behind me when I signed with North Carolina," Baggett said. "For my own best interests, I should have gone to Michigan State to start with. They didn't have a quarterback in 1972. If I would have been on that team maybe we would have had an opportunity to go to the Rose Bowl."

Michigan State's upset of Ohio State in 1972 indicated the Spartans had the overall talent to contend for the Big Ten title and a Rose Bowl trip. Ohio State topped Michigan to win the Big Ten title and went to the Rose Bowl despite the loss to the Spartans. If 1972 had turned out as promising as it looked in the preseason, might a rejuvenated Daugherty—only 57 years old at the time—have coached another year or two?

"Yep," said Baggett.

Years later, DeLamielleure still lamented the lack of a quarterback on the 1972 team when he reflected on that season following the death of Van Pelt in 2009.

"Honestly, Brad played the wrong position in college," DeLamielleure said. "He could have been our starting quarterback because he could throw the ball a mile. Brad also had an offensive player's personality. We spent my entire college searching for a quarterback. If Brad had played quarterback, we would have won a lot more games. He was a natural athlete who looked smooth in everything that he did. Unfortunately, George Perles and Hank Bullough pulled him away (from quarterback) to become the big playmaker for our defense."

Michigan State's decline in the win-loss column began with the 1967 season following the departure of All-American talent combined with drastic turnover on his coaching staff. Head coaches rely on their assistants in the recruiting game, and Daugherty's staff underwent drastic changes from 1967 to 1972. He lost some of his best recruiters when coaches moved on to head coaching positions or jobs in the professional ranks. The exodus started with John McVay, who helped recruit the star-studded 1963 recruiting class, leaving in 1965 to become the head coach at the University of Dayton. Danny Boisture departed to become the head coach at Eastern Michigan University in 1967; Vince Carillot, head coach at the University of Tulsa, 1969; Cal Stoll, head coach at Wake Forest University, 1969; Hank Bullough, NFL assistant with the Baltimore Colts, 1970; and Al Dorow, head coach of the Canadian Football League's Hamilton Tiger-Cats, 1971.

Daugherty also had lost a step in the recruiting game at the same time that 39-year-old Bo Schembechler arrived in Ann Arbor to bring new direction to the Michigan's program. If Daugherty returned in 1973, he planned to let go of two assistants who told him to back off on four players in the 1968 recruiting class—future Michigan stars Reggie McKenzie and Billy Taylor and future Notre Dame stars Mike Kadish and Clarence Ellis. All four players were taken early in the 1972 NFL draft.[1]

The post-1966 staff was not a good fit of personalities. There was resentment that Stolz joined the staff in 1971 at a higher pay and with the title of defensive coordinator. Daugherty, trying to find new energy on his staff, had been encouraged by old friend Harold McClure to hire Stolz. McClure was the head of McClure Oil Company in Alma, Michigan, and Stolz was a successful head coach at tiny Alma College.[2]

George Perles had taken over as the defensive coordinator role in 1969 when Hank Bullough left for the NFL, but Perles ignored Stolz's title in 1971. Perles ran the defense until leaving to join the Pittsburgh Steelers in 1972.[3]

DuPree said he and the offensive linemen saw a sign of dysfunction on the coaching staff in 1971 when Daugherty brought in an old friend to coach the offensive linemen, Buck Nystrom. He had played for Spartans under both Biggie Munn (1953) and Daugherty (1954-55) and coached one year under Daugherty (1958). Nystrom had a nice resume as an assistant that ultimately included three national championship teams. He was an assistant at North Dakota State (NCAA College Division, 1965) and Oklahoma (1968). Later he won a third national championship at Northern Michigan (NCAA Division II, 1976). But Nystrom got off to a bad start with the Spartans' linemen in spring football.

"We had the big, heavy oak sled we had to push," said DuPree, who as a tight end was grouped with the linemen. "DeLamielleure, another guy, and I moved our ends, but the other end wasn't moving. Buck was yelling and kicked a guy right in the rear end. We knew Duffy hoped Buck would be a shot in the arm for us, but that set the stage for us. We knew the kind of coach Buck was going to be."

The 1971 Spartans were 2-1 and coming off a 31-14 win over Oregon State when DuPree said Nystrom addressed the players in a meeting room the week of the Notre Dame game.

"He had decided by then that we didn't like him," DuPree said. "He said, 'If you guys don't get your asses in gear and don't beat Notre Dame, I'll quit on you.'"

The Spartans lost 14-2 at No. 4 Notre Dame. Nystrom left the Spartans after the one-year stint, although he returned to coach at Michigan State under Perles from 1983 to 1986.

Daugherty's post-1966 frustrations had deepened after 1969. Hannah left the school that year to take a position as the head of the United States Agency on International Development. Athletic director Biggie Munn suffered a stroke in 1971.

The football cutbacks frustrated Daugherty, who claimed Michigan State was at the bottom of the Big Ten in funding with Northwestern. He also had feuds with university vice-president Jack Breslin and faculty representative John Fuzak.

Dan Daugherty said his father felt undermined by Breslin. As the search for a new coach unfolded, Duffy learned that both he and new athletic director Burt Smith, a longtime Daughterty assistant, would not play a role in selecting his successor.

The final interview committee comprised Breslin, Fuzak, new president Clifton Wharton, and assistant athletic director Clarence Underwood.

Smith presented as finalists Oklahoma offensive coordinator Barry Switzer, Louisville head coach Lee Corso, and Iowa State head coach Johnny Majors. Switzer would go on to win three national titles at Oklahoma, while Majors captured one crown at Pittsburgh. Corso later served as Indiana's head coach, but he became better known as an ESPN commentator following his coaching career.

Daugherty favored Switzer.

The committee picked Stolz.[4]

"My Dad never would have recommended Denny Stolz as head coach, but Michigan State did not listen to him," Dan said. "He was not happy when Denny Stolz got the job—and then Denny Stolz got them on probation."

"Hindsight is everything, but my Dad stayed at the party too long. All of a sudden he didn't have the staff or the money, the program went downhill and Jack Breslin wanted him fired. My Dad was a great ambassador for Michigan State, but in 1972 they only paid him $29,000. My Dad should have left when John Hannah left."

Notes

1. *Spartan Seasons*, p. 20.

2. *Ibid.*, 24.

3. *Ibid.*, 19.

4. *Ibid.*, 25.

19

Bear Took a Pass, Got a Pass

"Momma called Duffy. She was assured it was a four-year deal. When she asked if I was going to be a quarterback, Duffy said, 'He'll be a quarterback until he decides he's not a quarterback.' That's a loaded statement as I found out. He said what coaches say, but my mom accepted it. My parents put me on a train in downtown Fayetteville and 36 hours later I was in East Lansing."—Jimmy Raye

Maybe if University of Alabama football coach Paul "Bear" Bryant had met Jimmy Raye's mother on the recruiting trail in an encounter similar to Michigan State coach Duffy Daugherty's experience, Bryant would have joined Daugherty in pushing the pace of integration of college football. By the time Bryant finally caught up to the rest of the union in 1971, half of the Southeastern Conference schools had integrated their football programs ahead of Alabama.

Peggy Raye was a forceful woman who inspired and motivated Jimmy and his four siblings to graduate from college. She, and her husband James Arthur Raye Sr., saw that America was changing for their five children. They wanted them to pursue opportunities denied their generation. Peggy Raye pushed her children; she wanted the best for them.

Bryant, as a recruiter, was known for winning over mothers first, but Peggy Raye was no pushover. She would have had specific questions for Bryant. Maybe her queries would have pushed Bryant to think more about the injustice of segregation. She would have told Bryant her son was worthy of the same football scholarship opportunities he provided his white players. Bryant, with his famous southern drawl mumble, would have had a tough time with his rejoinder.

Daugherty, Bryant's close friend in the coaching fraternity, learned about Peggy's steadfastness the hard way. When the famous coach, pictured on the cover of *Time* magazine, offered Jimmy his athletic scholarship, Peggy first had questions that needed to be answered. She dialed Daugherty's number at his office in Jenison Fieldhouse. Jimmy Raye sat quietly at the family kitchen table and nervously awaited the outcome.

"My momma called Duffy," Jimmy said. "She was assured the scholarship was a four-year deal. When she asked if I was going to be a quarterback, Duffy said, 'He'll be a quarterback until he decides he's not a quarterback.' That's a loaded statement as I found out. He said what coaches say, but my mom accepted it. My parents put me on a train in downtown Fayetteville and 36 hours later I was in East Lansing."

If Daugherty had botched his interrogation, Jimmy Raye would have still earned a college degree and played college football. Fortunately for Bryant, and unfortunately for black athletes in the 1960s, Bryant never met Peggy Raye. Bryant's inaction delayed the dream of Jimmy Raye and players like him to play for their home-state university for another decade.

It's difficult to tell the story of the Underground Railroad in the Civil Rights era without telling the stories of Duffy Daugherty and Bear Bryant—two icons on opposite sides of the issue of when to integrate college football. Daugherty agreed with Martin Luther King Jr. that time was neutral—he would not wait for the "right time" in the eyes of the alumni. In the 1960s, Bryant told Fred Horn, a prominent black Alabama high-school coach and later an Alabama state senator, "the alumni were not ready for black players."[1] Daugherty was a progressive man and Bryant a man dragging his feet, but the contrasts are told here not with malice but as examples of how men influence the future.

As late as 1965, Bryant protégé Gene Stallings, then the head coach at Texas A&M and later a national championship coach at Alabama, said recruiting black players would create disunity on the team. His comment was in response to Southern Methodist signing Jerry Levias as the Southwest Conference's black scholarship athlete.

Bear Bryant told Michigan State assistant coach Vince Carillot a similar story when he met Bryant for the first time at a clinic in the late 1960s. They were in Daugherty's hotel room waiting for him to take a shower and get dressed.

"Bryant said, 'Coach Vince, do you play gin?'" Carillot recalled. "I told him I did and we played gin. I was agape—this was Paul Bryant—but I asked about all the black players in the South and if one of these days he was going to recruit them.

"He said, 'I'm waiting to get the alumni ready. It's going to happen. It will happen, but the alumni are not ready for it yet.'"

Bryant waited until Alabama's high schools desegregated in the late 1960s and black players were playing at previously all-white high schools. He also might have been prodded by bitter in-state archrival Auburn having signed James Owens as its first black football player in 1969 (he made his varsity debut in his 1970 when freshmen were ineligible by NCAA rules). Bryant followed Auburn's example and signed Wilbur Jackson a year later from a desegregated high school. Jackson made his varsity debut in the 1971 season with junior college transfer John Mitchell.

Another layer can be peeled from the myth of the 1970 USC-Alabama game with the play of Jimmy Jones as the Trojans' starting quarterback. The anticipation and experience of Jones's performance should have been a revelation to Bryant (rather than the hindsight-created myth that Bryant staged the game to teach Alabama's fans about Sam Cunningham's play at fullback). In 1970, Jones was a junior and known quantity—a returning starter. Cunningham was a sophomore making his varsity debut in an era of freshmen ineligibility.

Yet Jones's play and leadership did not convince Bryant it was time to recruit a black quarterback for the Crimson Tide. In that same 1970 season, Conredge Holloway was a senior in Huntsville, Alabama. Holloway wanted to play for Alabama but picked rival Tennessee after Bryant told him he would recruit him but not as a quarterback.[2] After playing on the Volunteers' freshman team in 1971, the Alabaman was a three-year starting quarterback from 1972 to 1974, the first starting black quarterback in the Southeastern Conference.

As the South's most preeminent coach, Bryant wielded significant power that could have opened doors, but he remained on the wrong side of history. His first and only black quarterback was Walter Lewis in 1980.

A lone southern voice who acknowledged Bryant sat on the sidelines is Paul Finebaum, who built a hugely popular sports talk radio show in Southeastern Conference markets and began hosting an ESPN Radio show in August 2013.

"I don't buy the argument that Bryant couldn't have done more," Finebaum said. "He had more power than any football coach in the South, maybe in the country, and any public declaration from him would have helped enormously. I honestly wish he'd have forced integration a couple of years earlier. It would have enhanced his legacy."[3]

Paul Bryant grew up a poor country boy in the backwater Arkansas town of Moro Bottom when he received an Alabama scholarship in 1932. He raised his station in life to become a coach and leader of men. "Football has never been just a game to me. Never," said Bryant in his 1974 book. "I knew it from the time it got me out of Moro Bottom, Arkansas—and that's one of the things that motivated me, that fear of going back to plowing and driving mules and chopping cotton for 50 cents a day."[4]

Bryant apologists claim he wanted to integrate his roster at Kentucky, where he was a head coach from 1946 to 1953. The same held true with his years at Texas A&M, where he moved on from 1954 to 1957. Bryant says in his autobiography that he told Kentucky president Herman Donovan he could be the Branch Rickey of the Southeastern Conference.[5]

Though he does not say it in his book, the explanation his apologists offer for his failure to integrate at Kentucky is that Donovan feared being kicked out of the all-white Southeastern Conference. It's a plausible explanation for the late 1940s and early 1950s. It would no longer be a plausible explanation in the 1960s at Alabama when Bryant became an icon in the South. Alabama's student body was integrated in 1963 and five Southeastern Conference schools integrated their football programs ahead of Alabama. Bryant coached 13 all-white teams in his 25 seasons at Alabama.

In 1965, Richmond Flowers Jr. was a white Alabama high-school football and track star who was one of the top recruits in the nation in both sports. His father, Richmond Sr., was Alabama's attorney general, and he favored integration and clashed with Governor George Wallace over Civil Rights issues. Flowers' father had endured abuse and threats from segregationists. The Ku Klux Klan burned a cross in the family yard. When Richmond Jr. competed in a meet in Mobile, his father's introduction was greeted by boos.

"That's why I'm leaving this state," Flowers told his father. "That's why I'm not going to play football for Alabama."[6]

David Halberstam, the late Pulitzer Prize-winning author who early in his career covered the Civil Rights movement for Nashville's *The Tennessean*, addressed Bryant's lack of leadership in a 2002 *ESPN.com* article. He wrote Bryant was "the South's signature coach on the subject of great importance, whether or not to go after black players despite racial prejudice." Halberstam added, "... the Bear was very late to the dance, especially because people are always talking about football coaches as leaders. In this case, he did not lead very well. We know that he was a divided man on this, and we know that he was slow, much too slow to act, and so here we have the real test of a man in conflict with himself..."

The imperious Bryant was held up as god-like in Alabama. Coca-Cola sponsored billboards along Alabama roads that depicted Bryant walking on water. In fact, a popular joke started with the image of Bryant on a fishing outing with his fiercest rival, Auburn coach Shug Jordan. They were on a lake when a storm blew in and capsized their small boat. Bryant splashed helplessly in the lake until Jordan pulled him from the water. "Listen, Shug," Bryant said to Jordan. "I'd appreciate it if you didn't let it get out to my folks back home that I couldn't walk on water." Replied Jordan, "OK, it's a deal, so long as you don't let my people know that I didn't drown you."[7]

Bryant's political power also was evident in a story told by the late Beano Cook, a legendary college football bon vivant and an ESPN college-football analyst after a career as a publicist for the University of Pittsburgh, Miami Dolphins, and for ABC-TV's college football broadcasts. ABC executive Roone Arledge, soon to become a household name after launching Monday Night Football in 1970, televised the first prime-time college football game in 1968. Mississippi's Archie Manning completed 33 of 52 passes for 436 yards in a loss to Alabama at Legion Field, the Crimson Tide's home field in Birmingham.

Beano Cook happened to be in Arledge's office when Arledge learned the lights at Legion Field were insufficient. A crew had returned from inspecting the stadium for a night broadcast. Cook recounted the phone conversation years later in an ESPN story by Ivan Maisel.[8]

"Coach," Arledge said, "we're not going to be able to do the night game because the candlepower of the lights is not strong enough. Do you think you could do something about it?"

"Don't worry about it," Bryant answered. "I'll talk to the mayor. If he won't do it, he won't be re-elected."

"Bryant talked to somebody," summarized Cook. "We sent somebody to check the lights again. They were good enough. We did the game."

As Maisiel wrote, "For the record, Birmingham returned Mayor George C. Siebels, Jr. to office in 1971."

Bryant not only took a pass on challenging segregation in college football, he has continued to get a pass with his legacy and iconic stature. Denny Stadium on the Tuscaloosa campus was renamed Bryant-Denny Stadium. A statue of Bryant stands outside the stadium.

Coaches of far less stature than Bryant, and without statues erected to them, showed more courage by taking a stand against segregation. Maryland was the first school below the Mason-Dixon line to integrate its football program in 1963. Lee Corso was a 27-year-old assistant coach at Maryland on the staff of head coach Tom Nugent. In 1962, Corso called Darryl Hill of Washington, D.C., and convinced him to join the Terrapins as the first black player in the Atlantic Coast Conference.

Hill arrived at Maryland with a roundabout path. He was the Naval Academy's first black player in 1961 in a class that included future Heisman Trophy winner Roger Staubach, but Hill left Annapolis after his freshman year when he decided military life wasn't for him. He considered Notre Dame and Penn State as a transfer destination until Corso called and told him, "We've decided you are the guy we'd like to have break the racial barrier in the ACC." Darryl Hill initially expressed reservation, but Corso came back with a challenge he couldn't turn down.

"If you don't do it now, it might be another three or four years before it happens," Hill says Corso told him.[9]

Hill spent 1962 as a redshirt transfer at Maryland and broke the ACC color barrier in 1963. Bryant let those three or four years Corso didn't want to get away last eight years until his first integrated team in 1971.

Hayden Fry, best known for his years at Iowa (1979-1998), was only 32 years old when he accepted a job offer from Southern Methodist University in Dallas as the Mustangs' new head coach. His acceptance came with the condition he be permitted to recruit black players. Fry signed Jerry Levias in 1965 as the Southwest Conference's first black scholarship football player. That same year John Westbrook, another black pioneer, was a walk-on at Baylor University. They were the first two black players on a varsity roster as sophomores in 1966 in the defunct Southwest Conference.

"As a youngster, I had grown up with African-Americans in the West Texas town of Odessa," Fry said. "If we rode the bus they had to sit in the back of the bus. Well, about eighth or ninth grade it dawned on me something's not right. So I made a commitment if I ever got into a position where I could help my black friends I was going to do it. When I was offered the head job at SMU, I said, 'Yeah, I'll take it if you'll let me bring in some black players.'"[10]

Daugherty had similar enlightening experiences with two Syracuse teammates. Wilmeth Sidat-Singh was one of college football's first black quarterbacks. Marty Glickman was a halfback and track athlete who was Jewish.

Syracuse led reporters to believe Sidat-Singh was Hindu Indian based on his light skin and the surname of his step-father that he had taken. But when Syracuse played at Maryland in 1937, Sam Lacy, a prominent black sportswriter of the era, reported the story. Maryland informed Syracuse that Sidat-Singh couldn't play. In 2013, when Syracuse played at Maryland in as a new member of the Atlantic Coast Conference, Maryland honored Sidat-Singh's family at the game as a form of apology.

Glickman, who went on to a career as a famed New York sports broadcaster, played in the Maryland game, but he was victim of religious prejudice in 1936 at the Berlin Olympics. He had qualified for the United States' 400-meter relay team, but he was scratched from the foursome due to the anti-semitism of Germany under Adolf Hitler.

Bear Bryant's foot-dragging was not happening in a vacuum. Compare Bryant's leadership to the National Football League's preeminent football coach of the time, Vince Lombardi of the Green Bay Packers.

Rosters in the modern NFL had been integrated starting in 1946, but there were still racial issues at play. There were unspoken quotas on the number of black players on a roster. Blacks were only valued and kept on a team if they were starters. Blacks weren't given a chance to play the "white positions" that required thinking and leadership such as quarterback, center, and linebacker.

Lionel Aldridge, who was drafted by the Packers in 1963, told Lombardi he was engaged to his white college girlfriend and feared the consequences to his career. Aldridge died in 1998 and the story of his meeting in Lombardi's office was unknown until much later when told by Aldridge's former wife, Vicki Aldridge Nelson, and confirmed by Aldridge's friend and teammate, Dave Robinson.[11]

Vicki Aldridge Nelson says Lionel told her that Lombardi advised, "I don't care who you marry, as long as you play good football (and) you keep your nose clean."

This was 1963 and Aldridge was only a rookie—not yet an established star. Vicki Aldridge Nelson also told a story about Lombardi's response to Rozelle when the commissioner phoned Lombardi to object.

"Pete Rozelle, the commissioner of football, got wind of it, and to Lombardi's credit he said, 'This is my team, you can't tell me what to do with my team. They can do what they want as long as it's OK by me.' He just was amazing in the fact that if he believed in something, he fought for it."

Football coaches are a gossipy bunch, so Bryant had to know what doors to history were being opened at Maryland, SMU, and other schools in the South, and that Daugherty's Underground Railroad was gaining steam.

Bryant also gained experience helming integrated lineups when he was picked to coach college all-star teams such as the Senior Bowl. The time spent around an integrated roster failed to enlighten Bryant that black and white athletes could play together as a team.

Corso and Fry weren't the only coaches in the South who, although lacking Bryant's weight to throw around, nevertheless took a stance.

In 1958, Dean Smith was merely a 27-year-old first-year assistant basketball coach under University of North Carolina head coach Frank McGuire when he challenged segregation at a popular restaurant in the UNC campus town of Chapel Hill. Smith told the story for this first time in his 2002 book, *A Coach's Life.* He and Reverend Robert Seymour of Brinkley Baptist Church had a conversation about the need to do something to challenge segregation. Smith and a black theology student who was member at Brinkley Baptist sat down together at The Pines, a popular Chapel Hill restaurant. They were served without incident.

"You have to understand, Dean Smith wasn't Dean Smith in 1958," Seymour told John Feinstein in his book *One on One*. "He was an assistant coach. It wasn't out of the question that management might have complained to the university and he might have gotten in serious trouble. But he never hesitated to do it."

After learning the story decades later, Feinstein writes he asked Smith to comment on his bold challenge. The coach declined. Feinstein encouraged him, saying he should be proud of the moment in time.

"You should never be proud of doing the right thing," Smith replied. "You should just do it."

Dean Smith soon succeeded Frank McGuire as head coach in the 1961-62 season. His career started slowly, with students hanging him in effigy on campus. Before he gained the clout of his first ACC titles or even his initial Final Four trip and national title, Smith signed Charlie Scott in 1966 as the Tar Heels' first black scholarship player. Scott's first varsity season came as a sophomore in the 1967-68 season; he proceeded to lead the North Carolina to Smith's first Final Four. In October 1968, Scott helped the USA basketball team win an Olympic gold medal at the Mexico City Games. A black athlete could represent the United States in a red-white-blue uniform in 1968—but not Bear Bryant's crimson-and-white uniform.

In 1947, another then-unknown basketball coach, John Wooden at Indiana State, took a stand. Wooden's 1947 Indiana State team earned a bid to the National Association of Intercollegiate Athletics tournament in Kansas City, but he declined the berth when he was told he could not bring his black players. Wooden later gained clout as the "Wizard of Westwood," winning 10 NCAA titles in 12 years at UCLA from 1964 to 1975.

Alabama Governor George Wallace, who won election in 1962 on a platform openly spouting "segregation now, segregation tomorrow, segregation forever," saw the writing on the wall before Bryant and gave in to desegregation. On June 11, 1963, Wallace stepped aside from the school-house door in Alabama to allow Vivian Malone and James Hood to enroll as Alabama's first black students. The classrooms in Tuscaloosa were integrated, but Bryant required another eight years to integrate the football field.

Bryant's apologists say he was big on teaching, but the enrollment of Malone and Hood was only one of many teaching moments Bryant ignored. The apologists cite as evidence a quote from him that suggests he didn't have a segregationist's heart, "When folks are ignorant, you don't condemn them, you teach them."

But Bryant waited until the 1970s to teach, then added his first black player to his roster and invited USC to play at Alabama's Legion Field.

Other teaching moments lost on Bryant, ones he failed to impart to segregationists in Alabama:

1959: The first Liberty Bowl matched Alabama against integrated Penn State in Philadelphia. Bryant encountered resistance from Alabama trustees and local KKK members who wanted him to pull out of the game, but Bryant ignored them. There were no subsequent consequences for his defiance. A precedent had been set, but he didn't exploit it to play integrated teams or to integrate his roster for another decade.

1961: Syracuse halfback Ernie Davis became the first black Heisman Trophy winner. Davis was one of the first black players to face all-white Texas in the 1960 Cotton Bowl when No. 1 Syracuse beat the No. 4 Longhorns 23-14. At the end of the season, Alabama was denied a chance (that Bryant coveted) to play UCLA in the 1962 Rose Bowl in Pasadena. The West Coast media objected to the Rose Bowl considering an all-white team. UCLA's black players said they would not play against Alabama.

1962: The National Guard and Army troops were stationed on the University of Mississippi's campus. They were called in to restore order after protests against James Meredith's enrollment as the school's first black student.

1963: In March, Mississippi State University's basketball team ignored a state court injunction attempting to prohibit the Bulldogs from playing an NCAA East Regional game against Loyola Chicago. Mississippi State sneaked out of town to play the "Game of Change" at Michigan State's Jenison Fieldhouse in East Lansing. In August, Martin Luther King Jr. delivered his "I Have a Dream" speech at the Lincoln Memorial. In September, the bombing of the 16th Street Baptist Church in Birmingham killed four young girls and horrified the nation.

1966: Texas Western, with five black starters, defeated all-white

Kentucky and racist coach Adolph Rupp for the NCAA basketball title. Michigan State fielded fully integrated football teams and won back-to-back national championships in 1965 and 1966.

These Civil Rights signposts kept rolling by an oblivious Bryant. Ignoring the march of history was once eloquently explained by British Prime Minister Winston Churchill in a 1944 speech before the House of Commons this way: "Men stumble over the truth from time to time, but most pick themselves up and hurry off as if nothing happened."

The five SEC schools to integrate ahead of Bryant and Alabama were Kentucky, Tennessee, Auburn, Florida, and Mississippi State. Bryant once coached at Kentucky. Auburn was his bitter in-state rival. The SEC's black football pioneers and the year of their first varsity season in an era of freshmen varsity ineligibility:[12]

1967: Kentucky, Nat Northington
1968: Tennessee, Lester McClain
1970: Auburn, James Owens
1970: Florida, Willie Jackson and Leonard George
1970: Mississippi State, Frank Dowsing and Robert Bell
1971: Alabama, John Mitchell and Wilbur Jackson
1971: Vanderbilt, Taylor Stokes, Doug Nettles and Walter Overton
1972: Georgia, Horace King, Chuck Kinnebrew, Larry West
1972: LSU, Mike Williams
1972: Ole Miss, Robert Williams

Bryant's apologists say he wanted to be the Branch Rickey of football, but perhaps a more parallel legacy is Al Campanis. Bryant, Campanis, and Rickey were three major American sports figures born and raised at a time in American history when freed slaves were still alive—Rickey, 1881; Bryant, 1913; and Campanis, 1916. They came across descendants of slaves informally or formally and showed them acts of kindness.

Rickey, as a college baseball coach at Ohio Wesleyan, liked to tell the story of how he allowed the only black player on his roster, Charles Thomas, to stay in his room when Thomas was denied lodging on a road trip to face Notre Dame in South Bend. Years later as general manager with the Brooklyn Dodgers, Rickey said the incident was his inspiration to fight discrimination: "I vowed that I would always do whatever I could to see that other Americans did not have to face the bitter humiliation that was heaped upon Charles Thomas."[13]

Rickey signed Jackie Robinson to a minor-league contract with the Brooklyn Dodgers in 1946 as prelude to breaking Major League Baseball's color line in 1947. Campanis was one of the few Dodgers players who befriended Jackie Robinson during the 1946 spring training.

Bryant wrote about his black friends as a youth in Moro Bay. Billy Varner, a black man, served as Bryant's driver, bodyguard, and valet since the early 1960s until Bryant's death in 1983. Bryant said in his 1974 book that he had a black man dress in a red Alabama jacket and stand next to him on the sidelines during the Alabama-Auburn game that followed the Game of the Century between Michigan State and Notre Dame. He admitted it was an attempt to curry favor with voters from people on television seeing a black man on the Alabama sideline. He hoped No. 3 would vault to No. 1. A better method might have been to provide a young black athlete a chance to graduate and play for his home-state university.

Whatever sympathy Bryant and Campanis felt for their black friends, they never acted proactively to open doors for them and other black athletes when they gained positions of authority and power. Campanis saw his 20-year reign as the Dodgers' general manager abruptly end when, in a 1987 interview on the 40th anniversary of Robinson breaking the color line, he infamously told ABC's Ted Koppel on a *Nightline* interview that blacks lacked "some of the necessities" to be managers.

Bryant was never a Branch Rickey, a Duffy Daugherty, a John Wooden, a Dean Smith, a Hayden Fry, or even a Lee Corso. Bear Bryant was more Al Campanis.

Notes

1. HBO, 2008.

2. *Huntsville Times*, Feb. 20, 2011.

3. Barra, *The Last Coach*, p. 378.

4. *Bear, The Hard Life & Good Times of Alabama's Coach Bryant,* Bear Bryant and John Underwood.

5. *Bear*, p. 267.

6. Keith Dunnavant, *Coach*, ESPN, p. 250.

7. AP, January 1967.

8. *ESPN.com*, Oct. 14, 2011.

9. *100 Pioneers: African-Americans Who Broke Color Barriers in Sport*, Richard Lapchick, Fitness Info Tech, 2008, p. 291.

10. HBO, 2008.

11. HBO, *Lombardi*, 2010.

12. *Bowled Over*, p. 63.

13. *The New York Times*, April 14, 2012.

20

THE JOURNEY

"Burt Smith saved me by having Dick Proebstle work with me. He made sure Dick kept teaching me the fundamentals of the offense."—Jimmy Raye

Jimmy Raye broke away from the Tampa Bay Buccaneers' 2013 NFL draft preparations in early April for a quick visit to Michigan State's campus. He met with the university's Food Services Department to discuss "Jimmy Raye's Carolina Bar-B-Que Sauce," but they were not comparing recipes. The subject was scholarship funding.

Raye hoped to work an agreement with university officials to purchase his nonprofit product with proceeds designated for the George Webster Scholarship Fund and the Jimmy Raye Youth Foundation in Fayetteville. The Webster fund, established in 2007 in the name of the Spartans' College Football Hall of Famer, provides scholarships for Michigan State athletes returning to campus after their eligibility expires.

Raye's trip also included an invitation to speak before Professor Kami Silk's Communications 240 class. The subject was Diversity in the Workplace, held before 200 students assembled in an auditorium classroom at the Communications Arts and Sciences Building.

As Raye made his stops around campus and passed by Jenison Fieldhouse and Spartan Stadium, it gave him time to reminisce and collect his thoughts before Silk's class.

"I was driving across campus and I started to wonder, 'What possessed me to think I could leave little Fayetteville and come to this big school?'" Raye said. "I had never played against white players."

The answer to that question was the opportunity to break down racial barriers he faced in the Civil Rights era. Raye's first visit to campus was the recruiting invitation when he stayed at the Kellogg Center, the on-campus hotel that is the historic jewel of Michigan State's School of Hospitality and Business. Raye had crossed the Mason-Dixon Line into essentially a different country, but Jim Crow segregation was ingrained in his mind as he entered the Kellogg Center restaurant.

"I looked around and didn't know if I should sit down," Raye said. "When I did sit down, I kept looking around to see if someone would tell me to get up."

Raye returned to campus for the start of school in the fall of 1964. As a freshman, he was ineligible for the varsity by NCAA rules. Raye and the other first-year Spartans wandered down from their Case Hall rooms to the nearby practice fields located at the current Duffy Daugherty Building.

"They had a big green tarp across the fence so people couldn't see in," Raye said. "When we walked through the gate and looked out on the field, I said, 'Oh, my God. Look how big they are! What have I done?' I weighed 161 pounds when I arrived at Michigan State."

Raye was 748 miles from home as he learned to assimilate into an integrated environment, but his parents, James Sr. and Peggy, felt comfortable their son was in good hands with Duffy Daugherty.

"[Daugherty] was a warm, humble, jolly, and friendly man," James Raye, Sr. said. "In conversations with him you could always tell he was interested in the welfare and well-being of his players and not just their playing ability."

All freshmen confront a lifestyle change if they hope to survive college and graduate, but Raye faced more than adapting to the classroom and an integrated social environment. In some ways, his most important adjustment was on the practice field.

Jimmy Raye, more than players at other positions, benefited from the NCAA freshmen ineligibility rule. He had a year to learn an offense that was opposite in nature to the techniques and concepts he knew from high school. At E.E. Smith High, he directed an offense that was balanced between passing and running. In stark contrast, Michigan State was a run-oriented team. For three months in the fall of 1964, Raye drilled and drilled the new scheme's techniques.

"Burt Smith saved me by having Dick Proebstle work with me," Raye said. "He made sure Dick kept teaching me the fundamentals of the offense."

Proebstle had been the backup to Steve Juday in the 1963 season, but he suffered a knee injury and concussion that sidelined him for 1964. Smith invited Proebstle to help him coach the freshmen team.

"Dick was an exceptional character guy and a great friend and confidant," Raye said. "He taught me the nuances and technical aspect of learning how to run the belly option and the bootlegs. In high school we were a dive-football team. You didn't lead anything. There was more post-snap football at Michigan State than pre-snap football for me to learn. For a lot of guys, it's difficult."

In Michigan State's 1966 season opener on September 17, Raye made his first career start in a 28-10 win over North Carolina State that may well have led Wolfpack coach Earle Edwards to desegregate his football program a year later. Edwards was not from the South. He was a Penn State graduate who had once been a Michigan State assistant under Biggie Munn. On Munn's staff, he worked alongside Daugherty from 1949 to 1953; he had coached black athletes.

Edwards was named N.C. State's head coach in 1954 and had been held back by southern states' Jim Crow laws prohibiting black athletes, but there was a growing awareness on Tobacco Road times were changing by the mid-1960s. A story in the *Raleigh News and Observer* before the N.C. State-Michigan State game noted the irony of Raye, a North Carolina native, facing N.C. State despite not being recruited by the Wolfpack. In the article, Raye said he was interested in N.C. State, North Carolina, and Wake Forest, but his home-state Atlantic Coast Conference schools ignored him.

"Any one of those three schools would have been all right with me," Raye was quoted in the story. "But I didn't get the opportunity to go."[1]

In those days, newspapers avoided identifying athletes as black, or the subject of race in general, but the elephant in the room was segregation. There were no quotes from Edwards about segregation issues, a product of the media custom of the times rather than an accurate reflection of his thoughts.

In the game, there was no overlooking Raye's numbers. The signal-caller directed his offense to 396 total yards. Despite playing with a bruised knee and lower leg injury suffered a week earlier, he carried 10 times for 84 yards and scored on a one-yard run and completed 6 of 10 passes for 33 yards.

Michigan State's first score came on a 60-yard drive that Raye kept alive with runs of nine and 11 yards before Clinton Jones found the end zone on a 39-yard gain. On the second touchdown, Raye gained 30 yards to N.C. State's 37. Bob Apisa broke tackles on a run to paydirt on the very next play. Raye set up the third TD with a 22-yard run and scored himself from the 1. On the fourth touchdown, he completed passes of four, nine and eight yards on a drive that finished with a Frank Waters 1-yard TD run for a 28-3 lead.

"I think he did an exceptionally fine job," Daugherty said after the game. "The boys voted him the game ball. Every play in which he runs started out as a pass play. I've always said the threat of a pass is more important than if the ball is actually thrown. His play calling was good. He called practically all the shots."[2]

With the convincing victory, Michigan State was voted No. 1 in the first regular-season AP and UPI polls released the following Monday. The march was underway toward the November 19th Game of the Century.

Change also was afoot with the Wolfpack football program. N.C. State's all-white roster had been dominated by college football's first fully integrated lineup and a black quarterback from their backyard.

"I heard after that game that Edwards told people it was time for North Carolina State to start recruiting black athletes," Raye said.

In 1967, Earle Edwards signed his first varsity black player, Marcus Martin of Covington, who made his varsity debut in 1968.

Raye's parents were on hand to watch his first career start. They sat at the 50-yard line in Section 24, Row 16, seats 5 and 7 in the area reserved for players' family and friends. This was the first of several journeys to watch Jimmy play. The Rayes were accompanied on the 1,500-mile roundtrips to East Lansing by varying collections of old friends. Fortunately for James Sr. and Peggy, they had an eager driver in Monk Smith, the Seabrook Park director who was an early mentor to a young Jimmy Raye. Most times they traveled North from Fayetteville through Washington, D.C., toward Ohio and then into Michigan.

"Monk had a roomy green Pontiac station wagon," James Sr. said. "Although the car was not new and you could look at it and tell it had better days, my wife and I were glad to have a way to get to Michigan. It always took us there and back without any trouble."

On other trips they were joined by Dr. Watson Fowler, Milton Yarboro, and Pete Smith. Mary Catherine Farmer, mother of Jimmy's high-school sweetheart and future wife, Edwena, also made trips. The opportunity for them to see Raye as the starting quarterback at a major conference university was beyond their imagination.

"The trips were long, but with the men joking and talking about their experiences and dreams, no one noticed how long it was," James Sr. said. "I was riding high on pride as never before, yet anxiety was also gnawing at me because I was hoping and wondering if he was going to perform well."

He said they never encountered difficulties in the North en route to Michigan State's campus. "We stopped and rested and ate in many places without feeling of danger. Many times people in the northern areas actually seemed to go out of their way to make us feel comfortable."

Some of Raye's Michigan State teammates later in life gained an appreciation for the length of the trips. Steve Juday, Michigan State's All-American senior quarterback when Raye was his sophomore backup on the 1965 Rose Bowl team, stopped in Fayetteville en route to Florida vacations. Raye's mother-in-law cooked a meal for him before he hit the road again.

Michigan State's Sports Information Director Fred Stabley and his longtime assistant, Nick Vista, helped ease Raye into his role with the media when he assumed the starting quarterback role. Stabley is a charter Hall of Fame member of the Co-SIDA, the organization for the nation's sports information directors. Michigan State's press box, long ago dubbed the Stabley Hilton by *The New York Times'* Red Smith, was later officially named for Stabley.

"Fred and Nick were consummate sports information directors," Raye said. "Fred and Nick went to great lengths to educate me on how to take my time and breathe during an interview. Fred told me, 'When somebody sticks a mic or a camera in your face, take your time. Take a breath and sort out what you want to say.'

"That was never more helpful for me than at the airport coming back from our 11-8 win at Ohio State. A lot of people were there, and I was interviewed as soon as I got off the plane. A guy stuck a camera in my face. Fred and Nick served me well."

Such media preparation of athletes is customary now, but Stabley and Vista were ahead of their time. Stabley also lined up the Spartans' five All-America players—Bob Apisa, Clinton Jones, Bubba Smith, Gene Washington and George Webster—returning for the 1966 season in an iconic Michigan State sports photo.

In those days, newspapers avoided using posed photos that featured black athletes, but Vista said Daugherty never instructed or hinted to Stabley or him that they focus publicity on white athletes. As a result, the photos of Michigan State's five All-Americans and of Raye and Daugherty on the sidelines are frozen in time.

"It was business as usual for us," said Vista, who retired in 1988 after he succeeded his boss's retirement. "He never told us anything about how we should handle situations differently. Duffy was great to work with."

As Raye's Michigan State days moved into coaching after a two-year NFL stay, he established himself as both an X and O man and a recruiter. Segregation had ended by the time Raye began pursuing two of the top players in Virginia in the recruiting class of 1974, Tommy Graves of Norfolk and Larry Bethea of Newport News. Both players were black and pursued by southern schools in the newly desegregated South.

Raye, who still had name recognition in the region, beat out Virginia Tech for Bethea and bested Maryland and South Carolina for Graves. He sold both players on the opportunity to play for national championships in the Big Ten, an elite conference then more than now, with the added lure of the Rose Bowl, the college football's preeminent game, limited to the Big Ten and Pac-8 champions. Michigan State was also only eight years removed from its back-to-back national titles that included the Rose Bowl, and its annual schedule featured Notre Dame and Big Ten rivals Michigan and Ohio State. Those were valuable selling points in the pre-cable TV days when the NCAA limited national broadcasts.

Raye knew he had an advantage with Tommy Graves, whose favorite player was Brad Van Pelt, a 1972 Michigan State All-American, then with the New York Giants. Graves stood close to Van Pelt's 6-foot-5, 225-pound size and wore his No. 10 uniform number.

With Bethea, Raye presented Michigan State's tradition of defense. He sought assistance from Bubba Smith, one of the game's most famous defensive ends, and Smith and George Webster both called up Bethea (an accepted practice then but no longer permitted by the NCAA).

Jimmy Raye (middle) with two prime recruiting catches from Virginia: #88 Larry Bethea and #10 Tommy Graves.

"The other thing I told them is I had lived the experience as a player and a student at Michigan State," said Raye. "Other coaches could only tell them about their schools."

Graves was named second-team All-Big Ten as a freshman in 1974 season, helping upset No. 1-ranked Ohio State 16-13. Knee injuries prevented him from what Raye believed would have been an All-American career, but he recovered from missing 1977 with reconstructive knee surgery to earn first-team All-Big Ten as a fifth-year senior in 1978.

Bethea started as a tight end his freshman year, but switched to defensive end as a sophomore. He earned honorable mention All-Big Ten as a sophomore and second-team All-Big Ten as a junior. During his senior season in 1977, he was named the Big Ten's MVP—the first defensive player to win the Silver Football Award since Dick Butkus in 1963.

Bethea was drafted in the first round by the Dallas Cowboys. His athletic success was overshadowed by suicide after a tragic downward spiral from drugs, but his accomplishments won't soon be matched. He won the Big Ten MVP award playing for a team that finished *third* behind conference co-champions Ohio State and Michigan. He set school records of 16 sacks for the season in 1977 and 33 for career sacks, compiled in a remarkable three seasons. Both marks still stand 35 years later and counting; the next closest career total is 25.

Another future Michigan State player influenced by Raye's play for the integrated Big Ten school was his brother, Craig. Like Jimmy, he also had been a quarterback at E.E. Smith.

"Michigan State was embedded in me," says Craig Raye, now the assistant head coach/wide receivers on the University of Arkansas-Pine Bluff staff. "It was a goal for me just like it was at E.E. Smith."

Craig, 10 years younger than Jimmy, started his college career as a scholarship wide receiver at Austin Peay, but after a coaching change he transferred to Michigan State and made the team as a walk-on in 1976. Darryl Rogers was the Spartans' new head coach by then. Jimmy Raye had left for Wyoming after Denny Stolz was fired.

Craig sat out 1976 on the scout team as a transfer by NCAA rules before he earned a scholarship for the 1977 and 1978 seasons. He never earned a varsity letter in his backup role, but he has a 1978 Big Ten championship ring from his senior season playing with second-team All-Big Ten quarterback Eddie Smith and All-American wide receiver Kirk Gibson.

"Michigan State was a tremendous experience for me," Craig said. "I'm glad I made that move. It's a special place."

Craig's coaching career included a 10-year stay at NCAA Division III Wesleyan College as head track coach and assistant football coach. One of his football players was a nose tackle named Eric Mangini, who later became Jimmy's boss as head coach of the New York Jets. Craig also coached at Wichita State and Purdue before joining Arkansas-Pine Bluff in 2006. In 2012, Pine Bluff won its first Southwestern Athletic Conference title with 10-2 record.

"If you played quarterback in this state, at some point you learned about Jimmy Raye. It means a lot to me to come back to my home state and be a part of this event."— Colts offensive coordinator Pep Hamilton (left), a quarterback at West High in Charlotte, N.C. at the 12th annual Jimmy Raye Youth Foundation free camp. Photo by the author.

Football was now the family business. Jimmy's brother and his son, Jimmy III, followed him into the game. Jimmy III is now vice-president with the Indianapolis Colts as No. 2 in player personnel decisions to general manager Ryan Grigson.

All these years later in the football world, people still want to hear from Jimmy III about his father playing in the Game of the Century. "Because of my name, I get asked about the game about once a week when I see coaches my father's age," said the younger Raye. "I think the fact that people are still talking about it shows you the significance of the game. The game meant a lot on the field and with the social aspects. Michigan State had so many black stars and Notre Dame had only one black athlete—Alan Page."

One reason Jimmy II moved from college to NFL coaching during the 1970s was that it was an era when schools typically had one black coach on their staff for reasons other than teaching X's and O's.

"Early on my coaching career I made a decision if I'm going to be involved in coaching, I'm not going to be a social worker," Raye said. "I'm not going to be the guy they trot out for the parents to see they have a black coach. I'm not going to be the guy they call every time there is a problem with a black kid. I wanted to be the best football coach I could be expertise-wise."

His move to the NFL began an odyssey typical for the profession. As of 2014, he has coached 35 years for 10 teams, including two stops each at San Francisco, Atlanta, Tampa Bay, and the New York Jets. At each stop, particularly early in his career, the concern for Jimmy and Edwena was for their two children, daughter Robin and son Jimmy Raye III, to attend quality, diverse schools. There was personal sadness, too; Raye's mother passed away at halftime of a 1982 NFL playoff game between the Falcons and the Minnesota Vikings.

Jimmy Raye had coached about a decade before he put to rest his high-school dream of becoming a lawyer. When the Los Angeles Rams named him one of the first black offensive coordinators in 1983, his increased role in 1984 NFL draft preparations involved more of his time.

"I still had a passion to be a lawyer and wanted to prove to myself I could pass the LSAT," he said. "I had wanted to be a litigator and challenge myself in the courtroom. I thought it would be something I'd enjoy, but once I was a coordinator I had less time of my own to divide and devote to studying for the LSAT."

When Raye left the Los Angeles Rams for the Tampa Bay Buccaneers in 1985, Jimmy III was entering his senior year as a starting quarterback at Irvine High in suburban Orange County. The decision was made that Raye would move on to Tampa Bay on his own while Edwena stayed in California with Jimmy III in high school and Robin nearby attending Mount St. Mary's College in Los Angeles.

"He came to sports naturally," Raye said. "He was always with me at training camp as a ball boy and he had exceptional motor skills. When he showed interest, I got involved with fundamentals. I gave him fundamental drills for dribbling a basketball and throwing a football. We had a tire on a rope. He started with his set-up and throwing to a stationary target, and then throwing to a swinging tire."

Jimmy III was recruited as a wide receiver by San Diego State by Aztecs head coach Denny Stolz, the former Michigan State coach. The Aztecs won a Western Athletic Conference title his redshirt freshman year in 1986, but Stolz was fired two years later. Jimmy III finished his career under Al Luginbill, who ran an offense directed by Don Coryell protégé Dave Lay. Jimmy III caught 111 career passes—a figure that stood eighth all-time when he graduated in 1990.

Jimmy III signed with the Rams as a free agent in 1991, the same year his father returned to the staff as a passing game coordinator and receivers coach. By then Ernie Zampese, a former offensive coordinator under Coryell with the San Diego Chargers, ran the offense.

"That year was a great opportunity to coach my son and learn from Coryell disciples," Raye said.

Jimmy III played in the final two games that season and caught a 19-yard pass, but then bounced around the league attempting to make rosters as a free agent. When he was cut by Houston and San Diego, Jimmy Raye advised his son to give up the NFL dream as a player. "You can't keep training all year and then be one of the last cuts," said Raye. "I told him it was time to get on with his life."

Jimmy III spent one year coaching high-school football at his alma mater and then another year as a quality-control coach with the Kansas City Chiefs under Marty Schottenheimer. Raye had been encouraging his son to get into management rather than coaching when an opportunity that turned out to be better than expected presented itself.

Longtime NFL executive Les Miller hired Jimmy III to help him run the tryout camps in Atlanta as the NFL evaluated talent to disperse to its pro league in Europe. Chargers general manager Bobby Beathard, looking to sign a hidden gem among those NFL Europe players for the Chargers' upcoming summer training camp, saw the value of someone with such knowledge stored away. He hired Jimmy III as a scout.

"Later, Jimmy was scouting the Midwest for the Chargers and living in Kansas City when I was with the Chiefs," Raye said. "That was a good time for us because we were able to spend some time with him."

Jimmy III spent 17 years with the Chargers, rising up the ranks, and began to be viewed around the league as general-manager material when he was promoted to director of pro personnel as the No. 2 man to GM A.J. Smith. He interviewed for the GM position with the Chicago Bears in 2012 and had Smith's recommendation for the Bears, as well as his blessing as successor for the Chargers if he retired. When A.J. Smith was fired following the 2012 season, however, Raye was passed over. The Chargers attempted to keep Raye in San Diego. Instead, he moved on to Indianapolis.

Jimmy III has continued his quest to ascend to a general manager's role as his father's NFL career has winded down. Jimmy Raye and Edwena now live in a beautiful fairway home in a private gated community in Pinehurst, North Carolina, the historic and elite golf destination that served as site of the U.S. Open in 1999, 2005, and 2014. Raye first became a Pinehurst member before he bought property at the invitation of Dr. C. Mason Quick, a Fayetteville doctor who was one of Pinehurst's first black members.

"He was the one who got me involved in golf," said Raye. "When I was still a kid in Fayetteville, the only black people allowed in Pinehurst were the caddies. I had no reason to believe I would own a Pinehurst home. The idea was about as remote as being a black quarterback in the NFL in the 1960s."

However, Raye did beat the odds as a black quarterback in college in the 1960s. As he delivered his talk nearly a half-century later on Michigan State's campus for the Communications 240 class, he saw white, black, Hispanic, and Asian faces listening and staring back at him.

"I was struck by the amount of diversity in the auditorium. I noticed how easily they interacted with each other in that setting. I had a flashback to my freshman year when I entered an auditorium in the Natural Sciences Building. I was one black kid in a room with 299 white people. I had no idea what they were talking about in the class, but because of the structure Burt Smith had in place for us on the freshmen team, I acclimated. I learned to become comfortable in that setting."

By the time Raye finished his four-year stay on Michigan State's football team, he was like the Communications 240 students in the classroom auditorium he spoke to nearly a half-century later—a face that fit in regardless of skin color.

Notes

1. *Raleigh News and Observer*, Aug. 26, 1966.

2. *Lansing State Journal*, Sept. 18, 1966.

21

How Long Have You Been a Black Quarterback?

"I can remember when we were down in Bloomington and a sportswriter asked me, 'How long have you been a black quarterback?' I told him, 'As long as I can remember. I never played another position.'"—Jimmy Raye

Jimmy Raye hoped to receive a scholarship offer when he took a recruiting trip from North Carolina to Michigan State in July 1964. The first player he sought out upon arriving on campus was Jim Garrett of Columbia, South Carolina. Garrett was a well-known name to Raye and anyone who followed black high-school football in the Carolinas.

"Jim Garrett was the best quarterback in the eastern part of South Carolina in high school," Raye said. "I thought if he's not playing quarterback, something is wrong. I wanted to find out what was going on. When I talked to him, he said, 'Don't come here. They won't let you play quarterback. They'll switch you to another position.'"

Garrett believed skin color was the reason he was moved from quarterback to halfback. He played on the freshman team in 1962 in the era of NCAA freshman ineligibility and was a halfback by his first varsity season in 1963.

Another black quarterback on Michigan State's roster in July 1964 was Eric "Ruben" Marshall of Oxford, Mississippi.

Marshall drilled with Michigan State's freshman team in 1963 and was set to join varsity in 1964, but an ankle injury forced him to the sidelines in both the 1964 and 1965 seasons. Jimmy Raye raised the same questions with Marshall he had asked Garrett.

"He said don't come here," said Raye.

William Carver, a young assistant coach at E.E. Smith during Raye's senior year and later the school's head coach and the athletic director at Fayetteville State University, first met Daugherty and Stoll at a clinic in segregated Washington, D.C. When the Spartans recruited Raye, he said he felt they viewed him as an athlete rather than as a quarterback. He expected them to switch him to defensive back.

"They liked how competitive Jimmy was," Carver said, "but I didn't think they would let him play quarterback."

Raye was undaunted by the caution signs.

"They didn't know I had already made up my mind," Raye said. "Maybe it was ignorance on my part. I didn't want to hear they weren't going to let me play quarterback."

The alternative was to return to the South to play for one of the historically black schools. Raye respected their history and their coaches, and there was no questioning the talent at such colleges that had turned out so many National Football League players in segregated times, but his heart was set on proving he could play in the Big Ten.

In 1960s college football, no coach did more than Michigan State's Duffy Daugherty to push forward integration. But, there was a price to pay for the progressive stances Daugherty championed. He endured ignorant and ugly racial slurs from his own fan base—not to mention elsewhere. One year Daugherty spoke at an alumni meeting about the upcoming season when he was interrupted by a fan in the back of the room he described as a drunk.[1]

"Hey, Duff, how many niggers are you going to start this season?"

Daugherty replied, "First, before I answer that question, if the clown who asked it is man enough to come up here, I will do my very best to punch him in the nose."

The meeting was not an isolated moment for Daugherty. He described another time he was angered at a party attended by Michigan State alums and boosters.

"Duffy, you've been using a lot of niggers lately," one person told him. "You know, the minute you start four of them in the same backfield, you've lost me."

"Then I've lost you right now," replied Daugherty, who left the party with his wife Francine.[2]

A fourth black player in the backfield intimated a quarterback.

Daugherty does not state what year the alumni incidents took place, but the latter incident might have been 1965, Raye's first year as Michigan State's sophomore backup quarterback, or 1966, Raye's junior season as the school's first black starting quarterback.

Prior to 1961, black athletes believed there was an unwritten rule that called for a white halfback opposite a black halfback. Daugherty knocked down that taboo in 1961 with two black halfbacks, Sherman Lewis and Dewey Lincoln. They continued as a tandem in 1962 and 1963.

In the 1965 season, Steve Juday was a white starting quarterback with Raye his backup. There were two black halfbacks, Clinton Jones and Dwight Lee, and one black fullback, Eddie Cotton, behind Juday. Cotton, a native of the Bronx, New York, was supplanted by Samoan Bob Apisa on his way to an All-American sophomore season.

In 1966, Jones, Apisa, and Lee returned intact and Raye made history as Michigan State's first black starting quarterback. But Daugherty held off promoting Raye to starter in 1966 until late in fall camp, even though in 1965 Juday and Raye were the only quarterbacks to take snaps. His elevation to second-string in the fall of 1965 behind Juday also was late, even though he had been the freshman team MVP and the MVP of the 1965 Green and White spring game. Many times during the spring drills and fall camps leading into the 1965 and 1966 seasons Raye began to wonder if Garrett had provided him sound advice back in June 1964.

Questioning whether Daugherty stalled his promotion as a quarterback is a difficult subject for Jimmy Raye to discuss. How do you doubt a man who became your lifelong friend and mentor?

"It would be outlandish of me to suggest racism," Raye said. "I think he was conflicted, but that would be speculative on my part. He already had so many black players and he received so much hate mail and pressure from the alumni. Now he had a black quarterback at a time when sophomores didn't play that much."

Some integration puzzles are more complicated than others. The jagged pieces of a jigsaw puzzle ultimately snap together into a clear picture. But the last college football integration piece among players was the black quarterback. Finding a place for that piece was anything but a snug fit.

Michigan State assistant coaches Vince Carillot and Hank Bullough, the last two assistant coaches alive from the mid-1960s staffs, said Raye's race was never raised in coaches' meetings. Whatever alumni pressure Daugherty faced or second thoughts he had about starting a black quarterback with increased television exposure in the 1960s, he kept his own counsel. Dan Daugherty was attending high school and Michigan State during the 1960s. He spent time with the team in practice and on the sidelines of games. He said his father never discussed Raye's race as a quarterback candidate and was also never far from hearing ignorance on the subject of playing a quarterback.

"This is a true story, and I won't mention names, but my father always had the coaches and some fans over to the house on Saturday night after the games. One guy was a lobbyist for a utility company. He was a fair-weather fan who only came after wins.

"This supposed friend says to my Dad, 'Steve Juday is graduating and I hear rumblings you're going to start Jimmy Raye at quarterback. I just want you to know, you start a black quarterback and we're no longer friends.' My Dad says, 'We don't have to wait until he starts. We're no longer friends as of this second.'"

It's important to remember the role of television in the 1960s. Teams were limited to regional games once a year and a national game twice over three years. Raye could play backup quarterback to Juday in 1965 and enter regular season games without his skin color drawing attention. Television cameras were not present to show his face to unaware fans.

The Rose Bowl, though, is a national TV ratings bonanza for any school. Plenty of people watched when Juday struggled, and Daugherty was confronted with when to substitute him with Raye.

"The game reflects the culture," Jesse Jackson said. "When I was at Illinois in 1959, there was not one black person in a position of leadership in the entire athletic department. That was the culture. There also was a time when the black athlete did not play linebacker or center.

"The coaches used to take the fastest guys and they made them a halfback, a flanker, or a cornerback. Now you have guys in the NFL like Michael Vick and Robert Griffin III who are the fastest guys and they are quarterbacks. That has changed the game."

Raye entered spring drills in 1965, optimistic that he was well-positioned to earn the No. 2 job behind Juday, the returning starter for his senior season. In the fall of 1964, Raye had been named the MVP of the freshman team. Freshmen often practiced against the varsity, and Raye had earned the respect of the varsity players during those sessions.

Freshmen coach Burt Smith ran workouts on Old College Field next to Jenison Fieldhouse where the baseball, softball, and soccer stadiums now stand. The varsity practiced on fields adjacent from Case Hall where the Duffy Daugherty Building, Skandalaris Center, and practice fields now stand. There were no freshmen games to play, but adrenaline flowed when the first-year Spartans saw Daugherty drive his car from the varsity field down to the freshman field.

"Practice would get to a certain point, and we'd watch for that green-and-white Thunderbird to come snaking down the hill," Raye said. "He'd say, 'Hot shot, Jimmy Raye, get over here. Bob Apisa, get over here. He'd pick a group of us and we'd have to follow behind his car up the hill. We'd practice against varsity guys who were mad they didn't play on Saturday or varsity guys who were mad that they had to practice against us. When he called your name, it was a good and bad thing. Those were meat-grinder practices. The varsity players took out their frustrations on us."

Raye survived the meat-grinder practices and entered 1965 spring football optimistic he would receive plenty of work after Daugherty excused Juday from spring football to play for the baseball team. As freshmen team MVP, Raye felt he no longer had to worry about the haunting comments he heard from Jim Garrett and Ruben Marshall on his recruiting trip.

Another reason he felt optimistic was Daugherty's reaction to an invitation Raye received to come out for the basketball team. Raye had scored 50 points in an intramural game and word got back to John Bennington, newly promoted to head coach for the 1965-66 season. Bennington posted a message for Raye to contact him, but Daugherty took down the note and tossed it.

Nevertheless, early in the 1965 spring drills, with no forewarning from Daugherty or his assistants, Raye was devastated when he thought that his "Jim Garrett fate" had arrived. He was told by an equipment manager to join the defensive backs for practice.

The black players in particular noticed Raye unexpectedly joining the defensive backs.

"There was a silence that came over us," said Ernie Pasteur, an offensive lineman. "We wondered what was going on."

The surprise bordered on anger for some, including George Webster. Before Webster grew into a two-time All-American roverback and team captain, the coaches already understood he was a leader that had the pulse of the team. Webster walked over to speak with Carillot, the defensive backs coach.

"George was the one who made sure I wasn't switched to defense," Raye said. "George Webster asked Vince Carillot what I was doing with the defensive backs. I don't know what else was said, but the next day I was back with the quarterbacks. That was the last time they put me at another position."

Raye returned to quarterback, but he did not receive playing time in the first two scrimmages. Spring ball lasts only a month, with four scrimmages and the Green and White game. Jim Garrett's fate again crept into Raye's mind following the second scrimmage. He walked with dejection and a clean uniform back to the Spartan Stadium locker room from the varsity practice fields.

"After the success I had as a freshman, it was deflating emotionally," he said. "I was walking down the street to the stadium locker room. I had my head down, pouting and mad. I felt this hand come across my shoulder. It was Vince Carillot. He said, 'Get your head up. You'll have your chance.' That gave me impetus going into the next week."

By the third week of 1965's spring drills, Raye finally took his first snaps in a scrimmage when one of the quarterbacks ahead of him went down with an injury.

"When I did get in, it was against the No. 1 defense that in 1965 turned out to be the No. 1 defense in the nation," Raye said. "It was Bubba Smith, George Webster, Charlie Thornhill, Don Bierowicz, Buddy Owens, and Ron Goovert. It was be careful what you wish for."

Raye, playing with other practice-squad players referred to as White Rocks, managed to move the ball with some passes, but mostly he broke off gains running for his life.

"Hank Bullough got mad at the defense," Raye said. "I think that added to the identity I was more a runner than a passer. I was known as a passer in high school, but I was fighting for my life in the scrimmage.

On the pass plays, the White Rocks couldn't block the No. 1 defense in the country. I dropped back into a black hole. They decided I was a better runner than passer, but at least I got my foot in the door against the No. 1 defense. I left encouraged. I could have floated back to Wilson Hall."

For the fourth scrimmage, Raye arrived to his locker room cubicle to find both a green jersey and a white jersey. Confused, he asked equipment manager Ken Earley which jersey to wear. Following Daugherty's instructions, Earley told Raye to put the green shirt on first with the white shirt on over the top. With the white jersey, he directed the White Rocks against the No. 1 defense.

"I moved the ball with the white jersey," Raye said. "Then the manager told me Duffy wanted me to take the white shirt off and quarterback the green team going the other way. I was with the starters now and we went down and scored. I'm trotting off the field and manager throws me the white shirt. I have to go back out there to go the other way. I was afraid he was trying to get me to quit."

Raye's concern was not unfounded. It was a common practice throughout the nation then for coaches to try to run off players.

Jimmy Raye's frustration during that same spring of 1965 was agitated when he noticed another sign Jim Garrett might have been right. James "Shack" Harris, a black quarterback from Monroe, Louisiana, made a recruiting trip and visited a Michigan State practice. Raye recalled Harris standing near a seven-man sled with his high-school coach when an errant pass sailed his way. Harris reached up to spear it with one hand. Michigan State's coaches talked with Harris about his great hands, which in his mind confirmed suspicions the coaches wanted to switch his position.

"The coaches made the statement, 'You'll make a great wide receiver,'" said Raye, who served as Harris' recruiting host. "Shack and I went back to our teenage years when he came to Fayetteville with his family. When Shack left he said to me, 'I'm going back to Louisiana and I'll be on the cover of Sports Illustrated.'"

Harris attended historically black Grambling State University in Louisiana to play quarterback for Eddie Robinson, the coaching legend. Robinson had turned out many NFL players in his career, but he told Harris if he came to Grambling he would be the school's first black quarterback in the NFL.

The prediction came true: Harris made NFL history as a black quarterback in a 13-year pro career. He was one of the first black quarterbacks in the NFL, the first black quarterback to start an NFL playoff game, and the first black quarterback voted to a Pro Bowl.

Raye was not surprised Harris wanted no part of Michigan State and being switched from quarterback to receiver. A quarterback is a special breed, a player who requires physical talent, intelligence to read the defense, and the intangibles to lead a team. There are not very many of them—even today in a country of 300 million people—and quarterbacks do not give up the reins easily.

Harris' appearance at Michigan State gave Raye more pause, but he knew when he left Fayetteville he would have to remain dogged if he expected to break barriers. The frustration he felt never overwhelmed him on the practice field.

When the lineups were announced for the 1965 Green and White spring game, Raye was with the green jerseys—the No 1 unit. Raye played so well, he won the Green and White spring game MVP award, adding to his freshman team MVP distinction from five months earlier. It seemed reasonable to presume whoever emerged No. 1 in spring drills while Steve Juday was with the baseball team would be slated as Juday's backup when fall camp opened.

Raye returned home to Fayetteville, where he preferred to spend the summer. He was from a tightly knit family, he could work a summer job at Seabrook Park, and he felt his conditioning benefitted from workouts in the North Carolina heat.

Street and Smith Sports Annual's preseason issue was the bible of college football at the time. The information listed was fed to the magazine editors from college sports information departments, relaying reports they compiled from the head coach.

"I couldn't wait to get the magazine when it came out," Raye said. "I read Juday was the starter and the backup was unsettled. I was deflated again. I was the MVP of the freshmen team. I was MVP of the spring game. I assumed I was the backup."

When the 1965 fall camp opened, Raye and John Mullen, who was entering his junior season, split repetitions with the second-string unit. Raye was finally designated as Juday's backup one week before the season opener against UCLA.

"John was older, and maybe Duffy wanted to make sure he gave

Mullen his shot," Raye said. "Sophomores really didn't play back then and I came upon the scene so suddenly, but it was hard to understand. Duffy had such a track record with black players at other positions. Willie Thrower played there when he was an assistant coach."

As the 1965 season unfolded, the only quarterbacks Daugherty trusted to take snaps were Steve Juday and Jimmy Raye. Juday completed 95 of 186 passes for 1,253 yards, seven touchdown, and seven interceptions to earn first-team All-Big Ten and All-American honors from AP. Mullen finished his career without any quarterback statistics.

Raye played when Juday struggled or when games were decided and thus only threw six passes, completing three for 43 yards with one touchdown and one interception. He also ran the ball 30 times for 196 yards (6.5 per carry) and one touchdown.

The Big Ten champions then played in the Rose Bowl, where by the end of the game Raye seemingly solidified his position as Juday's heir apparent. When Juday struggled, Raye entered with less than seven minutes to play and nearly rallied the Spartans from a 14-0 deficit.

Raye's frustration with Duffy Daugherty and the depth chart resumed when the 1966 spring drills opened. He learned Daugherty considered quarterback competition open between Raye and five others. Mullen was getting another shot at quarterback as a senior. His junior year, he was listed as a quarterback but he also played backup offensive end and flanker. The other four quarterbacks included three sophomores, Charlie Wedemeyer, Bill Feraco, and Bob Super. The sixth candidate was junior Ruben Marshall, who entered his fourth year in the program after missing the 1964 and 1965 varsity seasons with injuries. A *State News* story at the start of spring football also mentioned that Raye may be switched to halfback.

"I've always said privately if I had never played in the Rose Bowl I would have never started at quarterback at Michigan State," Raye said. "Duffy went with Juday for so long at the expense of losing the game, if I had not played and played so well someone would have beaten me out in 1966."

Bubba Smith, George Webster, Clinton Jones, and Michigan State's other stars considered Raye the heir apparent after the Rose Bowl. They were disappointed Daugherty had not turned the Rose Bowl over to Raye earlier in the game.

"Jimmy could have started for us his sophomore year—he was that good," Clinton Jones said. "But Juday was a senior and returning starter, so that wasn't going to happen."

In 1966, Daugherty waited to name Raye his starter until one week before the season opener.

"I think he anguished over my plight as the starting quarterback," Raye said. "He had this great team and his best quarterback was a black guy. He had the pressure of the alumni, but he also was taking a chance of getting George and Bubba upset. He never sat me down and explained why it was an open competition. He was taking a chance on getting the team chemistry upset. We could have been talking about a great failure with that team.

"I don't know why he made it so difficult. I had taken all the steps to earn the job and I had come out on top. For me personally, there was never an air of racism in my time there, but he was making life miserable for me."

Once the 1966 season unfolded, Daugherty gave almost all the snaps to Raye. He was 62 of 123 for 1,110 yards with 10 touchdowns and eight interceptions. He was the second-leading rusher to Clinton Jones with 122 carries for 486 yards and five touchedowns.

Wedemeyer was only 4-of-16 pasing for 83 yards with no touchdowns and two interceptions, and Feraco 5 of 10 for 51 yards with no touchdowns or interceptions.

Feraco was a backup to Raye his junior and senior seasons in 1966 and 1967, and then in 1968 he was a backup to sophomore Bill Triplett. Among the six quarterbacks in the 1966 spring drills open competition, only Raye proved to be a Big Ten quarterback during their career.

"Jimmy was important to our team," Jones said. "People have underestimated how great Jimmy was on our team."

Raye quickly settled into his role leading a national title contender. By the ninth week of the season the 8-0 Spartans traveled to Indiana University in Bloomington. The rarity of Raye as a black starting quarterback might have been the reason an Indiana sportswriter oddly phrased a question the day before the Michigan State-Indiana game.

"I remember when we were down in Bloomington and a sportswriter asked me, 'How long you have been a black quarterback?'" Raye said. "I told him, 'As long as I can remember. I never played another position.'"

That same question sparked an infamous if apocryphal Super Bowl incident two decades later, allegedly asked of Washington Redskins quarterback Doug Williams as he prepared to become the first black starting quarterback in a Super Bowl. Some reporters present at the interview session later disputed the question was phrased that way to Williams. Still, the line continues to be remembered (if misremembered) every year by writers looking for Super Bowl punch lines.

Williams led the Redskins to a 42-10 Super Bowl rout with one of the finest performances of his career.

Raye also followed up the odd question with a big day—the best passing game of his career.

Michigan State beat Indiana, 37-19, as the Spartans improved to 9-0 and did their part to set up the Game of the Century the following Saturday. Raye completed 7 of 9 for 173 yards and three touchdowns. One of the two incomplete passes could very well have been a fourth TD of 64 yards.

Reported the *Fort Wayne News Sentinel:* "Raye, given all the time in the world to pick his targets, looked very tough against the Hoosiers and even threw one near the end of the first half that traveled 50 yards in the air before Gene Washington grabbed it and then stumbled to lose a T.D. That must have made the Notre Dame scouts shudder."[3]

Raye's historic season as Michigan State's first starting black quarterback and the first black quarterback from the South to win a national title also included earning honors as a second-team All-Big Ten pick. As the quarterback of an unbeaten Big Ten champion, he might have been named to the first team in other seasons, but in 1966 that honor went to standout Purdue University senior Bob Griese, an All-American, Big Ten MVP, the Heisman Trophy runner-up, and a first-round NFL draft pick by the Miami Dolphins.

What mattered most to Raye is that the Spartans defended their Big Ten title and won a share of the national championship from the National Football Foundation with the MacArthur Bowl Trophy. He also had broken a barrier. He had shown skin color should not matter at quarterback any longer.

By 1994, Tony Banks faced no such hurdles as a black quarterback to earn the starting job, even though he was a junior-college transfer new to the program. Michigan State lacked a Big Ten quarterback on the roster when head coach George Perles recruited Banks out of Mesa College in San Diego. Perles told Banks and his junior-college coach he would have to say in the media it was an open competition, but he assured Banks he faced no legitimate threat. Banks was a two-year starter under Perles in 1994 and Nick Saban in 1995.

Raye returned as the Spartans' starter his senior year in 1967. In two years as a starter and one as a backup, Michigan State never lost a game to Michigan or Ohio State, faring 3-0 against the Wolverines from 1965 to 1967 and 2-0 against the Buckeyes in 1965 and 1966 (the schools did not play in 1967). Raye was the backup when the Spartans beat the Notre Dame Fighting Irish in 1965, the starter when they played to a 10-10 in 1966 and missed the 1967 game with a rib injury when Michigan State lost to Notre Dame.

Raye remained a quarterback throughout his college career, one of the most successful and significant in Michigan State's history. As he told the Indiana sportswriter, "I never played another position."

Notes

1. *Duffy*, 1974, p. 29.

2. *Ibid.*, 30.

3. *Fort Wayne News Sentinel*, Nov. 14, 1966.

22

THE CURSORY HEAD COACH INTERVIEW

"I thought Jimmy Raye and Sherman Lewis both suffered in their chances to be a head coach because of their race. I know my Dad would have been very, very happy to have seen either one of those gentlemen named the head coach at Michigan State."—Dan Daugherty

Sherman Lewis initially embodied Duffy Daugherty's legacy as an All-American halfback in 1963—the Michigan State coach's first Underground Railroad recruit to earn such a distinction. Lewis continued to represent his mentor another 36 years as an assistant coach in college and the National Football League.

Jimmy Raye proudly did the same with Daugherty's legacy as a quarterback and then 40-plus years as a college and NFL assistant.

Tyrone Willingham, who was a walk-on in Daugherty's final recruiting 1972 class, exemplified his first coach in college and the NFL for 33 years. He was the first black college coach to win a Division I-A bowl game, the first black coach to lead his team to a Rose Bowl, and the first black coach in any sport at Notre Dame.

"Duffy's legacy has endured through our associations with him," Raye said. "Because Duffy gave me the opportunity to come from North Carolina to Michigan State, I played in the limelight of a championship team with some of the greatest players in the history of the game. My association with him is the most important thing that happened in my life."

Lewis, Raye, and Willingham received their starts as Michigan State players and assistant coaches and then crisscrossed the map for jobs. It comes with the profession. But a pinnacle that they never ascended was as head coach at their alma mater. "I thought Jimmy Raye and Sherman Lewis both suffered in their chances to be a head coach because of their race," said Dan Daugherty, whose father died in 1987. "I know my Dad would have been very, very happy to have seen either one of those gentlemen named the head coach at Michigan State.

"The ones that got the job instead of them, in my opinion, ran the program into the ground. I think the guy they have now, Mark Dantonio, is probably the best they've had since my Dad."

Willingham, who did land head-coaching jobs at Stanford, Notre Dame, and Washington, raised the inflection of his voice—which is akin to shouting for him—when the subject turned to Raye and Lewis.

"No. 1, they both deserved to be head coaches," Willingham said. "They system malfunctioned by not allowing them that opportunity. There are many young men—black, white, brown, green... whatever—that were deprived an opportunity to be tutored by these two men. And that's the shame that is. That's what segregation or racism is guilty of. It costs the overall public opportunities for a lot of very talented people."

Lewis, who owns four Super Bowl rings with San Francisco (three) and Green Bay (one), coveted one head-coach position more than any other throughout his career.

"The Michigan State job would have been the greatest thing that ever happened to me," Lewis said. "I love that place so much. I felt I could have recruited, hired a great staff, and done the job. I've always thought it was a great institution with great facilities. It's the most beautiful campus in the country. They just needed to recruit better. I felt we could be playing for national titles again."

Daugherty found Lewis when one of his Flagut High coaches in segregated Louisville used a connection to Michigan State athletic director Biggie Munn. Lewis had hoped to play at Notre Dame, but his love affair with Michigan State began with a spring 1960 recruiting trip to campus. He learned many years later Notre Dame did not commit to recruiting black athletes until the Irish signed five black players in their 1968 recruiting class. (As for the myth Bear Bryant steered Lewis to Daugherty, Lewis was only 11 years old when Bryant coached his final season at Kentucky in 1953 and left for Texas A&M.)

Lewis was a two-sport star whose All-American season in football included finishing third in the voting to Heisman Trophy recipient Roger Staubach. In track and field, he won Big Ten track and field titles in the long jump and the 300-yard dash. Lewis played two pro football seasons with the New York Jets before he coached a year at his high-school alma mater in 1968 and then jumped at a chance to return to his college alma mater in 1969.

"Duffy called me, and I was gone," Lewis said.

Lewis was one of the first black assistant coaches in the college game. He stayed at Michigan State 14 years through three head coaching changes—Daugherty to Denny Stolz (1973-75) to Darryl Rogers (1976-79) to Muddy Waters (1980-82). Ordinary coaches do not survive such turmoil unless they are trusted to provide transition stability.

When Rogers bolted to Arizona State following a disappointing 1979 season, Lewis hoped to be considered for Michigan State's 1980 vacancy. He was 38 years old and had just finished his 14th year with the Spartans. But Michigan State shocked its fan base when it named Muddy Waters, a 57-year-old man who looked 67 and possessed no major college coaching experience. He had played for Biggie Munn from 1946 to 1949, but he had spent his career at the small school level at Hillsdale College (1954-73) and Saginaw Valley State University (1975-79).

Lewis stayed on with Waters, but Michigan State predictably went into a tailspin with a 10-23 record in three seasons. Waters was fired, and Michigan State formed another search committee. George Perles, who had four Super Bowl rings in his time with the Pittsburgh Steelers, was positioned as the leading candidate in 1983 after having also been passed over for Waters.

Lewis joined Bill Walsh's staff in San Francisco and began his Super Bowl jewelry collection. In 1992, San Francisco offensive coordinator Mike Holmgren landed the Green Bay job and brought Lewis with him as his offensive coordinator.

After the 1994 season, Michigan State fired Perles and formed yet another search committee. By then the 52-year-old Lewis, in addition to his Michigan State background, had added to his resume three seasons as an NFL offensive coordinator. The day after Thanksgiving 1994, he flew across frigid Lake Michigan from Green Bay to Grand Rapids for an interview.

Michigan State's program was in dire need of stability after the second half of Perles's 12-year reign turned tumultuous and ended with NCAA sanctions. Recruiting fell off while George Perles focused on power plays to gain the dual role of athletic director and head coach. He finished 19-26 over his final four seasons.

For Lewis's interview, Michigan State assistant athletic director Clarence Underwood picked him up at the Grand Rapids airport to drive him to a nearby hotel for his interview. He met with university president Peter McPherson but only an abbreviated cast from the search committee.

Underwood, a pioneer African-American in athletic administration, felt an ominous foreboding. The interview was brief and the committee members did not remain in the room to discuss the candidate as they had for other interviews. McPherson got up to leave.

"I asked if we were going to discuss Lewis," Underwood said. "He said no. As it turned out, Lewis had absolutely no chance for the position and we should never have led him to believe he had a chance."[1]

Underwood said it was an awkward moment for him driving Lewis back to the airport.

Years later, Lewis learned more about the session. "I guess I was just a token interview," he said.

Upon returning home from Grand Rapids, Underwood received a call from McPherson. The president instructed him to inform Lewis and Jimmy Raye, whom McPherson had interviewed a week earlier, that they were no longer considered candidates. McPherson also told Underwood he would contact the other candidates, Penn State offensive coordinator Fran Ganter, Cleveland Browns defensive coordinator and former Michigan State defensive coordinator Nick Saban, Youngstown State head coach Jim Tressel, and Bowling Green head coach Gary Blackney.

Ganter was at one point considered the leading candidate with Penn State coming off a Big Ten championship, but he performed poorly in his interview. McPherson also flirted with trying to hire Nebraska coach Tom Osborne. Saban was finally named Michigan State's new head coach on December 12, 1994.

Willingham could have been a third candidate from Daugherty's legacy if the Michigan State had done advance homework similar to Stanford. Willingham had previously coached the Cardinal under Dennis Green from 1989 to 1991. When the job was open, Stanford brought him home from Green's Minnesota Vikings staff and named him head coach on November 28, 1994.

"I don't think anyone contacted me then; I wasn't a household name then," said Willingham, who added he reluctantly turned down Michigan State in 2000 and 2007.

By then, he was "a household name."

Lewis, with the benefit of hindsight, says he should have left Michigan State in 1980 rather than joining Waters' staff.

"Some people say if you stay in one place for too long, you get taken for granted, but I didn't want to go anywhere else," Lewis said. "I love the school. It was a mistake. If I had it to do over again, I would have left then."

Three times, Lewis interviewed for an NFL position as a head coach: Arizona, Chicago, and Dallas. The Dallas interview was for an opening in 1999 to succeed Barry Switzer. At the time, Green Bay was coming off a second straight Super Bowl trip, though it ended this time in a loss to Denver after defeating New England the previous season.

"I was coming in for an interview that I thought was undercover and all of the sudden these television camera lights flashed on me," Lewis said. "There were TV cameras everywhere. Everyone knew I was coming. I think that interview was just for show."

Dallas hired Chan Gailey.

"It's hard to say race was a factor when you can't substantiate it," said Lewis of his NFL and Michigan State interviews. "I had had some success in coaching on my resume when Saban got the job. There always are a lot of politics involved. I just didn't have the right people in my corner."

Similar to Lewis, Daugherty gave Jimmy Raye his start in coaching. The difference between the two was that Raye had no plans to enter the profession once his two-year NFL career as a defensive back with the Los Angeles Rams and Philadelphia Eagles in the 1968 and 1969 seasons ended with a compound fractured arm.

Raye returned to Michigan State in 1970 to complete his degree and planned to study for the LSAT to fulfill his high-school ambition to become a lawyer. Daugherty invited him in 1971 to coach the scout team and do advance scouting. After the 1971 season, he planned to return to North Carolina with his wife Edwena and two young children, but Daugherty had an opening on his 1972 staff.

"Duffy called me up and wanted me to come see him," Raye said. "He said he thought I would make a fine coach and wanted me to join the staff. He wanted me to start after the holidays. He didn't really ask me—he told me what he wanted me to do. I said OK."

Michigan State now had two black assistant coaches with Lewis and Raye, but they were still among college football's first black assistants.

"Jimmy was a welcome addition," said Lewis, who was entering his fourth season with Daugherty in 1972. "He was intelligent, had played quarterback and had the added perspective of playing defense in the NFL. He was a great recruiter. We grew together on the staff until we went our separate ways, but we have been close ever since."

Raye was a Michigan State assistant through 1975, until Denny Stolz was fired after his third season over an NCAA recruiting scandal. Raye, drawn to the warmer weather of California, planned to accept a San Jose State job offer in 1976. But Daugherty, with contacts everywhere and an eye to his protégé's futures, told him "you're going to Wyoming."

Daugherty explained new Wyoming coach Fred Akers, a former assistant to Darrell Royal at Texas, would be a head coach at Texas or Arkansas (his alma mater) in a year or two. Akers hired Raye as his offensive coordinator and Wyoming shared the 1976 Western Athletic Conference title with Brigham Young. Royal retired following the 1976 season, Texas hired Akers and he brought Raye with him to Austin.

"Wyoming turned out to be one of my greatest experiences in coaching," Raye said. "I was concerned about taking my family to a city with only one other black family, but we really enjoyed Laramie. My wife was involved in civic activities. I used to drop my kids off at school and wondered what I had done to them with my selfish coaching desires sending them to a school where no other students looked like them. But my kids enjoyed the school. They didn't really want to go to Texas."

Raye recruited for Texas in the winter and coached a spring football roster that included 1977 Heisman Trophy winner Earl Campbell. He had an immediate impact with Texas recruiting. The Longhorns integrated their football program in the 1970 season (the campus desegregated in 1950), but the doors to black athletes in the "Golden Triangle" Houston-Beaumont-Port Arthur area had remained closed.

"Darrell Royal said in 1963 he could win national titles without black players, and the coaches in the Golden Triangle didn't trust him with their players," Raye said. "The coaches trusted me. I was able to get kids to visit and we got a couple of commitments."

Raye had a foot in the door of the Golden Triangle as an African-American coach. More importantly, he had name recognition as a Michigan State teammate of Bubba Smith, the son of legendary Beaumont Pollard coach Willie Ray Smith.

Raye looked forward to coaching Texas' talent roster in 1977, but fate intervened after he spoke at a high-school clinic in San Antonio. Los Angeles Rams offensive coordinator Ken Meyer also spoke and took note of Raye's presentation. Meyer was about to be named the head coach of the San Francisco 49ers, and he called Raye with a job offer to join his staff.

"I never expected to coach in the NFL, but I talked to some people and they said it was not an opportunity that would come around often—particularly for a black coach," Raye said. "I made the decision and went to San Francisco."

Meyer only lasted one year in San Francisco before general manager Joe Thomas fired him, but former 49ers coach Monte Clark took Raye and other assistants with him when he landed the Detroit job in 1978. Clark had been a Don Shula disciple from his time with the Miami Dolphins.

"That was when I learned all the things in the NFL that made me a good coach the rest of my career," Raye said. "I attribute it all to Monte Clark."

Raye moved on to Atlanta in 1980 when Falcons head coach Leeman Bennett made him an offer, but Bennett was fired after the 1982 season despite an overall winning record and playoff trips in 1980 and 1982.

Jimmy Raye had been the only black assistant coach on the staffs at San Francisco, Detroit, and Atlanta. Suddenly he was out of work in a business built on connections and with few minorities in the pipeline. But Raye landed his biggest break in 1983 with the Los Angeles Rams. John Robinson left the University of Southern California and was largely bringing his USC staff with him. Robinson needed an NFL assistant familiar with the league. One of Robinson's USC assistants, John

Jackson, recommended Raye. Robinson took the advice and brought Raye aboard, naming him one of the first black offensive coordinators in the NFL.

Coach Robinson with Jimmy Raye.

"Not many guys would have done that," said Raye. "John was way ahead of his time. He allowed me to be the coordinator. He didn't get in the way or intervene with play calling. We had a great relationship."

Robinson said it was an easy decision once he interviewed Raye. "He had an encyclopedic knowledge of the NFL. We would talk about trying something and he'd say, 'Well, Detroit tried that in 1978' ... or he'd say 'If we try this, they'll cover it this way.' These days you can call everything up on a computer, but in those days it was mostly in a coach's mind how a team would react. He was a very smart guy and knew the ins and outs of every team."

The previously downtrodden Rams returned to the playoffs in the 1983 and 1984 seasons with a running game powered by Eric Dickerson. He was the 1983 Offensive Rookie of the Year and set an NFL rushing record in 1984 that still stands with 2,105 yards.

But then Leeman Bennett landed the Tampa Bay job in 1985 and offered Raye the Buccaneers' offensive coordinator role at a substantial pay raise. At the time he viewed it as a chance to enhance his resume. If he could turn around Tampa Bay following playoff teams at Atlanta and Los Angeles, he was better positioned to become a head coach.

Jimmy Raye also was a hot name in the mid-1980s. The media focused attention on the NFL's lack of a black head coach since Fritz Pollard in the 1920s. Raye was mentioned among the most likely candidates to break the barrier in national publications such as *Sports Illustrated* and *Pro Football Weekly,* along with Tony Dungy, Dennis Green, Johnny Roland, and Billie Matthews.

Raye possessed the most important distinction between an assistant coach and a head coach, John Robinson opined. "He would have been a good head coach because he knew exactly what he wanted to do. He was never uncertain. A lot of times people who get in leadership positions all of the sudden get insecure. It's easy for an assistant to have ideas, but when you're the head coach you're responsible for the culture of the team and it is a little harder. I don't think Jimmy would have ever had any problem leading. He would have been exact and his players would have followed him. He had a lot of integrity and ethical judgment on what was right."

Raye gained his first interview for an open head-coach job in 1986 with New Orleans Saints general manager Jim Finks. By then Raye had experience as an offensive coordinator with the Rams and the Bucs. He was pleased with the interview, but Finks hired Jim Mora. Finks explained Mora was coming off a United States Football League championship and could bring his staff with him.

"Jim told me I had the qualifications," Raye said. "He said he had heard so much about me and Tony Dungy, he wanted to visit with me for himself. He told me he thought of me as a leader of a pro football team. The Jim Finks interview was a legitimate deal."

But Raye's calculated move to show he could turn around Tampa Bay's offense backfired. He never coached quarterback Doug Williams, who left for the USFL when his pay-raise demands as the lowest-paid starting quarterback in the NFL were not met. Then the Bucs squandered the No. 1 overall draft pick in the 1986 draft on Bo Jackson, who signed a baseball deal with the Kansas City Royals. Instead of Tampa Bay featuring an offense including Williams, Jackson, running back James Wilder, and tight end Jimmie Giles, the Bucs posted back-to-back records of 2-14 in 1985 and 1986.

"I made a mistake," Raye said. "The only thing that matters in the NFL is winning. I was with a winning team in Los Angeles. We were having success and I thought I could do the same thing at Tampa. I was betting on myself that the powers that be would look at me as someone who won in Atlanta and Los Angeles and did it again in Tampa. But in the NFL, it doesn't matter how good of a coaching job you do if you don't win. The owners have to sell a winning coach to their fans."

Raye said he interviewed one more time as an NFL head coach candidate in Green Bay in 1988, but he does not consider that a serious interview. The Packers hired Lindy Infante.

As it turned out, Art Shell became the NFL's first black head coach midway through the 1989 season when Los Angeles Raiders owner Al Davis fired Mike Shanahan. Minnesota subsequently hired Dennis Green in 1992 and Tampa Bay introduced Tony Dungy in 1996, the first black coaches hired after a full interview process against other candidates.

By the 1990s, Raye was firmly viewed as an NFL coach, but he would have returned to the college ranks for Michigan State. He received his first opportunity with the Spartans in an interview shortly before Thanksgiving 1994 at a hotel near the Detroit Metro Airport with President McPherson and his committee.

During McPherson's search, it was recommended to him he consult retired Notre Dame coach Ara Parseghian, but McPherson needed the College Football Hall of Fame coach's identity explained to him.[2]

For the 1986 New Orleans Saints job, Raye had been interviewed by Jim Finks, a man with the credentials to be inducted into the Pro Football Hall of Fame Class of 2013, and judged to be head-coach material.

For the 1995 Michigan State job, Raye had been interviewed by McPherson, a man who deemed Raye unworthy to fill the seat of head coach at his alma mater. McPherson was a man with little football knowledge and less understanding of the combined legacy of Daugherty and former Michigan State president John Hannah. McPherson had also given Sherman Lewis only a cursory interview.

In retrospect, Raye believes his best opportunity to have landed the Michigan State job was in 2000, when Saban abruptly departed after the 1999 season for more money at LSU. But the job never really came open. Bobby Williams was promoted to interim head coach for the Spartans' Citrus Bowl win over Florida. The coaching staff and players both lobbied for Williams, who was named by McPherson as Michigan State's first black head coach.

Williams was fired after the 2002 season and Michigan State initially considered a black coach as a leading candidate, though not Jimmy Raye. Then-athletic director Ron Mason pursued longtime NFL defensive coordinator Marvin Lewis until Lewis opted to stay in the NFL and was named the Cincinnati Bengals head coach. Marvin Lewis's credentials were unquestioned, but the school overlooked obvious concern—as it had eight years earlier with Nick Saban—was that he would use the job as a stepping stone rather than provide stability.

Mason interviewed Raye for the 2003 job, but he subsequently picked Louisville head coach John L. Smith in a hiring so badly botched that word leaked in the middle of the Louisville's GMAC Bowl game loss to Marshall. Louisville players were seen on the sideline phoning friends about the news. Smith, a head coach at Utah State and Idaho before Louisville, had a tumultuous three-year run at Michigan State. He was fired at the end of the 2006 season in part for his lack of Big Ten background and Big Ten recruiting contacts.

Raye was with the New York Jets when Michigan State conducted another coaching search for the 2007 season. Mason flew in to interview Raye and stayed at New Jersey hotel, but a snowstorm hit the area. Raye said Mason wanted to interview him on the phone rather travel to the Jets' base at Hofstra University in Long Island.

"I don't think I ever had a legitimate shot," Raye said. "When he said he didn't want to come out to Long Island, I said, 'Don't worry about it. If that was the extent of your interest, it was in the best interest of both us not to pursue it any further.'"

Willingham, who is not given to hyperbole, is unequivocal on Raye's credentials.

"He would have been a fantastic head coach," Willingham said. "I don't merit being in the same conversation with what Jimmy Raye has done. When you look at what he has accomplished, how long he has been in the business and what he had to go through in the business, it's amazing—even from my perspective."

As Michigan State's coaching carousel continued turning, Willingham established himself as one of the top coaches in college football.

Willingham arrived at Michigan State from Jacksonville High in

Jimmy Raye in 2014. Photo by Ray Black.

North Carolina, a school he entered as a junior when it desegregated. The first 10 years he attended segregated Georgetown, a 1-through-12 black school in Jacksonville. He was a star quarterback, but with his 5-foot-7 height he had no illusions about a scholarship. He wrote 100 letters seeking a walk-on opportunity. Michigan State and Toledo were the only two to answer him. Daugherty and Raye offered a walk-on opportunity.

"Without Jimmy Raye, I probably don't get to Michigan State," Willingham said. "I knew about Jimmy and Michigan State from the Game of the Century against Notre Dame. Michigan State registered with me, and Jimmy was gracious and followed up on my contact letter."

Willingham, a quarterback and wide receiver as well as a baseball player for MSU from 1972 to 1976, began his coaching career as a graduate assistant with the Spartans in 1977 under Darryl Rogers.

"Tyrone reminded me of Tony Dungy," said Lewis. "They were both very mature for their age. Tony always handled himself so well, and Tyrone was the same way. There were like much older men."

Willingham made a similar impression on Jud Heathcote, who arrived for his 19-year tenure as Michigan State's basketball coach in the 1976-77 season, two years before his NCAA championship team with Magic Johnson in 1978-79.

"Tyrone used to always call me, Sir," Heathcote said. "I told him, 'No, you don't have to call me Sir.' Tyrone was a very serious, very dedicated and a very intelligent person. I don't think people gave him enough credit for that. They didn't hire him at Stanford because he was an idiot."

Willingham moved on to Central Michigan and Michigan State, and took a side trip to the NFL, before he launched his head-coaching career in 1995 at Stanford. In Willingham's second Stanford season, the Cardinal defeated a Michigan State team coached by Saban, 38-0, in the Sun Bowl. He was the first black coach to win a Division I-A bowl game. In his fifth season, he led Stanford to its first Rose Bowl in 29 years, although the Cardinal lost to the Wisconsin Badgers.

When Stanford hired Willingham, Condoleezza Rice was the university provost overseeing athletics. She was a long-time college football fan who signed off on Willingham's hire. Rice, the former U.S. Secretary of State, and Willingham also were named to the 13-member panel formed to select teams for the 2014 debut of the four-team College Football Playoff.

By 2002, Willingham was named the first black head coach in any sport at Notre Dame. In a sad irony for Michigan State, Willingham is now more closely associated among college football fans with Stanford and even Notre Dame.

Willingham, a private man who avoids discussing how job offers played out, was contacted twice by Michigan State once he had established his reputation as a winning head coach. He was contacted for the 2000 and 2007 jobs but not in 2003 after his successful first season at Notre Dame.

In 2000, Tyrone Willingham was fresh off Stanford's Rose Bowl trip. Willingham committed to remain with the Cardinal, and Michigan State subsequently lifted the interim tag from Bobby Williams.

The second time Michigan State contacted Willingham was after the 2006 season when he finished his second year with the Huskies.

"Michigan State knocked on my door twice, but the timing was never right," Willingham said. "It's difficult for me to say that because it's my alma mater. I love it and I want to do things for it because it was really good to me. But the timing was just not right."

MSU hired Dantonio for the 2007 season. At least this time Michigan State had passed on one of its three Daugherty legacy coaches for a choice who turned around the program and provided stability that had been lacking in East Lansing. The Spartans won a share of the Big Ten

Jimmy Raye with Tyrone Willingham during his tenure as Notre Dame head coach.

title in 2010, the Big Ten Legends Division title in 2011, and won the
2013 Big Ten title and beat Stanford in the Rose Bowl to finish No. 3 in
the polls.

Raye continued coaching around the NFL, including stints as an
offensive coordinator at Kansas City (1999-2000), the Oakland Raiders
(2004-05) and San Francisco 49ers (2009-10). He was fired in 2010 by
San Francisco head coach Mike Singletary, who, ironically, Raye first
met in 1977 when he tried to recruit him to Texas. Tampa Bay coach
Greg Schiano soon hired Raye for his 35th NFL season as a Bucs offensive assistant in 2012.

Raye missed the 2013 season following back surgery and the death
of his older sister, Pat. She had provided key assistance to organizing
Jimmy Raye Youth Foundation events. In 2014, Raye accepted a position
as NFL Senior Advisor to NFL Vice-President of Operations Troy Vincent.

"I spent my time trying to be the best coach I could be and that was
satisfaction for me," Raye said. "I'm more disappointed I never coached
in the professional ranks' biggest game—the Super Bowl. Sherman has

four Super Bowl rings and five Super Bowls. He has more legitimacy when you say he should have been a head coach.

"The times I was on a winning team, it didn't happen for me. When you're on a losing team, it doesn't matter. And then to be a minority doesn't help. I've had great rapport with the people I've coached. I look at this way: The chance I didn't get to be a head coach is the NFL's loss."

Not to mention his alma mater. Michigan State broke barriers with black athletes under Munn and Daugherty, but future administrations with varying degrees of understanding Michigan State's football history chose not to break barriers in the coaching profession with alums from Daugherty's historic Underground Railroad. The three accomplished coaches carried the Daugherty legacy longer and higher than the school that benefitted greatly from the late coach's progressive view of the world and his powerhouse football teams.

Notes

1. *Greener Pastures*, p. 266

2. *Spartan Seasons II*, Lynn Henning, p. 104.

WHERE DO WE GO FROM HERE?

By David Cornwell and Jimmy Raye

"The NFL has a responsibility to provide access and a welcoming approach to minority candidates, but the candidates also have a responsibility to learn career and networking skills."—David Cornwell and Jimmy Raye

The absence of a minority hire as a head coach or general manager for the 2013 NFL job cycle was discouraging, but it's not a reason yet to wring hands, lose faith or remain frustrated, not as long as the NFL responds as it did in the offseason to the lack of minority hires. NFL commissioner Roger Goodell demonstrated in the offseason a recommitment to past league programs that were designed to fill the hiring pipeline with qualified candidates—minority and white aspirants alike.

My name is David Cornwell, and I serve as executive director of the NFL Coaches Association. I work with Jimmy Raye, the president of the association and a pioneer among minority assistant coaches. We are both African-Americans, but we are committed to serving our constituency of both minority and white NFL assistant coaches.

Jimmy's NFL coaching experience spans five decades from his first job with the San Francisco 49ers in 1977 to his position as a senior offensive assistant with the Tampa Bay Buccaneers. When Jimmy joined the 49ers' staff, there were only three other black assistant coaches throughout an NFL that at the time numbered 28 teams. Six years later he was one of the first black offensive coordinators when Los Angeles Rams head coach John Robinson appointed him for the 1983 season.

My experience addressing NFL minority opportunities dates back to Pete Rozelle's tenure as the league's commissioner. I was hired in 1987 as assistant general counsel and director of equal employment, and I continued in that role with Rozelle's successor, Paul Tagliabue, until 1993.

In the 2013 offseason, when none of seven openings for a head coach or eight for a general manager were filled by a minority candidate, the NFL and Goodell took action. The league re-established a three-day NFL Career Development Symposium in May 2013 at the Wharton School of Business in Philadelphia and again in June 2014.

The NFL symposium originally ran from 1998 to 2008, and alumni from those symposiums include current minority head coach Ron Rivera (Carolina Panthers) and former minority head coach Leslie Frazier (Minnesota Vikings), as well as current white head coaches John Harbaugh (Baltimore Ravens), Chuck Pagano (Indianapolis Colts), and Mike Smith (Atlanta Falcons).

Discontinuing the symposium was a mistake. Reestablishing the symposium was a significant step that hopefully duplicates its success in the future.

The NFL has a responsibility to provide access and a welcoming approach to minority candidates, but the candidates also have a responsibility to learn and develop networking skills. We want to see the best person for the job hired, but without the NFL Career Development Symposium, there are fewer avenues for minority candidates to access the pool.

The symposium teaches career skills to assistant coaches and junior executives that aspire to be named a head coach or general manager. The instruction takes place in the presence of NFL owners and executive personnel.

At the 2013 symposium, Goodell was joined by team owners and presidents Robert Kraft (New England Patriots), Woody Johnson (New York Jets), Dan Rooney (Pittsburgh Steelers), Shahid Kahn (Jacksonville Jaguars), John Mara (New York Giants), and Michael Bidwell (Arizona Cardinals). They participated on panels and in breakout sessions.

The environment provided mingling opportunities and such networking fosters a pool of candidates. Ideally, we want candidates to place their name in circulation from what they've learned and who've they met.

Let's say I'm an assistant coach and my goal is to become a head coach. When I attend the NFL symposium, I have the opportunity to meet Jacksonville Jaguars owner Shahid Kahn. During the season, then, when my team faces the Jaguars, I'm sure to be out on the field early to see if there is a chance to say hello to Kahn. That's how networking through the NFL symposium pays off. When jobs come open in the off-season, hopefully I've made a lasting impression on NFL owners and general managers I've met.

We feel this approach differs from the Rooney Rule and the Fritz Pollard Alliance, which were both established in 2003 to promote minority hiring. The important distinction is we want to see a "numerical measurement" of minority candidates rather than a "measurement goal."

Let me explain. What this means is we prefer a numerical measurement that identifies the number of qualified minority candidates fed into the pool.

This approach differs dramatically from a measurement goal. A measurement goal requires a team to interview at least one minority candidate. This dangerously crosses the line to a quota—a word Jimmy and I don't like to see used.

The Rooney Rule and Fritz Pollard Alliance no doubt played a role in getting folks interviewed, but I'm not sure they played a role in getting folks hired. That, of course, is the objective. The Fritz Pollard Alliance, unfortunately, has developed into a clearinghouse. We should not have a single entity identifying candidates. That isn't the way teams find white coaches.

When the Rooney Rule and Fritz Pollard Alliance were established in 2003, the objectives were explained at a conference for sports lawyers that I attended. The goal was to establish a rule that requires teams to interview a black candidate. I spoke up and said, "Don't do it. You're establishing a ceiling instead of a floor." I was concerned teams would only interview one black candidate and then move on. That, as we've seen, was precisely what happened.

With the Rooney Rule/Fritz Pollard measurement goal, a minority candidate's name is provided to a team. But that club may not have the proper background on the candidate to learn if the name fed to them was the right fit for the job. The name provided might be a defensive coach, but the team prefers to hire an offensive coach.

A measurement goal misses the point of building a pipeline to replenish the pool with a variety of candidates from year to year.

The numerical goal, which the NFL symposium develops through networking and career skills, is needed to provide a stocked pool. The owners and their search committees are made aware of the minority candidate's qualifications before the formal interview takes place. If they're focused on an offensive coach, they'll find an offensive coach to interview—or vice versa.

From 2010 to the 2013 offseason—a period of time when no NFL symposium was staged—there were 23 openings for a head coach, but only two black candidates were hired. The Oakland Raiders promoted Hue Jackson from offensive coordinator in 2010 to head coach in 2011, but fired him at the end of the season. The Kansas City Chiefs promoted Romeo Crennel from defensive coordinator to interim head coach late in the 2011 season. The Chiefs removed the interim tag in 2012, but they fired Crennel at the end of the season.

The Rooney Rule/Fritz Pollard Alliance served a purpose to raise awareness of the lack of minority coaches in the NFL, but Jimmy and I don't believe either program possesses the tools to fill the pipeline with minority candidates as effectively as the NFL symposium and future programs that could be developed.

If we look back 20-plus years to the first black head coaches hired, they benefited from the media placing their names in circulation. In the mid-1980s, national publications such as *Sports Illustrated* and *Pro Football Weekly* and local newspapers reported on the NFL's abysmal minority hiring record. The stories shined a light on promising candidates that included Art Shell, Dennis Green, Jimmy Raye, Tony Dungy, Johnny Roland, and Billie Matthews. Essentially, the media built the first pool of candidates with stories that raised these names as coaches who deserved an equal opportunity.

Shell, Green, and Dungy were provided a chance and those pioneer black head coaches led their team to playoff berths. In the 1995 season, Ray Rhodes was voted the NFL Coach of the Year in his first year leading the Philadelphia Eagles. By the 2006 season, we had progressed to the point where we saw two African-Americans on opposite sidelines in Super Bowl XLI when Tony Dungy's Indianapolis Colts defeated Lovie Smith's Chicago Bears.

In the last eight seasons, Super Bowl titles have been claimed three times by teams with a black general manager—the New York Giants' Jerry Reese (XLII and XLVI) and the Baltimore Ravens' Ozzie Newsome (XLVII)—and twice by a black head coach—Dungy (XLI) and the Pittsburgh Steelers' Mike Tomlin (Super Bowl XLIII).

Following the Dungy-Smith breakthrough in Super Bowl XLI, the next six seasons featured at least one of the teams with a black head coach or black general manager. In addition to the teams that won, black coaches in the Super Bowl despite suffering a loss were Indianapolis' Jim Caldwell (XLIV) and Tomlin (XLV). But the success of pioneer black head coaches and general managers hasn't translated into a growing pool of candidates. The NFL remains decades behind the NBA in terms of identifying candidates. At the start of the 2012-13 NBA season, there were 13 African-American head coaches among the 30 basketball teams. In addition, coaches such as Doc Rivers, Byron Scott, Lionel Hollins, Maurice Cheeks, and Mike Brown—to name a few—have been hired, fired and rehired for another job.

Without a growing pool of candidates, we risk another 2013 shutout of minority candidates. The explanation most commonly given for the shutout was owners sought offensive coordinators (that doesn't explain the lack of general managers hired), while most black coordinators are on the defensive side of the ball.

We recognize and accept that there are trends that appear in NFL hiring cycles. Teams opt for offense or defense, motivators or disciplinarians and experience or fresh energy. But understanding there are trends serves to place an increased need on building pools.

Another recent trend in the NFL has seen teams hiring venerable retired general managers as consultants. If Ernie Accorsi, Ron Wolf, and Bill Polian are to be opinion makers and resources for teams in hiring, then minority coaches need to find their way into their networks.

We cannot assume every time a black man doesn't get hired, it's because he's black. But we also can no longer accept that the only way a black man can get hired is if there is special program, such as the Rooney Rule/Pollard Alliance, for black coaches.

The point is to create access and then build relationships. That's what everybody has to do. That's how you get jobs. Our job is to make sure the playing field is level for minorities—and not unfair to non-minorities.

The NFL can help raise the awareness of qualified candidates through the media with its own NFL Network. In the context of new technology, there is a thirst for information. We would like to see the NFL Network use NFL assistant coaches—black and white—to appear as spokesmen to discuss issues such as safety rules, other initiatives, and team-by-team looks. That's not a minority program, but it includes minorities in it. We want the NFL to use our assistant coaches to help it continue to grow.

When I worked in the NFL office, Reggie Roberts, now the vice president of communications for the Atlanta Falcons, and I would write a story on a black candidate and send it out to national writers. They would use it in their news and notes. We created a buzz around coaches.

We see emerging candidates in Mel Tucker, the defensive coordinator with the Chicago Bears; Ray Horton, the defensive coordinator with the Tennessee Titans; and Pep Hamilton, the offensive coordinator of the Indianapolis Colts. Terry Robiskie has been an interim head coach twice (2000 at Washington and 2004 at Cleveland) and has been the assistant head coach/wide receivers coach with the Atlanta Falcons since 2008.

The ability to lead an NFL team requires expertise, work ethic, communication skills and decisive decision-making. These are characteristics that are not limited to offensive or defensive coordinators or skin color.

As demonstrated by the NFL's decision to restart the NFL Career Development Symposium, you can be assured the Commissioner Goodell has this issue on his radar screen.

There is reason to be optimistic. When you emerge from the emotional aspect of this issue, you see we still have a ways to go. But the objective is being addressed.

UNDERGROUND RAILROAD RECRUITS AT MICHIGAN STATE, 1959-1972

A list of Duffy Daugherty's Underground Railroad recruits from the South from 1959 to 1972, according to Michigan State rosters:

1959: 56 players, 11 black, 0 from the South (Clifton Roaf was on the freshman team)

1960: 1 Southerner: Clifton Roaf, Pine Bluff, Ark.

1961: 3 Southerners: Clifton Roaf; Earl Lattimer, Dallas Lincoln; Sherman Lewis, Louisville (Ky.) DuPont Manuel.

1962: 5 Southerners: Clifton Roaf; Earl Lattimer; Sherman Lewis; Daniel Grimes, Newport News (Va.) Carver; Robert Moreland, Richmond (Va.), Maggie Walker.

1963: 4 Southerners: Earl Lattimer; Sherman Lewis; Robert Moreland; Jim Garrett, Columbia (S.C.) Johnson.

1964: 8 Southerners: Jim Garrett; Eric Marshall, Oxford (Ms.) Central; Ernie Pasteur, Beaufort, N.C.; Bubba Smith, Beaumont (Tex.) Pollard; Jimmy Summers, Orangeburg (S.C.) Wilkinson; Charlie Thornhill, Roanoke (Va.) Addison; Gene Washington, Baytown (Tex.) Carver; George Webster, Anderson (S.C.) Westside.

1965: 11 Southerners: Jim Garrett; Eric Marshall; Ernie Pasteur; Bubba Smith; Jimmy Summers; Charlie Thornhill; Gene Washington; George Webster; Jess Phillips, Beaumont (Tex.) Pollard; Maurice Haynes, Baton Rouge (La.) Southern; Jimmy Raye, Fayetteville (N.C.) Smith.

1966: 12 Southerners: Maurice Haynes; Eric Marshall; Ernie Pasteur;

Jess Phillips; Jimmy Raye; Bubba Smith; Jimmy Summers; Charlie Thornhill; Gene Washington; George Webster; Clinton Harris, Beaumont (Tex.) Pollard; William Ware, Beaumont, Tx; plus 6 freshmen: Frank Foreman, Ken Hines, Jack Pitts, Kermit Smith, Tody Smith, Frank Traylor.

1967: 11 Southerners: Maurice Haynes; Eric Marshall; Jimmy Raye; Jess Phillips; William Ware; Frank Foreman, Louisville Dupont Manuel; Ken Hines, Stroud, Okla; Jack Pitts, Decateur (Ga.) Trinity; Kermit Smith, Baytown (Tex.) Carver; Tody Smith, Beaumont (Tex.) Pollard; Frank Traylor, Beaumont (Tex.) Pollard.

1968: 11 Southerners: Frank Foreman; Ken Hines; Kermit Smith; Tody Smith; Frank Traylor; William Ware; Earl Anderson, Tifton, Ga.; Ronald Joseph, New Orleans St. Augustine; Tommy Love, Sylva, (N.C.), Sylva-Webster; Errol Roy, New Orleans St. Augustine; William Triplett, Vicksburg (Ms.) Temple. Honors: 2 Honorable Mention All-Big Ten, Tommy Love and William Triplett.

1969: 10 Southerners: Earl Anderson; Frank Foreman; Ken Hines; Ronald Joseph; Tommy Love; Errol Roy; Kermit Smith; William Triplett; Eric Allen, Georgetown (S.C.) Howard; Billy Joe DuPree, West Monroe (La.). Honors: 2 honorable mention All-Big Ten, Tommy Love and Frank Foreman.

1970: 10 Southerners: Eric Allen; Earl Anderson; Billy Joe DuPree; Ronald Joseph; Tommy Love; Errol Roy; William Triplett; Kennith Alderson, Baytown (Tex.) Sterling; Ernest Hamilton, Greenville (S.C.) Beck; Frank Timmons, Winter Haven (Fla.) Jewett. Honors: 1 second-team All-Big Ten, Eric Allen.

1971: 7 Southerners: Kennith Alderson; Eric Allen; Billy Joe DuPree; Ernest Hamilton; Ronald Joseph; Errol Roy; Frank Timmons. Honors: 1 All-American (and All-Big Ten), Eric Allen; 2 additional second-team All-Big Ten picks, Billy Joe DuPree and Ernest Hamilton.

1972 (Daugherty's final season): 13 Southerners (4 freshmen, 1 transfer): Kennith Alderson; Frank Timmons; Ernest Hamilton; Brendon Barber, Georgetown (S.C.) Winyah; James Cordery, Louisville Flagut; Charles Gordon, Fort Myers (Fla.) Dunbar; Cheadrick Harriatte, Conway, (S.C.), Whittemore; Larry Jackson, Clermont, Fla.; Charles McKinney, Clermont, Fla.; Otto Smith, Columbia (S.C.) Washington; Ray Smith, Dallas Pinkston; Tyrone Willingham, Jacksonville, N.C.;

Charlie Baggett (redshirt transfer), Fayetteville (N.C.) Smith. Honors: 1 All-American (and All-Big Ten), Billy Joe DuPree. (*Note: The is the first year the NCAA allowed freshmen to play on the varsity.*)

THE POEMS OF PAT GALLINAGH

What is a Spartan?

by Pat Gallinagh '67

The Aggie logo served its turn as long as MSU was still
A small Midwestern college geared to teach the farmer's skill
But as its mission grew in time, a new image was desired
One with such universal fame its bearer's surely be inspired.

The new name would be the Spartans, a warrior class who knew no fear
Who pledged their lives and honor to causes they held dear
State's athletes would be held to a much higher standard now
To play their heart and souls out til the last drop of sweat ran from their
  brow.

But the Spartan mascot encompasses more than just the athletes of the
  school
Every member of Michigan State's family carries this title proudly too
But what exactly was this new image meant to symbolize
In a world where reputation and achievement are still a treasured prize

A Spartan is a fighter, a fearless soldier for a cause
Who compete with strength and courage without asking for a pause
A Spartan is a guardian, a protector of the trust
Of the precious gift of liberty for which all humanity does lust

A Spartan is a dreamer who asks why things cannot be done

And sees a better future with projects yet begun
A Spartan is a doer, a pragmatist at heart
Who uses skill and knowledge to tackle problems from that start

A Spartan is a thinker, one who ponders and dissects
Philosophies and edicts for faults they might detect
A Spartan is a scholar, a student of the land
Who seeks a better understanding of Providence's grand plan

A Spartan is an artist, a creative soul and muse
An architect of beauty, song and verse for common use
A Spartan is an activist who speaks out when they see wrong
Who combats ignorance and hatred with truths buried far too long

A Spartan is a worker, one who's not afraid to sweat
While moving towards a vaulted goal labors without regret
A Spartan is helper, an altruistic being we're told
Providing comfort for the homeless and shelter from the cold

Above all, a Spartan is a champion no matter what the final score
Who's intensity and spirit produces feats of storied lore
For they know that sports are but a game to teach the survival skills
    of life
For a real world which beckons them filled with challenges and strife

A Spartan is a compendium, a sum of all these much sought parts
Combining the grace and wisdom of Athena with Hercules' strength
    and heart
Tho few are blessed with all the gifts of these mythical deities
All Spartans strive to reach these heights within their own realities

Spartans now span the globe and carry forth the torch
To light the darkest corners of this earth while steering a
    progressive course
But no matter where they wander, be it near or be it far
They bear the Spartan title proudly as they keep reaching for their star

© Copyright 2005 Pat Gallinagh

A Tribute to Hugh "Duffy" Daugherty

1915 – 1987

by Pat Gallinagh '67 © December 1, 2007

From the hills of Pennsylvania came a man with a lofty dream
Tho small in size and stature, he wasn't lacking self-esteem
He was a natural born leader, a captain of his team
He set his course and worked like hell until his goal he did redeem

Neither a broken neck nor a world war could block the path he set
He came with Biggie to Michigan State tho some felt it was a bad bet
But they built such a football dynasty that the Big Ten would soon relent
And let the Spartans in, for they had proved their standards they had
    met

With Biggie, they reached the Rose Bowl, National Championships and
    more
Duffy's toughies were the key, and a brighter future was still in store
When Biggie Munn had to hang it up, he picked Duffy to carry on lore
A job the redhead relished, to make State's football fortunes soar

For nineteen years he led the Green & White thru good times and some
    bad
Rose Bowls, Big Ten titles and national championships were had
The cover of Time, Coach of the Year and Halls of Fame made his family
    glad
His tenure and his record made his successors revere him like a dad

His heritage was Irish and of this no one could deny
And yes, he had an Irish temper that could flare when his directives
    didn't fly
He could be tough as nails but on occasion was not afraid to cry
But he also had a soft and tender heart that would make any mother sigh

His family was his lodestone which his players were part of too
When in need, if he could help, there was nothing he would not do
It didn't matter what string they played or if their playing days were thru

He used his power to cut the knot in hopes that things would soon
    improve

He knew how to keep things in perspective, win or lose or tie
Sportsmanship was what he taught and would never stoop to spy
He knew football was just a game upon which life did not rely
For when the battle was over, the stars would not fall from the sky

He never ran from trouble, he faced it like a man
He'd fight with all his Celtic heart and was not afraid to take a stand
Sometimes he won, sometimes he lost but never would complain
Of unfair calls or bad bounce balls for there was nothing more to gain

He was more than just a football coach, he was a humanitarian that
    cared
He fought racism and bigotry so the gifts of freedom could be shared
He sought to make things right in life and damaged souls he'd repaired
Time did exonerate his fight for civil rights and on how his idealism
    fared

He had his faults but who has not so let's not dwell on them
His strengths were loyalty and helpfulness that came from deep within
When other schools came courting, their chance of landing him were
    slim
For his heart and soul were anchored, Michigan State was part of him

He knew the most important part of the game he loved was not the final
    score
That future generations would soon forget, that and so much more
It was the friendships and the memories that the heart and mind did
    store
That would bring both tears and laughter at reunions welcomed door

So now let us pause a moment to ponder Duffy's legacy to all
The building that bares his name, his clinics, and the men he helped
    stand tall
His spirit still envelops the football program that he helped overhaul
His standards would boost all Spartans, be they big or be they small

A Tribute to George "Mickey" Webster

by Pat Gallinagh '67

Nov. 25, 1945 – April 19, 2007

His given name was George Webster but just Mickey to his friends
He was modest and soft-spoken but had athletic talent without ends
He hailed from South Carolina where the Civil War did start
And after Reconstruction collapsed, the races sadly drifted farther
apart
In his era in the south, segregation still ruled the day
And great black athletes had to make a hard choice where they wanted
to play
Go north of the Mason-Dixon Line in search of fame and glory
Or stay home with their loved ones and risk becoming another forgot-
ten story
He was one of the greatest football players to come out of the Deep
South
He choose East Lansing thanks to Duffy, where his pads spoke louder
than his mouth
Some bigots derisively called Michigan State the Grambling of the
north
But the truth be told, it was effort and ability that determined who
played this sport
For three full seasons he cast a giant shadow across the stadiums of the
Big Ten
His jarring tackles were the stuff of legends as the Spartan turf he did
defend
He'd zero in on running backs with laser-like precision
And coaches who dared to send one his way, often lived to regret that
decision
He helped lead State to two of its greatest seasons ever
And his number was retired in recognition of this immense endeavor
He was a captain, All-American and a number one pick
But to his teammates he was just one of them which his fame could
never nick
For his success in football, he still had a higher goal

To graduate from college and for those who followed show
That they came there to get an education, not just to play a game
For they'll be done playing before they know it, then reality the name
It took years of summer school and effort but graduate he did
And once he retired from pro ball a new mission he did bid
To help younger players make their way thru the college maze
So they could hang up their diploma for all the world to gaze
For ten years he fought the turf wars of the NFL
Until injuries and Father Time his football career did quell
The opponents he faced later in life were both cruel and merciless
They attacked him with such ferocity that they put his mettle to the test
Heart disease and cancer teamed up to rob him of his health
And disability and mounting medical bills stripped him of his wealth
Tho his situation was depressing he never cried about his plight
For he knew he had done more in life then most men have a right
His courage in the face of adversity was something to behold
And when told his time was short, he shrugged and smiled and let it all
unfold
For he had accomplished more than most of us could ever hope or
scheme
All-pro selections, halls of fame and the honors of he held in high
esteem
He's one of the brightest stars in the Spartan football galaxy
And the scholarship which bears his name will ensure his legacy
The barriers that brought him north have since crumbled into dust
The chance of another great one coming here from there is probably a
bust
He left us much too early but his life was not in vane
He was a role model for humility and a credit to the game
For those of us who knew and loved him, we are still a bit in awe
Knowing we played with one of the greatest the game has ever saw

About the Author

Tom Shanahan is an award-winning sportswriter who has written for the *San Diego Union-Tribune, Voice of San Diego, Chargers.com, Rivals.com,* and the Internet service Gameday Central. He has won multiple first-place awards from the San Diego Press Club and first place from the Copley News Service Ring of Truth Awards. The National Football Foundation/San Diego Chapter presented him its Distinguished American Award in 2003 and USA Track and Field's San Diego Chapter its President's Award in 2000. Shanahan grew up in Big Rapids, Michigan, and graduated from Michigan State University with a journalism degree in 1978. He lives in Cary, North Carolina, with his wife Taosheng and daughter Jai Jai.

Made in the USA
Monee, IL
10 January 2022